TELL ME A STORY

AN ANTHOLOGY

WRITE NOW WRITERS' GROUP

Light's Scribe
Books

CONTENTS

POETRY

GENERAL FICTION

SCIENCE FICTION & FANTASY

PREFACE
MICHAEL SPENCE

IN MEMPHIS, Tennessee, there is a building on Union Avenue bearing a plaque that identifies the downtown area as the setting of John Grisham's early novel *The Firm*. Other locations in literary history bear similar renown—one can find, for example, the pub in London where C.S. Lewis, J.R.R. Tolkien, Dorothy L. Sayers, and the other Inklings met to share their works in progress.

The Living Word Christian Center in Brooklyn Park, Minnesota, may never bear a similar distinction...but then, short of omniscience, one dares not say "never."

On the first Monday of each month (subject to quirks of the calendar), the Write Now writers' group gathers at the LWCC as it has done for the past sixteen years, to share the fruit of current labors and to provide critique and encouragement. For further suggestions as to how the typical meeting goes, I refer the curious to Laura Shrake's "Passion Pursuit" and Christine Prueher's "True Purpose."

The genres in which we write vary almost as widely as our subjects. In these pages you will find memoir, eulogy, science fiction, poetry, comedy, high and low fantasy, and fable. All represent our desire to use our God-given talents to bear faithful witness to his truth, for his glory. And to entertain you in the process.

Enjoy.

INTRODUCTION: TELL ME A STORY

C.J. WELLUMSON

I BELIEVE it to be innate in all people that we enjoy stories, whether we tell them, write, read, or listen. Throughout human history, stories have been crafted and shared. Our need to do this is ongoing and likely never to cease. We do love them.

Our fascination started from the earliest known times with the first cave drawings, stories painted or scratched in stone. First, there was a simple horse, not yet a story. Later, came a horse with a rider chasing a deer. Over time, these visual stories joined with verbal storytelling. As people sat around evening campfires, they shared stories in an oral tradition, person to person or person to groups. I like to imagine the most serious tellers of stories, those who made sure their words were retold exactly as intended. They insisted the retelling should maintain original integrity.

You may have heard of the "Telephone Game." Line up ten people, then the first one whispers a sentence or story into the ear of the second, then number two whispers it to the third, and so on. Finally, the tenth person repeats what he or she heard to the first. It may be similar, but it certainly comes out changed from the original.

Little chance of remaining true. We can appreciate why those oral-tradition crafters insisted on accuracy. They became important historians, and their stories began passing down accurate facts, myth, and knowledge.

Today, we have paper and ink, the printing press, and computers. These tools have advanced for us a heightened ability to keep our stories as intended.

If your intention is to be a novelist, *Story* must be the number one concern. We may be impressed with the literary gymnastics of writers, the highbrow musings or pretty, poetic prose, and artistic alliterations. We also can work toward success in the high art of humor or the imaginative field of science fiction. Whatever genre you choose to work in, Story must be first and foremost, or readers will not keep turning your pages. Great turns of phrase can go only so far.

Imagine looking at a large tapestry on a castle wall. Next, look at it through a hollow straw. Visible is only a small sample of some of the vivid colors, and maybe a tiny pattern or two in the threads. You will not see the artist's entire and intended story. Now, what do we call a tapestry without the artist's story?

Give up?

We'd just call it a rug. Loop after loop of fabric that may be a beautiful show of color by itself, but hang it next to one depicting a horserace, farmers cutting hay, or a king knighting a blacksmith, and tell me which one will demand your attentions and remain in your memory.

In fact, Story does matter.

What is Story? Try this exercise: "The cat sat on a mat." You, the reader, do get an image, but no story. Next version: "The cat sat on the dog's mat." This is the beginning of a story. The reader is drawn in by a hint of danger and a question raised: What might happen next? That is what all authors want and work toward: reader involvement.

Mr. Hemingway illustrated this well when writing, in his own words, the world's shortest story: "For sale: Baby shoes. Never worn." The story begs of the reader, "Why never worn, and why for sale now?" This is good storytelling, as it invites the reader's participation.

When I was a small boy, I liked to plead with my mom, "Tell me a story." When staying at my cousin's house, I would pester my uncle to tell us again and again about Oscar, a favorite character in a chain of his stories. "Don't stop," we'd beg. "Tell us more."

Remember when the teacher would wheel in the film projector—or the TV cart, or plug a laptop into the classroom's flatscreen? This always brought me and fellow students relief and excitement. We knew we'd be seeing a story. It may have only been a narrative on how they built the Hoover Dam, but a story, nonetheless. Far preferred to the droning of a semi-bored educator who sometimes wanted to be running for the parking lot as much as we did.

Years later, when I had become a father, my three-year-old daughter would sit on my lap as I read to her from the *Berenstain Bears* or selections from our library of Little Golden Books. When a passage stirred her, she would twitch and tighten and sometimes reach to turn a page before I could. She was learning, growing her vocabulary, and imagining new and exciting visions. A beautiful event to witness. The gift of Story, I realized, is one we appreciate from a young age.

Wherever you find them—in a book, at the movies, on the radio, in a magazine, or told by a friend—stories pay off that craving for a getaway from everyday tedium, provide a rest from problems, offer a bit of excitement, or add to our knowledge. They open imaginative doors to places we've never known, teach us how to relate to those different from us, and show us what we need to navigate our lives.

They can soothe us and awaken courage, inspire, and edify.

A great gift, these stories. One of our greatest. All this and more describes what Story is. They can be a blessing, too. We can share them as if from our own hands.

Feed yourself on them often, give them to others, and always create them when inspired to do so.

Long may they remain close friends.

OUR STORY

PASSION PURSUIT
LAURA SHRAKE

Type a chapter in a passion pursuit too big for you,
When a call to write comes knocking, what else can
    you do?
At times it seems unspiritual or frivolous at best,
But storylines and characters will not let you rest.
First monthly Monday finds you at the Write Now group
    to share,
To hone your skills, give feedback, and help the group
    prepare.
You cut cliches and adverbs, too, to make the story flow,
Then, add another plot twist to make the reader say,
    "Oh no!"
Next, it's time to edit, trimming the story to the bone,
Transcribing redlines into your laptop all alone.
Then, hand it off to Bridgett for some polish and pizazz,
Before the book is printed and you are totally jazzed.

TRUE PURPOSE

CHRISTINE PRUEHER

Editor's note: Believe it or not, this was an actual meeting. While I don't believe these specific surprises have ever been repeated, our group is sufficiently diverse that one should never assume what we will find.

"I THINK you are all going to be blown away by what I have written," he said.

This was such a bold statement from someone who was about to share an excerpt from his manuscript with a roomful of strangers. Most of us were cautious about letting anyone hear what we had written for fear of ridicule. Not this guy. He was all out there, ready to wow us.

The person in charge told him to go ahead. The next few minutes, which seemed like hours, became one long stream-of-consciousness with few stops along the way for such trivial matters as punctuation. A good edit job wouldn't have helped, because the content was so confusing.

Descriptions of a hitman, a machine gun, and the typical violin case housing a weapon were all there. As he read, I tried to visualize what he said, but just as an image would form, the next words would erase it like a violently shaken Etch-A-Sketch.

There was a lot of blood, maiming, and murder. Just dangling pieces of information that made absolutely no sense, and I wasn't the only one not getting it. He would read the names of characters who would appear and exit quickly, just because they could, for no reason at all, and without any depth.

I looked at the other faces around me, which all wore deep frowns. We all wanted to like it and were trying to find a shred of something to cling to. Right as I thought it was taking a turn for the better, he would plunge us back into a dark area of nothingness. Random pieces of scenes and fragmented sentences with no substance kept on coming.

My mind couldn't take the search for understanding anymore. Instead of a sample reading, it felt like I was undergoing a form of brainwashing, where I was supposed to make sense of what he was presenting and accept it. He had set the stage by saying this was right up there in excellence with Moses reading the Ten Commandments. What was I not getting?

When he uttered his last sentence, he said, smiling brightly, "Isn't it great?"

I looked to the ceiling to avoid eye contact, as he was seated across from me. I was trying to give the impression that I was deep in thought, when really, I was trying to recover from the mental assault we had all just experienced.

The silence in the room was like none I had encountered before. Throats cleared and people swallowed hard as we all tried to come up with a response. This was why we were here, after all.

We met weekly in a classroom at a church as fellow writers to discuss what we were working on. The goal was to get feedback on how to improve and where we were hitting the mark perfectly.

This guy was expecting us to comment, and no one could think of anything positive to say. I could tell that the man running the group was calculating some thought, as was I.

The only thing that came out of my mouth was, "After hearing it out loud, how do you think you did?"

It was a clever trick I had seen Randy Jackson use as a judge on *American Idol*. When singers were at their worst, he would turn it around and have them explain their views rather than give his opinion. It created a way to discuss without causing any harm, and none of us wanted to make him feel bad. He thought what he had put down on paper would be the next *New York Times* bestseller.

"I think I could clean it up in a few places," he said.

"Like where?" I asked.

"I could take out a few of the killing scenes, because that got to be a bit much."

I was out. Someone else, though, picked up on that and began to explain how to improve. Another attendee pointed out another aspect where he could rearrange some things for better meaning.

Instead of taking in the ideas gratefully, he got angry, hastily put away his manuscript, and said, "You don't get it."

That was the first thing he'd said all evening that I understood. We were the problem, not him.

As I went to more of these sessions, I noticed that the best writers had extreme difficulty exposing what was on their pages. That's how I felt, like I was letting reckless people look after my children. I recall one woman reading the most enchanting children's story with a timid voice.

"I don't think it's my best," she stated at the end.

"Why?" I asked. "It was so well done."

"It sounds boring."

"How many times have you read it?"

"Too many."

"That's why," I said. "Put it aside and come back to it later. It will be brand new to you then."

She sighed. "I feel like something is missing, though."

"While you were reading it, I kept seeing it as a pop-up book, where each page is three-dimensional versus flat."

She sat up straighter, grinning. "Oh! I like that idea! I already have an interested publisher. I just felt like I needed it to stand out in the crowd from other material like this, and that would help."

On another occasion, a woman gave us a glimpse into her recent work. Without much fanfare, she led us into the world of a man who had committed a crime and was on a prison bus, pondering his existence. It was easy to get caught up in the storyline, and her words were vivid. We could feel the anxiety of this character coming right through, along with his deep regret.

We all were awestruck at her talent. She was very unassuming in appearance, with her hair half-combed, a dirty, stained T-shirt, and stretchy pants that had seen too many days. She and I had discussed her background as a single mom who was struggling, like I was at the time. I had listened, then told her that what she was going through would have a good outcome, having no idea she housed such a gift inside.

"That was amazing," the group's leader said.

"Really?" She raised an eyebrow. "I thought you wouldn't like it. I almost threw the whole thing away yesterday."

"No. I think you should keep going with it and see where it leads you," he said. "You have the start of something great."

"I usually don't write about topics like this." She shrugged. "I write erotic romance novels."

It was one of those moments where you think you heard wrong, and inwardly you are saying to yourself...*huh?*

The look on our leader's face told me I had heard correctly.

Stumbling over himself, he said, "Go in this direction. See where God takes you with it."

"I guess so," she said. "Writing smut is easy for me."

It was like being punched in the chest.

He looked at me to add help to the situation, and I was thinking, *You are in charge, buddy, not me.*

"Smut just flows off my pen," the lady said.

I cringed inside. This was turning into an after-hours 1-900 phone chat. Before she could get into any further details, I said, "Maybe God wants you to do something else. What you have been doing was just for a period of time until you got to this point."

I was trying to tone it down and break the uncomfortable feelings I'd sensed all around me. She was being honest, so I didn't want to be anything but delicate in how I addressed it.

I had seen a lot of nonverbal reactions in my time, but the expressions around the table were unreal. Wide-eyed and pale, most of the members seemed shocked to their core. My goal was to get her to see she was better than where she had been, and she needed to embrace it.

"Your writing is from God," I said. "You know that, right?"

"I never thought of it that way," she said, widening her eyes. "I just did it."

"God wants you to be aware of the idea that you can tell a story you are given, and it will have deep meaning to many people. Maybe the genre you were writing in was limiting God's speaking through you."

No one in that room would have ever read what she said was her usual. Well, maybe one guy, but I could tell by the muted reactions that most wouldn't have touched it with a ten-foot pole.

"You have a choice," I said. "You can do what is easy, or you can move to where you have never been and see what you are made of."

She had been writing in a comfort zone where what she produced would show up without effort, but now she had to put some work into it with genuine feelings. Right away, she'd been ready to throw the entire thing into the trash because she believed it wasn't good. But when she got outward recognition and support, fellow writers telling her the truth, then she was willing to keep going.

Moving from one place of being into another isn't something most of us excitedly sign up for. We like safety nets and the false assumption that life will somehow change before us if we keep doing what we have always done. We cannot walk a higher road until we decide to get on another path. That is the scary part.

Leaving behind what is familiar to seek something that is calling us to unknown territory. Sometimes, we need another voice in our lives to tell us we can do it.

Many creative or spiritually gifted people hide their talents for fear of what others will think. Proverbs 29:25 explains, "The fear of human opinion disables; trusting in God protects you from that." (The Message)

There's that word again, *trust*. And if you have been criticized or hurt in the past, it's easy to want to protect yourself. So, you self-isolate and cut yourself off from the world.

The other illusion is that we are just a tiny drop in an ocean of others who are so much better than we are. What do we have to offer the world? We convince ourselves that we aren't anyone of value, so the painting goes undone, the book isn't written, the speech is never delivered, and the healing prayer is never spoken. It's just another way to keep ourselves safely tucked away out of the limelight. Yet, Proverbs 18:16 states, "A man's gift makes room for him." (NKJV)

So, instead of sitting on the sidelines, making excuses while God waits to do the best divine work ever in your life, be willing to step into the real reason why you were created and live out your true purpose.

Nonfiction

GOOD FRIDAY AND THE FLOOD

C.J. WELLUMSON

Editor's note: As we assemble this book, Stillwater, Minnesota, has been on alert for flooding. As serious as this promises to be, however, it is neither the first nor the most severe in Stillwater's history. For that, read on.

During Easter vacation of our college Freshman year, three buddies and I were joy riding in a friend's shiny new 1965 Oldsmobile Cutlass hardtop when an announcement interrupted the tunes blaring from the radio. The local rock-and-roll station broadcast a call for volunteers to head to Stillwater, Minnesota, and to get there fast. The St. Croix River was rising and threatened the historic riverside town with flooding. We all agreed to answer the call, then drove the thirty-five miles to face the emergency. It was April and Good Friday.

Once we arrived in Stillwater, officials sent us to the parking lot of Hooley's grocery store, adjacent to the riverbank.

A man greeted me warmly, handed me a shovel, and pointed toward a round mountain of fine brown sand. "Only three scoops per bag," he said. "They can't carry more than that."

A line began forming behind me—all young people, some maybe

junior high age, others looking to be in their older teens. They'd each hold a cloth bag open as I dumped in the three heavy scoops. Once loaded, they disappeared, and the next person stepped forward, somewhat like water instantly pouring in after scooping out of a cup.

Zick was the sound the shovel made when I thrust it into the dry sand. Aim, thrust, *zick*, turn, drop the load into the bag, repeat. Nonstop. Hour after hour. I'd sometimes need to tell a few of the smaller kids to hold the bag farther open, and once I'd loaded it, they would hurry over to the dike.

The high school let the kids out to help. The nearby Stillwater State prison allowed trustees to join in. Volunteers from other areas, who had worked six-to-eight-hour shifts, were given cots to sleep on in the Armory. American Red Cross and Civil Defense vans provided sandwiches and hot cocoa.

The dike, or levee, was five thousand feet long, nearly a mile. From my vantage, it only looked a hundred yards wide. The rest was out of my sight range. It was almost eight feet high when I started. Men walked on the top and yelled information about how high the river was. Civil Defense and Red Cross loudspeakers reminded us that we were only one sandbag ahead of the rising water. No one relaxed. Aim, *zick*, drop, run. An endless cycle. Large dump trucks would appear, deliver more sand, then make room for the next one.

Now and then, a young boy with a new bag would greet me with, "Hi again. I'm back," or something similar.

I might reply, "We're beating that river," or, "You're doing great."

The only other human sounds I recall came from the loudspeakers on the tops of vans. They'd remind us of the sobering news: the river hadn't yet crested. We all wished it soon would.

I somehow sensed how high and perilous that river was, though I never saw it, hidden behind the levee and our crowning rows of sandbags. I felt it, the power and potential danger. The sound of rushing water and the damp air contributed. The men walking the top looked straight out toward the water, not down. They also searched for any areas where the dike might let go.

If it did, where could we run? I imagined the rushing water coming after us. I'm sure we all did. Maybe we could make it to the roof of the grocery store, or up the hill that rose toward Main Street.

Officials instructed many of the store owners to fill their basements to the top with clean water. This would equalize the pressure if the flooding did gorge on their buildings, and it would keep them from collapsing.

I learned later that a rumor was spreading that the dam upriver at Taylors Falls might break. I was fortunate to have never heard that story, and thankfully it never did let go.

I was young and at or near my peak in physical strength. Manual labor for all those hours came easy, but sometime toward twilight, my forearms began to give out. I wouldn't be able to lift sand much longer.

Thankfully, someone soon told us, "Stop, we beat it."

We'd sandbagged high enough that the experts said, even though the river hadn't crested, it could no longer rise high enough to breach the top of our bags.

During those long hours, I'd lost track of my friends. We reconnected at the Red Cross truck and received sandwiches and pop. None of us spoke much as we ate. Our ride home was unusually quiet, but joyful. We'd done something to be proud of.

The St. Croix crested on Easter Sunday.

Years later, I learned much about that weather event. For example, none of the other dikes in Minnesota had held. Not one.

The National Weather Service in Chanhassen reported that the flooding resulted from a perfect storm of coincidences. They said heavy rains in the fall had saturated the ground to the point that it couldn't absorb more water. Add to that an extremely dry, cold winter with a frost depth that was tremendous. "Very, very, very deep," they said. And further, "Lack of a snow blanket kept the ground completely frozen. In March, unseasonably cold, twelve to fifteen degrees below normal, four snowstorms fell. The snowpack was almost twice as much as normal." A river of water waited in that snow. With April's warming, rains added to the water level, then came the melting that could only run above the still frozen ground.

Mark Seeley, a University of Minnesota professor and climatologist, said, "It was unbelievable. When you have a weather event of that magnitude, it stays with the residents for the rest of their lives." He added, "It's a convergence of all the right factors."

The National Weather Service ranks the spring flooding of April 15 through 18, 1965, as the worst Minnesota has ever seen. Fifteen people died.

I was fortunate to be with like-minded guys who answered the call for help. Funny thing is, I don't recall us ever talking or bragging about that day. I remain proud of our efforts, though, and happy to have the memory and the visions from it.

Today, as you drive into Shakopee, Minnesota, and cross the river, a sign stands next to the road that states, "High Water Mark— April 1965." A thick black line across the sign's white background indicates the water's height. It's above the top of my car. There are other signs, too.

Every time I see one, I'm reminded.

To this day in Stillwater, residents speak of "The Teenagers' Dike"—the eight-foot-high, mile-long levee that saved their downtown. Everyone got along...kids, adults, prisoners, too. The dirt that built the dike was later used to make ball fields and tennis courts at Lily Lake.

Today, any of those teens still remaining could be grandfathers like myself. I hope they tell their youngsters the story—how, day after day and united in spirit, ragtag groups of kids, including ours, held back a mighty river.

JUST JUMP
BRIDGETT POWERS

"C'mon, just jump!" my cousin Donna taunted from below. "Your feet are closer to the ground than your eyes are."

I shook my head. "Uh-uh."

In our six short years, she'd told me plenty of other things, too. Things that hadn't worked out the way she'd said. Like, if you thread a straight pin just beneath the skin of your hand, it won't hurt.

It had.

Oh, I'd watched her and her sisters and neighborhood friends jump off that porch a dozen times each. They were all fine, still running and riding and skipping rope—no broken bones. But I wasn't like them. They rode ten-speeds and played softball and wandered the alleys and backstreets of their neighborhood with no adults around to make sure they didn't get lost...or run over by a car... or eaten by the Doberman they'd never see coming.

I wanted to do those things, too. I looked down at the carpet of green stretched deceptively soft below me. Could I?

"I'm serious!" Donna shouted. "It's not that far. It just looks like it because your head's way higher than your feet."

Not *that* much higher. When you're the smallest kid in your class, so nearsighted you have to use schoolbooks bigger than you are, and have no depth perception, three feet may as well be three miles. I mean, it took four tall, concrete stairs to reach this slab of gray I was standing on. From the ground, my head would barely poke above the porch. And that ground wasn't as soft as the springy grass growing on top of it.

Just then, my aunt squeaked through the storm door and stopped beside me. "What're y'all doing?" she asked.

Aunt Lou always seemed to get me. I could talk to her. Except, I couldn't say a word.

"Trying to get her to jump off the porch with us," Donna said. "She's scared. Tell her, Mom. Her feet are closer than her eyes."

"She's right," Aunt Lou said. "You'll land on your feet. I'm right here if you want to try."

Well, if she said it wouldn't hurt...

My heart would probably jump to the ground before I did. I swallowed half the air in the yard, closed my eyes, and...

That split-second held within it a future of leaps yet to come, some of which Donna again instigated—like tricking me into riding my first loop roller coaster—while others would fulfill more lasting purposes. Imagine me, legally blind and going off to college in a city of strangers...or flying for the first time, alone...or after decades of preparation, leaving behind the career I'd planned for since before that day on the porch, to enter a world of uncertain heights and vast empty air—becoming an author.

My hair blew back from my face, I flailed my arms, and...*oof*. My knees buckled, but I didn't even fall over.

I straightened to the sounds of Donna's clapping and yelling, then looked around, unable to believe the world was still the same.

"Well?" Donna said.

I grinned and ran back up the steps.

I'm still climbing.

However out of reach the next goal might appear, God always reminds me to just jump. My feet are closer to it than my eyes.

25

For more information on Bridgett's books, visit her website: BridgettPowers.com.

RIDING THE RAILS
MARIAN CANFIELD NEWGORD, AS TOLD TO MARY ANN LENARZ

"Papa, Mama, hurry!" I shouted, jumping into the back seat of our old Buick touring car. "Let's go! It's a long way."

I fidgeted with the folds of my dress...white, as always. In all my eight years, Mama had seldom let me wear any other color—from my dresses to the giant bows she tied in my black curls—and I had to dress up *all the time*. Boys were lucky. Still, we were leaving for our annual trip to Mason City, Iowa, where Mama's sister lived. If my parents moved any slower, though, it would be 1920 before we got there.

At last, they came out of the house. As Papa cranked the motor, Mama put a picnic lunch in the back with me. The motor caught, and Papa got in as the car rumbled and shook. He turned around and smiled.

As he put the car into gear, it lurched ahead, and Mama held onto her hat.

"Oh, dear," she said, "be careful!"

He just laughed and kept on driving. That old car chugged away, and I laughed, too. I loved Papa so much and wanted him to be proud of me. He always made me smile.

I couldn't wait to get there. Sometimes, I got to stay overnight at my friend Jeannette's. Uncle Charlie was a lot of fun, too. He was an engineer for the railroad and let me do almost anything I wanted. He and Aunt Mary lived with my grandma, and though I had no cousins, I always had a good time with them.

I couldn't wait to stay in their big house again, with its winding staircase and window seat by the fireplace in the parlor. The back yard was enormous, and people came from miles around just to see Grandma's beautiful rose garden.

I sat in back alone, watching the scenery throughout the tedious auto trip. It took six hours in that old Buick, along some pretty awful roads. We drove from the city to the country, passing cows and sometimes horses. Big red barns dotted the countryside, adding splashes of color to the fields of wheat and corn.

We had to stop three times. Once for a flat tire, another for our picnic, and then for the mud. The ride was dusty and bumpy in dry weather, but when it rained, the road turned slick, and we got stuck. When it got too bad, Mama pulled the isinglass curtains.

When the rain finally cleared, Mama opened the windows, and I tried not to fidget. Then, I saw it coming...

"Papa, a train!" I stuck my head out and waved. "It's going the same way we are."

The wheels clickety-clacked on the rails as the engineer pulled the whistle and waved back. The long train took forever to pass us, with its passengers and the freight cars at the end. Then, the caboose came, and another train man waved. I sighed as the train disappeared.

I sat down, smiling. "Papa, do you think that was one of Uncle Charlie's trains?"

"I don't know, honey. You'll have to ask when we get there."

As we pulled into Mason City, I stared out the window at the apple trees lining the boulevards. In Minneapolis, we had elm trees, but on our street, they were very small. Papa had planted the first little elm in front of our house.

When we arrived, I jumped out of the car and ran past the roses into Grandma's arms. Aunt Mary met us on the porch, and the smell of Grandma's fresh bread made my mouth water. Even though we'd stopped for a picnic lunch in an empty school yard along the way, I was famished. Fresh, warm bread with butter melting on it was always a special treat.

When Uncle Charlie came home from work, he gave me a bear hug and said, "I'm happy to see you all, especially my favorite niece." He looked at Mama and Papa. "Tomorrow's my day off. I'd like to take Marian down to see the trains."

'"Will you really, Uncle Charlie?" I squealed. "Really take me?" I wanted to jump up and down, but that wasn't ladylike.

Mama gasped. "Why, Charles, she'll come home filthy dirty!" she said, as if that would be the worst thing that could happen.

"Now, Anna," Uncle Charlie said, "every child needs a little dirt now and then, but I'll do my best to keep her clean."

I looked at Papa with pleading eyes. He was on my side, surely. "Oh, Papa, can I go? I want to go. Please say yes."

In the end, Papa and Uncle Charlie won out. I was going to see the trains in the roundhouse! I went to bed that night, more than anxious for morning and my big adventure with Uncle Charlie and Papa. It took a while, but I finally drifted off to sleep.

✒

Next day, I was scrubbed and shining. With my little hand in Uncle Charlie's on one side, and my other in Papa's on the other, we walked the short distance from the house to the rail yards.

The place was enormous, noisy, and dirty, with steam engines belching their sooty smoke into the air. The roundhouse was just that—a huge, round, red brick building where the trains came to be checked and maintained. Each locomotive would drive onto a large track on a turntable, where it rotated until it came directly even with a length of track over a pit. It ran onto that short track, where a mechanic could service it.

Uncle Charlie took me around to meet his friends who worked for the railroad. "This is my niece, Marian," he said, "from Minneapolis."

As we walked through the yards, he pointed out a big, black locomotive, hissing and steaming, getting ready to drive into the roundhouse. He waved at the engineer, and the next thing I knew, Uncle Charlie grabbed me and handed me up into the engine. I forgot about my white dress, white stockings, and silk bow. I was riding the engine!

My heart raced as I pulled the whistle cord and the engine chugged into the roundhouse, with me in the driver's seat. It settled neatly on the turntable. The engineer laughed at my obvious excitement, and I could hardly sit still. Uncle Charlie chuckled, too, when he retrieved me from the cab of the locomotive.

"Why are you laughing, Uncle Charlie?" I asked.

"Oh, Mari," he said, as he flicked my chin, "you should see yourself. Your mama is going to have my hide. By my soul, you're as sooty as the coal man." And he let out a roaring belly laugh.

Behind him, Papa was laughing, too. He dabbed at my nose and cheeks with his big white hanky, brushing at the black smudges. I didn't care how dirty I was. I couldn't wait to get back and tell everybody about my great train ride.

"Uncle Charlie," I asked, "can I do that again?"

"Well, honey, I suppose sometime. We'll just have to catch your mama in the right mood, won't we?"

"Thank you," I said, and gave him a big hug. I wanted to sing and dance my way home. I'd just had an adventure I would remember all my life.

Mama didn't get too angry about the dirt. In fact, she seemed pleased that I had such a good time, but I had to clean up right away. "You can wait one more day to see your friend," she said.

As I snuggled down for the night in the big back bedroom, the breeze sent the smell of roses through my window. I would see Jeannette first thing in the morning and tell her all about today. I sighed when a train whistled in the distance. Maybe I'd be the first woman engineer when I was grown. I smiled and closed my eyes, already dreaming of steam locomotives and engineers.

ANXIETY: FINDING BEAUTY IN THE ASHES

SUSIE JONES

ANXIETY WAS my reality for over thirty years. It is the biggest thief you will ever meet. Count on it to steal your time, memories, and peace, then dictate what you can and can't do. It will come for your sanity and tear away at your soul until you no longer want to live. For me, ending it all wasn't an option, because my fear of death was worse than the anxiety. Still, I longed for an end to find peace. That elusive relief did come…at a time when *no one* would have expected it.

The account you are about to read gives you a glimpse into the war I waged between my relationship with God Almighty and the hell I was enduring at the hands of this thief, anxiety. In the heat of battle, sometimes all we can do is hope for a way of escape. I found mine and pray this story will give you the courage to keep fighting for yours.

I didn't come into a relationship with the Lord until my college years, so I guess you could say I was a late bloomer. Becoming a believer, however, provided another problem for me in dealing with anxiety. *Miffed* would be an understatement for how I felt when I encountered a massive contradiction between the promises in the Word and my experiences. I believed in healing and knew what Jesus did for us on the cross, so why had God abandoned me to this disease?

Let me first preface this account by saying: God deals with everyone differently. The one-fix-fits-all method doesn't apply to our Heavenly Father. Well-meaning preachers sometimes supply their solution for what ails us. Meaning, they blame *us* for our failure to get healed, but they haven't walked in our shoes, nor are they God. How God comes to your rescue is between you and Him. He knows each person's heart, what they can take, what they will accept, and what they believe. Scripture reminds us that God will not give us more than we can handle, so remain fierce through the struggle and hold on, no matter what.

I've known nothing so terrible as anxiety—it's a horrible and debilitating disease. The origins of mine are unclear. I don't recall a specific circumstance or event that served as my trigger for terror. All I knew was, my soul felt shredded and grated like cheese as I battled for serenity every day.

There are no English words sufficient to describe what a giant monster this mental health issue is, but I will try to show you. We can't truly appreciate the victory, after all, until we've lived through the battle. Come along with me for a peek into a typical few days.

The workday begins. I close my eyes, hoping not to faint. I still have work left undone, and the kids at the childcare center need my attention. No one here knows how terrified I feel all the time. The days last forever, holding me captive to paranoid thoughts. I busy myself, looking for more to do, fighting through the dizziness and lightheadedness. Idle time would be worse. I tell myself over and over, *There is nothing to fear here. You are okay. You are safe.*

A sudden pain stabs at my head, while pinpricks race across the top of my skull, creating waves of nausea. My heart beats faster as my vision distorts, generating flashes of white light. I am *not* safe.

Something is wrong. *Not my brain, Lord,* I pray. *I can never let them put me in an MRI machine again.* My heart beats faster as I recall the last time.

My airways narrow and tighten. Breathe…scan the room…find a focal point. *Breathe! In, out, in, and out.* It's no use. The walls close in, regardless. I am trapped with no way out. My mind races with irrational thoughts hyper-focused on every pulsing, pounding, and stabbing sensation my body is undergoing.

What's about to fail? Is this the day the panic seizes my life? My chest tightens, an invisible hand grabbing at my throat, leaving me gasping for air. Trembling legs and muscle weakness make my knees buckle. The room has disappeared. Only black circles containing specks of light remain.

I've tried all day not to take medication. I want to be brave, but Xanax will quiet my mind and body.

A half hour stretches out like days before the medication will bring peace. Who hears my tortured cries? Who knows that it will take everything I have to get through this day and not die? I must watch the time to make sure I don't take the next dose too late and allow the torment to start all over again. Maybe now I can complete the day's work.

When work ends, I head for a home where no one will greet me. I miss being married and the calming warmth of physical touch. Having a companion helped. No other comfort has proven as effective for me. Being by oneself is terrifying. What if I die and no one finds me? Will I be able to call for help soon enough? What if my heart stops and my life ends?

I wish the fluttering in my chest would cease. The sensation frightens me. Sweat breaks out across my brow, and intense bubbles of heat push their way out. The Bible says what a man thinks in his heart, so he is (Proverbs 23:7). I can't stop thinking about dying. Fear circles me like a predator stalking its prey.

Once I finally get home, I pour some wine and take another Xanax to dull my senses. Bedtime nears, but I must wait a while longer. If I retire too early, sleep will be brief and the night will draw out with intensified panic.

To ensure the escape slumber brings—quieting these tormentors who hunt me without mercy—I take a couple sleeping pills. They slide down easy. I'm halfway there. One more hour to wait. Another glass of wine will take the edge off. Night can't come soon enough. Staying awake is terrifying.

I try to read but cannot focus. So, closing my eyes, I take a deep breath and exhale enough air to fill a pinhole. Chills crawl up my spine, sending shivers throughout my body. At a sudden jolt of pain in my chest, my eyes open. I wince. Maybe under the bed covers, in utter darkness, comfort will find its way to me.

Standing, I try to gain my balance, then turn off the lights and stumble across the living room. The lightheadedness has taken full control. The carpet acts like poison ivy against my feet. Another annoying side effect of anxiety, itchy skin. Often, a stiff brush relieves that. My arms start tingling and my hands go numb, like they are asleep.

After climbing into bed, I roll to my side and say, "Alexa, enable sleep meditation."

Mild pinpricks target my legs and arms, but I focus on the recorded voice guiding me toward sleep. Soon, if I am lucky, I will drift off...I pray...I hope. Tears stream silently onto the pillow. I petition the Lord for peace and ask him not to let my life be taken tonight. I have little hope for anything better tomorrow. The world is a scary place. I pull the covers over my head, wishing to stay here, always.

Morning arrives. What is the time? Have I really made it through the night? *Bitter daylight, how I wish you weren't here.* My heart palpitates and then quiets. Before I can open my eyes or step out of bed, I take an account. How bad is the fear? Am I able to take a deep breath?

Nature calls, but I don't want to move. That's how the anxiety monster awakens. Am I okay? No out of the ordinary sensations plague me.

I offer a quick prayer. "Please, God, don't let today be like every other day. Grant me peace."

Maybe He doesn't hear me because I am not truly His child. If I were, why would He leave me in this condition? I believe in healing, after all.

In His Word, He says, "Let not your heart be troubled, neither let it be afraid." (John 14:27) How? I am exhausted. I don't have the wherewithal to fight anymore. Will He end it, or must I take a chance at something worse and end myself to find peace?

I stand to use the bathroom but grow dizzy, and black spots fill my vision. I don't feel well at all. My stomach churns, and my colon sends an even more urgent request. I make a mad dash to the bathroom, where I nearly pass out.

I can't face another day. Crawling back into bed, where I feel safe, I request a meditation from Alexa. My heart races but calms when the meditation recording begins.

At its conclusion, I rise and move slowly through my routine, trying not to wake the monster any further. Maybe if I am slow and deliberate, I will go unnoticed. Staying home is not an option. That's when the enemy really has its way.

Talking to God incessantly during the day brings milliseconds of peace. Prayers for an end to this agony occupy much of my mind, but death must be the only escape because God has not answered. Thinking this way brings the walls in close, and panic hijacks my body. There's nowhere to hide. My brain holds me hostage. I still my breaths, waiting for my heart to stop, because now I want it to.

Since my heart insists on thumping away, I force myself to go about today's plans, picking up supplies for home. For some reason, a break comes. *Thank you, God, for this moment.* How beautiful the world is when the monster sleeps.

Chores and errands serve as a pleasant distraction. Driving is calming. The faces in the grocery store are more in focus than usual. I envy all the shoppers for how at ease they seem. If only I could be anyone else other than myself. I must hurry before the peace leaves. What are the odds of outrunning anxiety? Impossible...and breaks like this are few.

Meditation helps, but it lasts a short time and isn't strong enough to rewire my brain. Neural pathways that take me to the edge run deep. The monster has trained them well. Treatments such as brain spotting, EMDR, and talk therapy dominate my free time.

I even tailor my eating habits. Clinical studies claim nuts and fish help ease anxiety. Maybe if a person could eat enough of them. Then what? Mercury poisoning? No thanks.

Yoga offered a distraction until I tore my meniscus. The doctors never mention shock therapy or a frontal lobotomy. I wish they would. With all the methodologies I'm throwing at this thing, you'd think one of them might be forceful enough to cause a monster exodus.

After that brief dive into the battles I faced, you'll be happy to learn that my story begins to wrap up with this bit of revelation: When someone makes you a promise, there is nothing you need to do beyond receiving it. The same is true for gifts. When God is the one making the promise, the outcome *will* be favorable—because He never lies, and He does not break His oath—no matter what we do.

He says, "...seek and you will find; knock and the door will be opened to you." (Matthew 7:7, NIV) He will deliver—He doesn't know how to withhold. Be patient and wait, then trust. Restored health is His promise! Healed sicknesses and diseases are a done deal! Jesus took them on the cross.

Many times, I meditated on this, trying to keep hope alive. It's difficult to believe when daily life is a struggle or when you feel like an ineffective Christian and a failure. After all, that exact condition raged within me for over thirty years.

I did everything people suggested. I read scripture, claimed scripture, and prayed until I ran out of words. I prayed in the spirit, took communion, got counseling, and read self-help books. I depleted financial resources on essential oils, counseling, and pills. Sometimes, I did nothing...out of sheer exhaustion.

The books seemed to point out all the mistakes I'd made. When I changed my methods, still nothing helped. Despondency produced anguish, so I quit searching for an answer and accepted my lot in life. The lack of results had to be proof—nothing would change.

Then, something did. (Shh. You won't see this one coming. I sure didn't.)

In January 2021, ten days after my sixty-fourth birthday and still in the middle of all the changes the coronavirus pandemic had foisted on us, the Lord told me to do a self-exam. How did I know God spoke, you ask? Because it happened right after my morning prayer time, and that topic hadn't been so much as a blip on my radar.

He said, "You need to do a breast exam."

"Why?" I asked. To which I got no response. I am, however, positive an eye roll occurred—and it wasn't mine.

To make a long story short, I did the exam, found a lump, agreed to a biopsy, and received the dreaded diagnosis.

Cancer pandemic-style meant no contact with family and quarantining for fourteen days. I put my nose to the prayer and Bible-reading grindstone for two weeks, trying to get my faith in line with God's word. No surprise, my anxiety had risen to new heights once news of cancer hit and I was forced into being even more alone than usual.

On the morning of surgery, insanity had reached an all-time high. The monster held me paralyzed in bed. I turned on a healing video, trying to screw up the courage to drive myself to my daughter's. From there, she would take me to the hospital.

At the end of the teaching video, the preacher said, "An evil spirit has tormented someone who's watching right now in their mind for years. God is going to take it from you this minute."

I threw my arms into the air and shouted, "I receive that!"

In an instant, my entire body tingled with an unfamiliar energy. Then, something pulled away from my shoulders and let go. A peace came over me so profoundly, I broke into tears—a tranquility I'd never known in my life. My mind grew clear and quiet, and the colors everywhere shone brilliant.

I arrived at the hospital with no fear and a calm that held even through the two-and-a-half-hour wait to get into surgery. In the past, anxiety would have kept me away from the surgery center or forced me to leave.

I awoke from surgery to a voice saying, "I will restore you to health and heal all your wounds."

At first, I thought the nurse had said something, but she assured me she hadn't spoken. I knew that voice, the same one who'd told me to get tested.

Weeks later, test results proved God had made good on His promise. I didn't require any further treatments. That was February 24, 2021, and even now, anxiety is a distant memory.

Why my healing came when it did remains a mystery. The only thing I had changed was deciding to give up on being delivered—which certainly wasn't a demonstration of great faith. Everyone has a breaking point and fails, but God still cares. He doesn't give up, even if we do.

One of my pastors once said, "If you don't have faith, then ask for mercy."

During my walk with God, several notable miracles have happened. Four other times, I've received healing for incurable diseases. I know He is merciful, whether I am faith-filled or a blathering idiot with none. He is consistent and steadfast. God keeps His promises. He orchestrates all the details in your life that need fixing.

So, before you contemplate your end or stop hoping, remember that God will never leave you or forsake you. Not ever! No, *never*! So, don't give up! Because you never know—tomorrow could be your day of deliverance. Don't fear the future. God is already there.

While you sleep tonight, He will be putting together your solution. Believe that and look for it like a lost treasure. Grab every bit of hope you can find, make note of it, and wait for the fulfillment of God's promises. Don't settle! It's coming!

May whatever you are experiencing today become a distant memory, starting tomorrow, in Jesus's Name. Have faith in His name —it's that simple. Say it, "Jesus, Jesus, Jesus."

THE DATE

KATHARINE GRUBER

DURING CHRISTMAS VACATION IN 2003, my parents invited my family to visit the famous Dayton's of Minneapolis, eighth-floor Christmas display. We enjoyed immersing ourselves in that year's theme based on Roald Dahl's book *Charlie and the Chocolate Factory*. However, nothing prepared us for the cruel comments we heard later that day.

The display ended at the entrance to the gift store. My oldest eyed the brain teasers and books, while his brother gravitated toward the model dinosaurs. My Dad intercepted them before they reached their targets.

"How would you like to eat lunch at Applebee's?" he said while wrapping an arm around each one.

I mouthed a silent "Thank you" as my sons exclaimed in unison, "Yes!" They each grabbed one of Grandpa's hands and pulled him towards the elevator.

"Hey! Settle down, or we will go straight home!" Dad said. I'm amazed at how our rambunctious boys became calm and polite when threatened with losing the privilege of eating out with them.

Now at the restaurant, we ordered while the conversation flowed. Grandpa asked the boys which scene they liked the best. Jon, the youngest, loved the animated scene where Charlie repeatedly pulled out the golden ticket, thanks to the magical animatronics. Timothy wanted to float up in the air like Charlie and his grandfather or shrink to fit in the story's television.

I glanced out the window as a baby blue 1970 Cadillac Coupe de Ville pulled up to the door. How it shined, all clean and waxed. A man in his 70's emerged from the car, dressed in his Sunday best. He walked to the passenger side, opened the door, and began assisting his date. She shifted her legs to the side of the seat as the man unfolded her walker. He placed his hand on her shoulder as she stood and grabbed the device, her neck hunched. She pushed the walker, paused, walked two steps, then repeated the process.

Together they made their way inside to a table. Her date, a gentleman from a different era, helped remove her coat. Once she was settled in her chair, and the server recorded their orders, he left to park his car. When he returned, their drinks arrived within minutes.

I tuned into the conversation with my family as they discussed more of their favorite scenes from Dayton's display. Somehow, my ears caught snippets of conversations around me.

"I can't believe they came to eat at a restaurant. She can't even drink without spilling."

I turned toward the upper section where the comment originated when I heard the people behind me say, "Look, she's drooling, how disgusting."

My eyes widened, as I looked around and saw more people staring at the couple.

"She shouldn't be allowed to eat here." The comment came from my left.

I, too, glanced at the older couple. Yes indeed, she had spilled her drink. Her date signaled the server to bring more napkins and replace her drink, while he chased rivulets of water with several napkins. As he wiped the table, he spoke to her in hushed tones, with a smile that never wavered. She grasped the toppled glass, but her hand tremors caused it to drum a staccato rhythm as she struggled for control.

The man steadied her hand, and together they placed the glass upright. Next, he dabbed her mouth and chin with a dry napkin. This time, he held her glass as she sipped from a straw. I imagined them on a date as teenagers or college sweethearts sharing a chocolate soda.

More disgruntled comments pierced my daydream. I nudged my husband and parents to notice. While glancing around at those cruel offenders with scrunched-up noses, I wanted to shout at them, "Look, do you not understand what's going on here? This is love."

TIME TO MOM UP

KRISTA ZOERB

While pregnant with my third, a multitude of unfamiliar women crossed my path with the same message: "I wish I'd had one more child." Like any other overloaded, short-sighted, unorganized 'live for the moment' woman, I ignored the universe trying to keep me from future regret.

Sure, kids are loveable (mostly), cute, and entertaining, and I did want to be a mother of four. Yet clearly, these prophet moms were not aware that I was *so* not qualified for parenthood. My general state of reality nine years before was: "What are you supposed to do with these people-things? I know...stick them in front of the TV!"

After my firstborn spent her first three years fixated on innocent cartoon fodder, I came across studies that found...guess what... children under three should watch zero hours of TV. Those, they say, are the most critical years of brain development.

Oops.

New motherhood seemed so overwhelming that I would get asthmatic toward the end of the day just watching my two nieces and four-month-old daughter. What were they doing to stress me out? Climbing on furniture, playing with toys, coloring pictures, eating, taking naps, and watching TV.

Hey, don't judge me! Crafting babies into toddlers is an intense business. Well, it is if you are, like I was, the Homer Simpson of moms.

As instructed in Home Ec. during high school, I'd carried around the sack-of-flour baby wrapped in a blanket for a couple of weeks. They never said anything about making eye contact or talking to that precious ground wheat. That's how babies learn to speak, right?

They definitely *never* taught us that babies are sponges who absorb your facial expressions, tone, and words. So, always use positive words that build, *not* condescending words spoken from angry faces. That will create a lack of self-worth, which can carry through to the teenage years, causing them to believe they are unlovable and will never be successful. Now, *that* would have been valuable information. Oh my, the power of words!

Every aggravated mom, at some time, says, "I hope you have a child just like you when you grow up."

My response to that was always, "Me too! 'Cause she'll be *awesome!*"

Where my first daughter, Veronica, was an innocent dove, the Lord saw fit that not only should I have a child like me, but my second daughter, Olivia, should be me magnified by ten.

As a kid, when I wanted my way, I would quietly hide in my thoughts and craft how to accomplish my goals undetected. As Olivia was growing into her personality of energetic persistence, I discovered that the age-old method of screaming wasn't creating any self-control in my preschooler or toddler.

I stocked up on parenting books and read about setting boundaries, taking away privileges or toys, and withholding rewards as motivation to behave. What do ya know? The whole 'control your emotions, not control *through* your emotions' deal worked. Great! Just in time...baby number three was on the way.

Shortly after the arrival of Hannah, my husband left his

corporate job to start his own business. Overwhelmed by the thought of three kids and a smaller income, I decided we were done having babies. At this time, my parents sold their business, thus ending my cake job of watching my own children while doing bookwork. Before job hunting came daycare hunting.

Turns out that putting three children in daycare is like paying a second mortgage, an expensive option. My husband suggested I start watching other people's kids, so I could be home and still have an income. Sounded simple enough. Oh, wait. Remember that part of living for today and possessing absolutely no organizational skills? I went for it anyway.

My days became filled with morning walks, the girls still in fairy costumes and bubbling from our early morning sugar-infused tea parties, and teaching them to shop for the best deals. That's a skill, right? "Okay, nap time. You go sleep so I can read my books and magazines." Then, I finalized the day with making fabulous dinners, except when they were gross.

Ah...me, me, me. It was all about me. Did I have to actually *work*? Do you mean, be a responsible parent *on purpose*?

Before offering to watch other children, I had to research as if studying for college finals. I printed off some daycare schedules and activities while old memories washed over me. My mother was a hippie version of Mary Poppins (kind of still is). She would take us on walks and teach us about animal and plant life. We'd play in the rain, bake bread and cookies, read stories, have artsy crafts time, go to beaches all summer, then go sledding and build snowmen all winter. Those aspects of childhood were ideal, and somewhat missing from my own kids' experience.

Having lost sleep at the thought of all the responsibility, I had to squash my apprehensions of inadequacy and "Mom up."

The two children I started with were typical boys. I had typical girls, typical nieces, and no boy experience whatsoever.

While keeping the kids on a busy schedule of learning, crafts, exercise, singing, story time, and playtime, with me as referee of toys, I'd hear passers-by comment, "You've got your hands full."

My response was always, "You got that right."

At the end of the day, I'd literally pass out on the couch.

Sometimes in tears.

With girls, everything was Barbies, cookies, glitter, ballet, and unicorns. Boys were a culture shock. It was superheroes, cars, trains, and kung fu. Each day was an amusement park of emotions. After several months of daily time-outs and meltdowns (them and me), I was so grumpy and exhausted that I fantasized about quitting. Add to that, trying to prep Veronica for kindergarten—and she did not want to prep—and I imagined myself sunning on a private sandy beach, sheltered by palm trees as I watched my apron wash out to sea.

My husband constantly repeated the words of our Pastor, "If you don't quit, you win."

Sigh...Don't quit...don't quit.

It dawned on me one morning that the things I did enjoy about life streamed all the way back to early childhood. Could the same be true for their childhood experience? Was I shaping their lives simply with the attitude in which I approach each task?

As I struggled up the hill, pulling a wagonload of kids, a Grinch's heartwarming scene unfolded. I prayed, "Lord, if this is what you really want me to do...I will do it and be happy." I decided to force myself to focus on the pleasant parts of the day in the midst of the unpleasant moments.

A miracle happened. A neighbor asked me to watch her infant. Her friend wanted me to take her little girl as well. Every cloud became an ice cream rainbow! Right away, I ended up caring for the busy boys, convinced this new task would be *so* much easier. The limits of my ability had been stretched.

It occurred to me that these children-critters were with me nine hours a day, and with their parents about five waking hours. I considered myself as much a parental influence as their own. My new decision to approach their flaws with the attitude of how to help them grow up was leaps beyond my previous thinking of, *When will this day end?* That was, indeed, a miracle.

My girls partially liked having playmates, and partly resented sharing me. All the while, my heart toward those children started to grow into compassion for all children. I found myself cooing at unfamiliar babies when in public. As the first two families moved on to corporate daycares, I found more parents seeking care for their kids. Regardless of what my girls didn't like, they had no idea I'd become a more hands-on mom than I would have been with only them.

Neighbors asked me to watch their children, or the neighborhood kids would just see a safe place to play and mix in for a couple of hours. At times, I could be entertaining eight to ten.

At the time of writing this, I often have six or seven kids swarming around me on bikes. Others chalk up the driveway while I'm pushing an eager learner on a bike and shouting, "Don't give up. You can do it!"

Now, when neighbors say, "You've got your hands full," my smiling response is, "This is nothing." And now I know, even if I would've had that fourth child I wanted, this would still be "Easy, peasy, make my cake cheesy!"

Several years after writing the original version of this, I had that fourth baby, one more girl. She is delightful, and my life is full.

CAN FEAR BE CONQUERED? HERE'S MY STORY

SHARON ROSE

LIFE THREW a plot twist at me. It didn't even have the decency to foreshadow the event. Very rude. I had no time for this in the middle of launching a book! Ironically, my personal plot twist (a heart attack) touched on a theme from my upcoming novel—fear.

That's the beauty of fantasy stories. You can take a concept out of our everyday world, look at it differently, and gain new insights. But do those insights work in the real world?

After experiencing a heart attack, I can report that conquering fear works as well in practice as it does in a fantasy adventure.

You may have heard that heart attack symptoms can be confusing in a woman. True. Every woman that I've told this to asks me for the details, so I'll be complete, even though one detail is gross.

The first symptom felt like hunger. A few minutes later, diarrhea hit. I assumed I'd picked up a stomach bug of some sort. Then, a weird pain started in my sternum. Yeah, that's in the chest, but my bone hurt, not my heart. It wasn't even on the left. Then came the rush through both arms and up to the top of my head. Intense sweating next. It all ebbed and flowed, so I lay in bed, feeling awful and hoping it would go away.

After ten minutes, I called for an ambulance. (Copy me on this if you ever suspect a heart problem! DO NOT spend days hoping it will go away. That isn't how the heart works.)

At this point in telling my story, I usually hear, "That must have been so scary!" I don't fault anyone for thinking that. We are programmed to fear heart attacks. People die from them. People are debilitated by them. Good source material for fear, right?

Actually, I've been challenging fear for several years, and it gets easier with practice. So no, I was not afraid. I *was* uncomfortable. I *did not* want to face a heart attack or whatever this bad thing was. But fear simply had not occurred to me yet.

About the time I was being lifted into the ambulance, a thought went through my head. *This is really happening, and it's not good.* I don't do fancy prayers, but I know God loves me, so my silent prayer went something like: *God, I can't do anything about this, so I need you to take care of it for me.*

His answer? *I've got you,* along with a strong feeling of being safely held.

From that point on, I figured my one useful task was to rest, so I did. About halfway through the twenty-minute drive to the hospital, it dawned on me that any normal person would be afraid. *Shouldn't I be concerned? What ramifications lie ahead—what effect on my future?* I considered for a second, then decided, *No. Rest is working quite well. I'm staying with that.*

Please don't think I'm bragging. It took me a long time to even realize this was possible. Fear is common in our world, but it is not normal. It is not useful. It is *not* required. You DO NOT have to bow to fear.

Back to my story. I'll spare you all the details, though I must offer gratitude for the medical staff, friends, and family who supported me during a hard time. They were all wonderful. At the time of writing this, I'm three weeks past the big event, and I want to tell you the results of my non-normal approach.

First, enduring a health challenge without fear is far more comfortable than worrying all the way through it. I've tried both approaches. Rest is way better.

The heart attack was caused by a blood clot in an artery. Fun fact: I have unusually large arteries.

My cardiologist walked into my room the next morning with a huge smile and said, "You turned out to be really interesting!"

Huh. Well, at least she was smiling.

Within twenty-four hours of the first chest pain, I felt fine and still do. After many tests, the cardiologist reported that I have healthy arteries, valves, and heart muscle. I asked about damage to my heart, and she said, "*Very* little," with strong emphasis on *very*.

I was in the hospital for six days because of an IV blood thinner. Fortunately, the nurses showed me how to put the heart monitor on battery power, so I could get around on my own. I was released with no restrictions, and I'm back to my regular exercise.

Sound too perfect? I love how this worked out, and I won't apologize for it! Some call this a miracle. Some say my good results are from getting to the hospital fast. Both may be true. I'm just thrilled that I sailed through without fear.

I find one thing strange. When I've talked about having no fear, either during the event or in my ongoing activities, I've gotten worried looks and advice. "Be careful...be safe...abundant caution is best." They mean well, I'm sure.

Our society seems to believe that the absence of fear is denial. Fear is assumed to motivate wise actions. The reverse is true, but few realize it. If you stand against fear, expect pushback.

There are many challenges in life, and we will all go through some of them. Challenges may turn out well...or not. Fear never prevents them or makes them easier. It can make them worse. I will defy fear the rest of my life, no matter how many people think I'm wrong.

I've told you my story to encourage you. Fear CAN be overcome. It's incredibly freeing, so I hope you start your own anti-fear mission.

For more information on Sharon Rose's books, visit her website: SharonRoseAuthor.com.

WABS AND ANGEL

C.J. WELLUMSON

Poverty had bought me a summer of sleeping on my friend Jerry's couch. His upper duplex apartment in south Minneapolis was in Indian Town. That's what everyone called it. Fortunately, the residents tolerated the white-collar Irishman and me, his Norwegian carpenter guest. We all got along well.

I was young and starting a new business, carpentry and contracting for hire. I'd try anything that I could talk someone into letting me build.

My entire estate included a tool kit, clothes, a fine guitar, and a 1965 Chevy pickup. By personal survey, over half of those Chevy pickups were the same awful green color. This one didn't have a second gear. Only first and third worked, making smooth driving impossible.

It was ownership of that truck that kept me up and working one night until sunrise. Not only working for free, but ultimately paying for my generosity. This misadventure started late on a Friday afternoon.

"I'm off to work," Jerry announced. I worked days, but he was on nights.

"See you tomorrow," I said. "Let's play some music over the weekend."

He grinned. "Sounds good. Call Duffy, too. We're overdue for an all-night jam session, and Saturday's tomorrow."

I now had something to look forward to. I'd worked hard all week in the August heat, building a large and somewhat complex deck for my former high school Vice Principal. To say I was tired would be a start, exhausted gets closer, but that can't fully express it. I had staggered into a twilight place somewhere between punch drunk and delirious. That lumpy couch was welcome this night.

The living room was filled with early evening summer sunlight. Too tired to pull the shades, disrobe, or even eat, I lay on my back for mere seconds before falling into the arms of Morpheus and finding blessed rest.

Three hours or so later, haunting sounds reached me through a distant and hazy tunnel. *Boom...boom...boom!*

What was this invasion? In a semiconscious fog, I wished this intrusion would stop.

Reality returned suddenly. I sat up, but still was as much asleep as awake. Again, came the incessant pounding on the front door, along with the muted voices of Wabs and Angel, two young Native American kids I'd befriended. Or had they befriended me? They were about eleven and nine, a brother and sister who lived next door. I was fond of both.

"C'mon, open up," Wabs said. "Mom needs you to help us. C'mon, hurry!"

I groaned. "Wabs, that you, man? Hold on, I'll get the door. Wait up and don't pound on it anymore. Please stop it." Now on full alert, I forgot how tired I'd been a few hours earlier. The blessing youth brings to strength was helpful. I opened the door.

Wabs didn't give me time to take a breath. "Hey, my mom needs your truck, and you, too. We have to move over to Little Earth now, tonight. Let's go. She says come over, and you'll get paid, too, but come over now, quick."

Little Earth is an inner-city Native American community about a mile away from where we lived. It consists of modern townhomes that are rented to the local tribe's people.

"Give me a few minutes," I said. "I was sleeping, so tell her I'll be right there."

"Okay, I'll tell her you promised."

"Promised what, man?"

"Hurry up," he said, already turning away. "See you at Mom's."

He wasn't taking no for an answer. I didn't consider that their failure to plan ahead wasn't my problem. I only knew my young friends needed me, and that's what mattered. But why should I hurry? This sounded like a trap, or a trick, maybe something I shouldn't rush into. In spite of those misgivings, I sprang down the stairs and straight to their house. Maybe Wabs was kidding. Could be a setup. Would I get hit with water balloons or firecrackers?

Considering what happened that night, either would've been merciful.

Wabs's mother wasted no time explaining that she needed me and my truck to move them now, tonight. "Welfare will pay you," she said. "Here's my worker's name and number. Call her Monday, first thing. They pay sixty dollars. Call her, you'll see. Done this before."

"How much stuff do you need moved, Marjorie?" I asked. "And who's going to help me with the heavy things?"

"Wabs!" she bellowed. "Get your cousins over here. We gotta go. Get them fast."

I frowned. Were they sneaking out on the landlord? It didn't matter. I was going to do this. If caught, I'd plead stupidity.

We worked half an hour and got the first load on the truck. Not a cardboard box was in sight. They'd packed loose items into pillowcases or tied them in sheets or blankets. Somehow, my own level of poverty seemed luxurious.

At Little Earth, we unloaded, then headed back to where we began. We dispatched another load as fast as the first. I was getting tired again but figured we could make it in maybe two more. My reward would be the return to needed slumber. Thoughts of my promised wealth also energized me, but two unanticipated surprises were waiting.

"You have to go to my sister's house next," Marjorie ordered. "I have things there, too."

She wasn't someone I'd ever choose to cross. Everyone, adults and children, gave her grace. A Native American friend of mine, Gino, had advised me to respect the men but keep my distance from an angry Native American woman. I paid attention.

I hoped this trip to the sister's was going to be a short one, but that hope floundered when they showed me around. As much or more than we'd already moved awaited our attentions.

"I can't do this with just Wabs, Angel, and one cousin, Marjorie,' I said. "I need help, and lots of it."

"Wabs, get Trinka's kids going, now," she commanded. "C'mon, get them over here quick."

Wabs jumped to it, and thank goodness, he returned with two strapping lads as able as he. All were heavyweights for their age. Five of us crammed into the truck's cab and drove off, leaving others behind to pack.

"Wabs, here's the deal," I said. "I'll split half of whatever welfare gives me if all of you promise, and I mean promise, you'll stay with me till everything is moved. I'm tired again, and you guys can't quit."

"You promise we get half, right?" he asked. "That's about thirty bucks' sure thing money. Okay, we'll work all night if we have to."

"Deal," I said.

We made four more trips before it was over. The first sunrays were just breaching the eastern horizon.

I rubbed my eyes. "See you next week, kids. And thanks. We did it, and you were great."

Angel pleaded in a soft voice, "Don't forget."

I couldn't let her down.

I'm not sure if they were Dakota Sioux or maybe Chippewa. There are several tribes in our area. It didn't matter. I was happy I could do this, because I'd now seen firsthand the legacy of the government's treatment of our native peoples. I patted myself on the back for willingness to make some amends, if only in this small way.

By the time Monday arrived, I'd forgotten about calling the social worker. My routines required focused attentions. At last remembering promises to the kids, I called the lady late in the day. She informed me that the moving money program had been discontinued only a month before. There would be no check.

I drove home from work carrying heavy concerns. Wabs and Angel were waiting on my front steps. How was I going to tell them no one was getting paid?

They surrounded me with their contagious anticipation. Angel tugged on my shirt, while Wabs twirled around me like a dervish. No doubt, I was certain, they had their own designs for every well-earned penny.

"Sit down, guys," I said. "I have something important to tell you."

"It's payday, right," Wabs asked, sinking onto the top step.

Angel plopped down next to him. "I'm buying a new doll."

I stiffened. "I have to tell you guys something serious. Uh, okay... well...uh, here goes. There's no check. I mean, I only have just...cash!" I hollered.

We all jumped and twirled about. Angel's hugs were as welcome as tulips in April. Wabs couldn't stop grinning and punching me on the shoulder. The sight of them skipping and spinning down the sidewalk delighted my soul.

I've spent thirty dollars thousands of different ways since that day, and forgotten where every nickel went, but thoughts of that investment will forever bring joy to my spirit.

ROAD TRIPPING WITH MOM

SUSIE JONES

ALMOST EVERY OCTOBER, Mom and I would embark on an annual vacation. We had earmarked 2020 as our year of fresh starts and boundless opportunities—a year for personal growth and monumental transformations. However, our expectations took a back seat with the arrival of the coronavirus famously known as Covid-19.

Instead of beginning the new adventures we'd envisioned, we found ourselves grappling with shortages of toilet paper and disinfectant products. The onset of the pandemic halted travel plans, shut down businesses, and forced schools to close their doors. Remote work became the norm, and virtual classrooms replaced traditional ones. Social distancing measures severed our connections with loved ones, driven by the constant threat of contagion. Media outlets bombarded us with escalating death tolls, instilling widespread fear. Masks became obligatory attire in public spaces, subject to the whims of gubernatorial mandates.

Indeed, life had undergone a significant shift.

After enduring seven months of mind-torturing isolation and replenishing our supplies of toilet paper, groceries, and hand sanitizer, we reached our limit. With air travel, train journeys, and cruises off the table, we turned our attention to the grand old tradition of road trips. We brainstormed destinations we could explore within a week, eager to drive anywhere—even off a cliff if necessary.

While my daughter and I had no qualms about staying in motels, Mom expressed discomfort with the idea. Acknowledging the importance of her health, we unanimously ruled out overnight stays and opted instead for day trips. With that in mind, we focused our destination choices on Mom's cherished memories—Mason City, Iowa, her birthplace; Faribault, Minnesota, where she'd attended boarding school; and Morgan, Minnesota, home to her century-old farmland.

Our first stop was Mankato, Minnesota, for a much-needed shopping spree. Mom and I shared a fondness for the same store, so we made a direct path to Christopher and Banks. Considering the ongoing pandemic we were enduring, a wimpy retail therapy session wouldn't suffice. What we needed was a substantial money dump to alleviate our stress. Our shopping excursion proved fruitful. The store was like an empty settlement, so the clerks on duty were all too helpful in finding us traveling clothes. We drew the line at matching masks.

Our next stop: Morgan, Minnesota, just an hour-and-a-half away. Armed with Google Maps and Mom's beloved road atlas, we prepared for the journey. Mom had a special affection for her maps, relishing her role as designated copilot and map expert. We kept electronic resources handy as a backup in case of any misreads.

Our primary goal was to discover picturesque byways along the journey. Since our trip occurred in mid-October, we eagerly expected to find enchanting, vibrant autumn hues and breathtaking landscapes—hence the reliance on the atlas. Unfortunately, Google Maps did not grasp our intention, and I struggled to communicate the need for something other than the quickest route.

With my copilot having charted our course, we embarked on our journey. Before leaving town, we made a quick stop at the nearest Walmart to pick up a set of three-pound weights I'd need for my physical therapy session after returning home that evening. Reflecting on it now, I have to laugh at how well-prepared we were for any potential encounters with bandits or suspicious characters along the route. Our arsenal included a fly swatter for swatting, a bag of weights for slinging, and Mom's cane for bashing. Plus, we had a box of Rice Krispies and a bag of marshmallows in case of a food emergency—although I preferred to combine them into a delicious Rice Krispie bar later, my reason for buying them in the first place.

As we traversed the back roads, we encountered farms unlike any I had ever seen. Vast expanses of fields stretched as far as the eye could see—some freshly harvested, while others were dotted with people on equipment tending to them. The farms we passed were substantial operations, with an abundance of expensive machinery and storage silos for corn and beans dotting the landscape. Semi-trailers were parked in the middle of nowhere, and various pieces of farm equipment diligently played their roles in the crop removal process. Brilliant green hues adorned some plots.

"Those have been sown with cover crops to prevent soil erosion during the winter," Mom explained.

"Where do the owners and workers spend the winter?" I asked.

"Many opt for warm-weather vacations as soon as the crops are harvested," Mom said, "or leave shortly after the Christmas holiday and come back in the spring."

As I stared at the fields, I pondered how easy we find it to overlook the effort behind our food. We never consider the demanding work of the farmers who make it accessible to us. For a moment, pride swelled within me at the knowledge that Mom's heritage has played a role in this process for countless years. Although she doesn't personally farm her land, she has rented it to the same family for the past five decades—a family deeply entrenched in agricultural pursuits. While I'd heard about the farm and even visited it in my youth, I hadn't had the opportunity to see it as an adult.

The journey was serene, with minimal traffic aside from the occasional semi-trucks transporting their harvest. The autumn hues adorned the trees, contrasting beautifully with the endless fields of golden corn. As the day progressed, the wind intensified, its force palpable against the car, causing occasional sways as we navigated the winding roads.

Compared to the frantic city driving in Minneapolis, this was a welcome change. Country drivers seemed more at ease, adhering to speed limits and showing consideration for others on the road—a refreshing concept. However, amidst this tranquility, one impatient driver sped toward us from behind a semi-truck, attempting to pass it. This reckless maneuver forced me to slow down and veer to the right to avoid a head-on collision.

After muttering a few swear words, I turned to Mom and asked, "Do you think they were visiting from Minneapolis?"

As we approached Morgan, Mom said, "I'm not sure which turn leads to my land, but we always looked for a nearby farm as a marker."

"Is the road gravel or paved?" I asked.

"Gravel," she said.

Glancing around, I groaned. All the roads in sight were gravel!

After exploring several of them, we returned to the main county road for another attempt.

"It was roughly six miles outside of Morgan," Mom said.

Despite multiple tries, we remained unsuccessful. I suggested driving into town and seeking guidance from the courthouse, where the deed might be on file, or asking another local authority.

Mom laughed. "There is no courthouse in Morgan."

It dawned on me that Morgan's population was only around 850. "What county are we in?" I asked.

"We are in Redwood County," she said. "Redwood Falls would be the nearest town with a courthouse, about twenty minutes away."

I sighed. "Since we're already here, shall we see what we can find out? After hours of driving, I could use a bathroom break, anyway."

We pulled into the only gas station in town, situated across from a grain mill. Semi-trucks, lined up six or seven deep, waited to be weighed in at the mill. Since this appeared to be the only activity in the area, I couldn't help but wonder if someone here might have information about our farmer.

"The land is situated across from a cemetery," Mom said, "but I don't recall its name."

My attempt to search for Morgan cemeteries online yielded an overwhelming number of results, suggesting that there might be more deceased individuals in the town than living ones. Unfortunately, this information didn't help, as the church had been demolished many years ago.

After leaving the gas station, we drove along Main Street, which spanned about two blocks. I spotted the post office and decided to pull over and try to gather some information. Someone here must know the farmer who had tended the land for the past half-century. After donning my mask, I entered the post office and approached the clerk behind the counter.

"Hello, my name is Susie," I said, smiling at him. "I'm here with my 91-year-old mom from Fairmont. We've been searching for her farmland, but she's unsure of the exact location. We were hoping to obtain the address of the farmer who has been caring for it for the past fifty years. Is there any way you could check the phonebook for his contact information? I understand that most people these days only use cell phones, but it might be worth a shot. We need him to guide us in the direction of the farm."

He retrieved the phonebook, but Warren's name was not listed. I brought it out to Mom, asking her to browse through the first names under our farmer's last name in search of Warren's father. Strangely, there were several matches, but Mom couldn't find the right one. I returned inside, where the clerk had taken out a plat book and managed to locate Warren's name, address, and phone number.

After thanking him, I took down the information and returned to the car.

I entered the address into Google Maps, and we set off. The destination was only about ten minutes away. Ordinarily, I might have been hesitant to visit a stranger's house unannounced, but Mom was acquainted with him. Besides, my confidence had grown a bit after spending the last three months knocking on doors for the US Census.

Upon reaching our destination, we proceeded up the quarter-mile gravel driveway leading to the house. I let out a breath at the sight of a car parked out front. I walked up to the door and knocked. A beautiful, black-and-white dog of the Aussie variety appeared on the other side of the screen door and fixed his gaze on me without making a sound. What an unusual encounter! I had never met a dog that didn't bark. Periodically, he would glance to the left. Drawing from my experience with animals during the census, I interpreted this as a sign that someone was home but chose not to answer the door. Despite knocking several more times and waiting, I received no response.

When I returned to the car, I dropped my keys into the center console and told Mom, "Instead of leaving, I think we should try calling the Redwood Falls courthouse. They might be able to provide us with directions since the land is registered, right?"

"Not necessarily," she said. "Since the land doesn't have any buildings on it, it doesn't have a specific address."

I turned my gaze towards her, raising an eyebrow. How would we ever find this elusive field? "Well, let's give it a try," I said. "First, I'll call the farmer's number and see if whoever is inside will answer the phone."

The call returned a recording saying that the number was out of service, which didn't come as a surprise. Then, the person who answered at the courthouse in Redwood Falls stated that they had no records of the land in Morgan and suggested contacting Brown County.

While I was on the phone with Brown County, a semi-truck sped up the driveway at about sixty miles per hour, kicking up clouds of dust and swerving. I frowned. That kind of driving was a bit hazardous for country roads.

"Mom, I think someone is coming home, and it might be best if we stay in the car for now," I said.

Just as I ended the call with Brown County, the driver of the semi-truck approached my window, his forehead furrowed. As I rolled the glass down, he tilted his head to the side, eyebrows raised. In an agitated tone, he asked, "Can I help you with something?" He stooped to gaze farther into the car, focusing on the passenger seat. "Pat?" he exclaimed. "Well, Pat! What are you doing here?"

He pressed a cell phone to his ear and reassured someone on the other end that everything was all right. Shortly after, a young boy of around ten emerged from the house. A few minutes later, a black car sped up the driveway like the truck had earlier.

As it turns out, visiting the post office in Morgan sets off a town-wide alert. Warren's wife's best friend happened to be working in the back room and overheard my conversation with the clerk. She called her friend and relayed a slightly altered version of events, claiming, "Someone said they've owned your farm for the last fifty years and need your address to talk to you."

At the same time, Warren's son, Landon, had called to inform him that a stranger had knocked on the door and was sitting in a car in the driveway. Warren, who was out working the fields, had jumped aboard the semi-truck to investigate. Meanwhile, his wife was also rushing home, spurred by her friend's account, to defend her family and property. Landon was visibly unsettled by the entire ordeal, while the dog, Rosco, remained indifferent.

"I tried calling first," I told Warren, "but the line was out of service."

He chuckled. "You won't believe it, but I accidentally cut the phone line with the weed whipper just this morning."

Warren was much younger than I'd expected and had a pleasant demeanor. We enjoyed a delightful conversation and shared laughter as we recounted the events leading up to this unexpected encounter. As a precaution for any future visits, we exchanged cell phone numbers.

After spending about an hour with us, Warren drew us a map. He told us the cemetery that overlooked Mom's land and served as the final resting place for her parents—an additional reason for our visit—still existed. We bade Warren farewell, and although I was tempted to ask whether we should skip calling next time and simply announce ourselves at the post office, I refrained.

En route to our destination, we made a point of writing down any road markers or distinctive landmarks to ensure we could find our way back. Surprisingly, even in the countryside, there were numbered street signs to guide us. Thanks to our excellent map, we reached our destination without any trouble.

The wind had intensified even further, swirling sand and cornstalks across the road, reminiscent of a Minnesota snowstorm but with different elements. As I stepped out to capture photos of Mom's parents' gravesites and the land, I felt as though I might be blown into another county. If I had been wearing a wig, it surely would have taken flight! Despite the blustery conditions, we fulfilled our mission.

Our excursion to Morgan on October 14th, 2020, proved to be one of the most enjoyable day trips of the week.

On the drive home, Mom told me about one of Dad's trips to Morgan, during which he was accompanied by a group of Episcopalian vestrymen who were in search of a new priest. On their way home, they'd decided to take a detour to find the farm and inspect its crops. Despite facing difficulties along the way, Dad managed to reach the parcel of land. However, his traveling companions never let him forget the challenges they endured trying to find it.

"So, you see," Mom said, "we weren't the only ones to get lost."

I laughed. "That's reassuring. So, how did Warren's family end up tending the land?"

"The farmer who did so before Warren's father, Allan, decided to stop farming," Mom said. "We needed to find a replacement, so your dad made another trip to Morgan, where he asked around town and visited nearby farms to see if anyone was interested in doing shares with the land. A few people mentioned knowing someone suitable but warned that he was Roman Catholic, a minority in German Lutheran Morgan."

Following the next curve in the road, I raised an eyebrow. "What did Dad say?"

"Oh, he didn't care about religious affiliations. He pressed for more information. Good thing, too. That original farmer turned out to be sloppy. The search for our current farmer led Dad to the grain elevator, where he sought recommendations from locals and was eventually given Allan's name. Elevators and post offices in Morgan have proven several times to be great resources. Who knew?"

Warren and his family transformed the land, which the previous farmer had nearly ruined, into a stunning property that Mom takes immense pride in. More importantly, she has forged a deep and enduring friendship with this remarkable family. I am grateful for such kind and caring individuals who look after her and watch out for her wellbeing. We consider them part of our extended family and hope to nurture our alliance with them for years to come.

Gone are our vacation days. Mom now lives closer to me, in an assisted living facility nestled in a northern suburb of Minneapolis. It's a mere fifteen-minute journey between us, a stark contrast to the three-hour distance we endured back in 2020 and for the last thirty years before that.

While she may no longer take extended trips as she once did, the unusual mild winter temperatures of 2024 in Minnesota have allowed us to enjoy delightful excursions lasting several hours. At 94, she needs the aid of a wheelchair during our outings, as well as our attentiveness to the terrain. My oldest grandchild usually accompanies us on these outings, turning our adventures into cherished family affairs, often featuring food and occasional playground visits amidst the paved trails of Minnesota's State and County Parks. Remarkably, we've already enjoyed three picnics this year, even amid the chill of January and a February that has been almost balmy.

Equipped with a yearly pass to state parks, we will adapt our outings to suit Mom's needs this year, ensuring she can savor the beauty of each passing season from the comfort of my car. I count myself fortunate to still have her by my side, dedicating myself to crafting experiences that will brighten her days.

She may not always recognize me, recall the day of the week, or even know which town we're in, but that makes the trips we took in 2020 to places from her past even more precious. My love of her remains unwavering, and in the face of time slipping away, making memories for me and my grandson is what truly counts. Better yet, is creating adventures for her—even if, tomorrow, they only linger in my mind and that of my grandson.

LITTLE BOXES

C.J. WELLUMSON

The United States was in a post–World War Two building frenzy when we moved into an emerging suburb. A few homes on our West 55th Street had been built pre-war, and were occupied mostly by young families. Ours, completed in 1950, was built for us by our family of carpenters and builders.

As young kids, my friends and I would sneak into those nearby "under construction" homes after the workers left. The smells of lumber and glue, sawdust, and leaded paint drew us and kept us in. We'd play "Guess what room this will be" while walking among the forest of unclad, bare wood, stud walls.

I'd imagine a pretty young girl I hoped would soon move in. Of course, she'd fall only for me, as I'd keep the neighborhood riffraff away. Her mother was sure to insist that I spend most waking hours with them, while demanding I sample her endless array of award-winning baked goods. Those dreams were never fulfilled, but they did continue.

Everywhere, new homes were sprouting. In New York State, Bill Levitt became the Henry Ford of home builders. He cleared some large acreage of its potato fields and built Levittown on New York's

Long Island. Levitt built his homes the way Ford built his cars, assembly line style. Instead of cars moving along the line to the waiting workers, the workers moved from house to house. The excavators first, then concrete, followed by the framers, roofers, painters, and so on. Finish this one and revolve to the one next door. Keep moving down the block, eighteen finished in the morning, eighteen more in the afternoon.

First Levittown, Long Island, and its 17,000 homes, then Levittown, Pennsylvania. Eventually, 140,000 of his homes were planted all around the country. Levitt was called the "Father of Suburbia."

His ranch house, known as the "Levittowner," was 800 square feet and considered *modern,* an important buzz word in those days. If it wasn't such, you'd best make it so to help it sell. *New* was good, and *improved* could help, too, but *modern* trumped them all.

Having no garages, some came with a carport, and none offered basements. All were "Television Equipped by Admiral" for $7,990.

Bill Levitt called it, "Democracy in real estate, that every family in the U.S. is entitled to decent shelter." All well and good, but let's not forget that until after 1954, these developments were racially restricted to permit Caucasians only.

Army veteran Hal Lefcourt moved into Levittown, Pennsylvania. He said, "We were young, all of us who moved to Levittown, and we thought Bill Levitt was the greatest man in the world. Imagine it, $10 deposit, $90 at settlement, and you had a house of your own."

Suburbia was not just a community, but a new kind of world trying to develop. We had our own Levitts in Minneapolis, Vern Donnay and Orren Thompson. On the higher end, was builder Carl Hansen. Mile after mile of pristine rows unfolded until they either reached a river or some other natural or man-made barrier where they had to stop. The veterans, the weddings, and the babies just kept coming. Housing, in large part, drove the burgeoning economy.

Some considered these new homes something less than good quality products. "Built too fast...they use inferior materials...they'll never last." Detractors touted those and similar opinions, trying to create a suburban myth.

Time has proven those sentiments wrong. The structures, some now sixty years old, are still standing straight and true. Their Douglas fir floor joists, thick trim profiles, and striated cedar siding have stood, time-tested, through decades of Minnesota winters.

In 1962, a folksinger-songwriter named Malvina Reynolds wrote "Little Boxes," which became a minor hit record. A cutting satire about suburbia and its perceived middle-class conformist values, it knocked the "little boxes" we lived in. Her lyrics scoffed,

> *Little boxes on the hillside,*
> *Little boxes all the same.*
> *There's a pink one and a green one*
> *And a blue one and a yellow one,*
> *And they're all made out of ticky-tacky,*
> *And they all look just the same.*

And on it went.

Frankly, I never aligned with Malvina's vitriol, then or now. My friends lived in a red one, and my cousins a green. We picnicked in the backyards of the yellow ones and enjoyed warm cookies and kind smiles from the moms in the blue ones.

Don't get me wrong, I'm all for nonconformity when it can improve something; but first, Malvina, show us how to provide, as Bill Levitt said, "Decent shelter for 100 bucks down."

CAPTURED BY LOVE

SUSIE JONES

For those fortunate enough to experience the joys of being a dog mom or dad, the unconditional love of these fur babies is unmistakable. Pet owners grasp the bittersweet reality of how deeply these companions can touch our hearts. True dog lovers embrace an unparalleled commitment that spans a lifetime but feels all too brief. Such was the bond I shared with Samantha. This is the story of her journey.

I first met Sam, a beautiful German Shepherd with light tan and black markings and white legs, when she was five years old and I took on the role of her babysitter. Whenever my daughter and her boyfriend, Sam's human daddy, ventured out of town or for an evening out, I would step in to watch over her.

She and I had a myriad of rules in place. No climbing on the furniture or sneaking into the bed, no direct eye contact upon my arrival, and no table snacks, except for the *occasional* popcorn treat. She had to wait until you were out the door before moving, then she'd stay at your heels. Attempts to pet her often resulted in a playful game of chase, as she would pivot before you could touch her, offering only her rear. Samantha's idiosyncrasies didn't end there; she had an affection for using pine trees or bushes as back scratchers.

She might have looked like a police dog, but later in her life, one would discern that she was not the guardian but rather the one in need of protection. While she insisted on playing the fierce alpha in the presence of other canines—often displaying what we termed her *wolf face*—no dog parks would snare her. She needed isolation or to be on a leash, except when with her daddy.

Her most cherished pastimes all included outdoor activities. She loved chasing a ball, as long as it flew from a ball launcher, her speed comparable to wind. Swimming was another beloved activity, likely due to her upbringing as a poolside pup. After a refreshing dip, she would often visit the raspberry bushes for a treat, plucking her own. She also proved herself a mighty chipmunk hunter, frequently capturing her prey. A feat that used to infuriate us. She shredded the downspouts in her relentless attempts to access them. The women in the family often expressed discontent over the chipmunks' demise. In the yard, she indulged in playful antics—whether with a basketball, a giant log, or a two-by-four—attempting to toss them into the air despite their size surpassing hers twice over. Sticks and tennis balls were for wimps in her world.

Sam turned out to be an excellent duet partner during renditions of "Jingle Bells," harmonizing and maintaining perfect pitch until the final note. She showcased her talents further by joining in with the outdoor warning sirens each month, howling through the majority of the test.

As the years passed, her family expanded. With her daddy's marriage to my daughter, she gained a mommy, then a couple of human brothers years later, for whom she was an active participant in the gender reveal. She wore the sign that announced their gender. This marked my more permanent entry as Grandma Number Two, a.k.a. City Grandma.

After the arrival of the first brother, her little family settled into a more spacious home, where her mommy opened a business in the basement. It was in this home that she developed a severe health crisis. One evening as I was leaving, I noticed her struggling outside, clearly in distress. I alerted her daddy, who rushed her to the emergency vet, where we discovered that her stomach had twisted. She underwent emergency surgery just in time to save her life. If we had hesitated even an hour later the outcome would have been tragic.

After a few years, Mommy's career interests shifted, and she closed her business. Since the mother-in-law's apartment became available once more, I moved in with them. Sam often stayed with me in the basement, serving as both a companion and a fierce protector, especially against unwelcome visitors...like the flying squirrels who found their way inside. Once, after a lengthy visit to my mom's, I returned to find that seven of them had taken refuge in the basement. Sam was oblivious to the situation because she had remained upstairs while I was away. The squirrels chose the early morning hours to announce their presence, attempting to join me in bed! As soon as Sam spotted them, she sprang into action, darting from room to room in pursuit until Daddy had to come corral the last one.

During the summers, our routine consisted of extensive walks, covering about five miles, and refreshing swims at various parks' fishing docks. Twin Lakes stood out as our preferred destination, where we formed bonds with both human and canine companions. Surprisingly, Sam displayed reasonable behavior with other dogs in the water, until they showed interest in the stick I was tossing. At that point, she would issue a sharp bark, deterring any potential snatchers. Following her swim, she would enjoy breakfast in the back of the car with the hatch raised, while the humans socialized nearby.

Autumn was a season of abundance for her, in the form of apples. Anytime we passed an apple tree, she couldn't resist snatching at least one fruit off the ground for a morning snack. Her enthusiasm for apples knew no bounds, often leading to overindulgence and subsequent digestive problems. I had to regulate her intake, offering a half portion alongside her breakfast, sometimes accompanied by raw carrots.

In the backyard, everbearing strawberry plants tempted her, triggering impromptu foraging sessions. She seemed to lead a charmed life, surrounded by fruit-producing plants wherever she resided, whether our neighborhood's offerings or the abundance of raspberries at Country Grandma's property.

Winter was all about spending quality time outdoors with the family, and she *loved* the snow. She would bury her nose in snowbanks, roll on her back, and snatch big snow bites as we trekked through the woods. Her obsession with rolling in the snow led us to the amusing solution of outfitting her with a face mask to shield her ears from infection—a sight that never failed to elicit laughter. She embraced it, like her other outdoor attire tailored for various weather conditions; including a raincoat for wet days—though she often was hesitant about going out in the rain—snow boots, indoor socks with grippers, and her cozy blankets. She was always well-prepared for any of Mother Nature's events.

Sam's two quite different grandmothers delighted in spoiling her. Country Grandma's place was her getaway when her family traveled out of town. With twenty acres to roam and an abundance of berries to munch on, she would exhaust herself running and playing during her stays. After such vigorous exercise, she'd return home and not move for several days. On the other hand, City Grandma—yours truly—visited her home during the kids' absence. Though we, too, enjoyed walks and playtime, the activities were more structured, given our urban surroundings.

Whenever either grandma visited, Sam would express her excitement through whines, barks, and joyful dances in the entryway. If both were present, she'd overflow with too much excitement to manage. She didn't know whom she should herd first. Both grandmothers understood why she was so thrilled; neither of us was adept at enforcing her rules, allowing her to reign supreme during our times together.

Sam had many adventures and was a constant presence in her family's activities. In her younger days, she would cruise alongside Daddy as he rode his bicycle. No one would be surprised to find her in many of the family photos, and whenever there was an amateur photo shoot involving the boys, she made sure to be included. On one memorable occasion, she sported a Vikings T-shirt during the year the team finally made it to the playoffs, although her enthusiasm seemed somewhat subdued, as if she harbored doubts about their chances of winning. How rude!

When my second grandchild arrived, the family decided it was time to relocate again. After much deliberation, we agreed to head north to live with Samantha's daddy's parents in their spacious country home. Now blessed with a large backyard all the time, two grandmas, and a dog and a cat to get spicy with, Sam found herself in paradise.

Before the move, we had noticed changes in her gait. A visit to the vet revealed the heartbreaking diagnosis of degenerative myelopathy, which meant she would likely lose the use of her back legs within six months. After this, she spent all her time with me, as the uncarpeted floors in Mommy and Daddy's part of the house proved too challenging for her to navigate. We were lucky that Samantha did not get her diagnosis until later in life. We've since heard of others who contract the illness as early as three years old.

Despite the grim prognosis, she defied the odds, remaining upright for a year and a half before her back legs gave out. To aid her mobility, we resorted to harnesses and boots that protected her feet during walks and held her back legs up. As the disease progressed, we introduced a wheelchair, which proved to be a life-changer. It restored her freedom, allowing her to run, explore, and indulge in mischief—such as berry-picking—with newfound joy. But the anxiety the disease created made her fear many things she never had before, especially loud noises. She became distressed when I would leave the room and stuck by my side constantly.

Samantha continued to delight in all her beloved activities, especially swimming, which required much more effort. I set up a ramp for her to get into the car with the help of a special harness, and to transport her down to the lakeshore. Our lake outings often lasted a couple of hours. Despite her disability, she relished walking in the water and could paddle with her back legs. She found a new tolerance for furry companions sharing her space. People marveled at her boundless energy, refusing to believe her advanced age of fourteen. Upon returning home, we headed to the walk-in shower for a comforting warm rinse, a ritual she had mixed feelings about. Every few weeks, I treated her to a gentle scrub with doggy shampoo, restoring her to her former non-fishy-smelling self. Afterward, she would power nap for the remainder of the day.

We swam four times a week and shared morning walks around the property with the other grandma and her dog, whom Sam wolf-faced often. Some habits never die.

Sam's presence was a constant source of comfort to me; we shared a special bond. She exhibited a protective instinct towards me, always attentive to my movements. Even within the confines of the house, she made sure she was never far from my side. At times, her intense gaze made me feel self-conscious, which I took as a silent invitation for cuddles on her bed—a request I obliged, often countless times throughout the day.

She was in her wheelchair for nine months. The vet had told us the disease would progress to her upper body and could also affect her respiratory system. Her anxiety intensified, as was the case for all dogs who contracted this disease, perhaps because they didn't understand what was happening to their bodies. Eventually, our family had to decide to release her—allowing her to cross the Rainbow Bridge.

By now, the boys were six and three. The day was bittersweet. We took our last walk with her at Woodland Hills Park, then drove from there to Culver's for lunch and ice cream all around. Yes, Sam too. She enjoyed a feast of treats and her last meal of all her favorite things. We all rallied around her the rest of the afternoon, getting in our last hugs and kisses. The boys set up sleeping supplies next to her bed for a nap, while the rest of us gathered around as well.

We told her all day this was going to be the best day of her life—she'd be going home to be with Jesus. He would be waiting for her, and she would have no more fear and could run like the wind again.

The doctor arrived at our home around 3:30, and by 4:10 Sam was on her way to heaven. It had been a year or more since she had paid any attention to who came to the door, let alone sounded an alarm by barking, but when the doctor arrived, Sam bolted off her bed, scooted over to her, and stayed close. It was like she knew her redemption had arrived.

Dogs are so loyal; they just don't leave on their own. Sam lived an amazing life, and we miss her so much. But we know she will be waiting for us on the other side with her tail wagging, a basketball nearby, and a big smile on her face.

Editor's note: For a moving tribute to this lovable fur baby, see also "For the Love of Samantha" in the Poetry section of this anthology.

POETRY

YOUR STRENGTH IS MY PEACE

SHARON ROSE

When the tempests blow, I will rejoice,
For you quiet them.
When floods pass their bounds, I will praise you,
For you recall them.
When the earth trembles, I cling to you,
For you reform it.
Though storms rage, or the waves beat, or the earth spews
*   boiling rock,*
Still I will worship the One, for your strength maintains
*   my peace.*

––––––––––––––––––––––––––––

This poem is from the author's upcoming novel, To Weave the Wind. *For more information on Sharon Rose's books, visit her website: SharonRoseAuthor.com.*

LIGHT OF SALVATION

LAURA SHRAKE

The light of the Savior saturates my bones
In the truth of His word, I am never alone.
When weakness seeks to undo me, He is ever near
Holy Spirit speaks to me, when I have ears to hear.

INSECURE NO MORE
LAURA SHRAKE

The heavy woes and worries that self-talk brings,
they seek to fix my focus on worldly things.
In the process of magnifying me,
imaginings I don't want come to be.
When stress threatens to steal my breath,
shrugging shoulders, I say, "What's next?"
It continually stalks me—no rest in sight,
as I dig negative word pits with all my might.
Breaking bad habits that bring on my pain,
is harder than stopping a pounding rain.
When I turn to His love and rest,
He's kind and gentle—He's the best!
As soon as I'm willing to make the smallest shift,
He's there helping; Holy Spirit, the greatest gift.
I make time with Him top priority,
His love overflows so bountifully.
Vistas open before my eyes,
issues recede to proper size.
When my gaze is firmly fixed on Him, then I see,

In the spirit, not with eyes, as it's meant to be.
Then, I can do what Holy Spirit prompts,
share His love and truth to heal offenses.
To repair the hearts of broken,
lost people, like I used to be.

DEAR ME...

J.J. WILDER

Dear Me,

> It seems that grieving over memories I could have made in
>   my moments of weakness and stupidity
> Is the only grief more tragic than mourning over someone
>   who's moved on.
> I had no idea you were who you turned out to be
> For, you see...I'd forgotten this was your first time living as
>   well.
> You didn't walk into life knowledgeable on the power of
>   society, self-respect, or money
> The only thing left now...is to forgive you.
> Loving you blindly and loathing you silently
> Prove to be equally poisonous.

Sincerely,
Me once I remembered who I was
before I became what I told myself I should be.

PRECIOUS FATHER-IN-LAW

LAURA SHRAKE

A father-in-law who sees you and knows you,
How precious it is to be seen and known.
With smiles and hugs, he greets you,
An exchange of stories and laughter abounds.
After your parents have flown home to heaven,
He keeps the parental torch lit in their place.
So, when that father-in-law exhales his last breath,
What can a daughter-in-law do but rejoice,
Now with bodily struggles to breathe at an end,
Spirit and soul unite with Jesus in his heavenly home.

FOR THE LOVE OF SAMANTHA

SUSIE JONES

I wasn't sure, but now I know, for the Bible has told me so.
Perish forever, you will not. Jesus waits, no leash in hand
*   where you'll be caught.*
In the quiet hush of a painful goodbye, God's love lifts you
*   toward the sky.*
Our tears fall like gentle rain, as you embark on your
*   journey away from pain.*
Today marks your release, and the day Jesus gives you
*   peace.*
So as your soul is set free, hurry to God, to find lasting
*   eternal glee.*
Jesus awaits in your favorite places, where joy and peace
*   have no empty spaces.*
Your best-loved thrills imprinted in time, being held
*   together for your eternal rewind.*
In realms of memory, where time does freeze, treasured
*   things linger, with a cherished ease.*
As you ascend the Holy Mount, towards the eternal Son,
*   your legacy echoes in the wind's soft hum.*

*For you a journey walked, a destiny fulfilled, a mission
      complete, for us left behind a heart's layover, both
      bitter and sweet.*
*Run with the wind through fields and streams, chase after
      squirrels, and fulfill endless dreams.*
*Swim the lakes so crystal blue, sniff the grass anew, come
      visit us in our dreams, where love will be the only
      theme.*
*We're setting you free to be your best, your truest self,
      forever young and carefree.*
*Stop in from time to time, in dreams or space, where
      memories linger, for a familiar embrace.*
*Jesus can mend what we cannot, so in His arms, we know
      you'll find a lot.*
*Upon the sea, where death was denied, your covenant
      formed, in the ebbing tide.*
*Salvation's dance, a cosmic decree, He said all flesh shall
      witness a victory.*
*So, it begins for you, in divine jubilation, a symphony of
      hope, a celestial ovation.*
*So, close your eyes to this world's embrace, for in seconds,
      you'll find heavenly grace.*
*Someday, we'll snuggle, across the great divide, where
      mercy and love surely abide.*
*Wait for us in that distant space, keeping us close to your
      heart, in your new special place.*
*Go in peace, find the Savior's hand, and begin your
      forever in God's heavenly land.*
*Your precious face, and your curious ways, a snarky
      attitude are now part of heavenly days.*
*Play freely with others, our good girl, roll in the snow, and
      let joy unfurl.*
*Be the best you can be, a young dog again, upright and
      free.*

Fear and anxiety, now erased, your ears hear God's praises
    we've all embraced.
Until then, we'll hold our memories tight in our hearts,
    where love never takes flight.
Farewell for now, sweet furry friend, on the Rainbow
    Bridge, our paths will blend.
Perfect in every way, we will cross someday, eternally free
    and skipping with glee.
If only this world would fall away for one last look, a
    cherished memory, from your now closed book.
Just to see you dancing near a tranquil brook, a glimpse of
    heaven, now your sacred nook.
So, as your flesh fades, in this gentle sleep, know that
    resurrection awaits, to capture you while we all weep.
Your footprints will always linger on this earthly shore, as
    witness to a life that lives forevermore.
Wheels and harnesses are all done, the battle has ceased,
    you have overcome.
Love transcends, never fading away, in that one truth, we
    find rest today.
Forgive me, my dear friend, I don't mean to linger, it's just
    saying goodbye means you must ascend.
Thanks for giving your all, and never giving up, from the
    beginning to the end, you were our wonderful,
    loyal pup.

GENERAL FICTION

THOUGHTS OF AN AVERAGE MAN

J.J. WILDER

THE BLUE DOORS SLIDE OPEN. *Ping.* Something doesn't feel right. I step onto the train in slow motion, head down, unsure what's wrong with me. My thoughts churn faster than the people crowding past me onto the subway.

I'm not suicidal, yet I frequently dream of death. I know I'm lucky to be alive, and giving up halfway through would throw away several opportunities and put my parents in the grave. How would my sister survive that much loss? Shaking my head, I force myself to face some honesty as I squeeze between two people and grab onto a pole. They'd eventually get over my death, and decades from now, none of my kin will know who I was, what I did, or how I died.

The blue doors slide shut behind me. *Ping.* My conscience reminds me I don't ever plan on committing suicide. Living is pointless, sure, but not enough to throw it all away. I just always feel empty, like the cold, featureless pole I'm gripping.

Maybe I'm depressed? No, I still feel joy in little things or everyday interactions, but this pitted feeling always takes over after everything I do. Drumming my fingers against the frigid metal, I scowl. So, what's wrong with me? Am I bipolar? No, bipolar is different from simply feeling hollow. Maybe some other, undiagnosed disorder? Who's to say? Undiagnosed disorders are common among adults in today's society.

The subway train hisses as it comes to a halt. *Sssft.* I knit myself into the mass exiting onto the platform. As the doors slide shut behind us and passengers join the chaotic crowd, I stay on the green crossing line for some odd reason, overwhelmed with an emotion I can't quite name or comprehend. Looking around, I spot two siblings playing hide-and-seek between the pillars, a woman crouched on the stairs, crying, and an old Asian man on a bench, watching people pass. Then, something ticks inside me, and a weighted, sinking feeling settles in my chest.

I understand the problem now. I wake up early every day to stare at social media, live for my paycheck, socialize strictly on weekends with coworkers as my only friends, and don't have the time for a committed relationship. Nothing is wrong with me. My life just has no purpose.

"Excuse me," a hoarse voice says. "I'm sorry, but could you help me find my stop?"

I turn to find an old man in a yellow vest standing alone at the open doors. "Oh, sir," I say, pointing, "over there is an officer who can help you."

At first, he smiles toward the police officer, then his face goes blank. He lets his gaze wander as he fidgets with his hands before turning back to me. "Excuse me. I'm sorry, but could you help me find my stop?" he asks again.

Poor old man. I give in and follow him back onto the train, then stop dead. It's empty. Blinking, I shake it off and help him sit down. The next instant, the scent of tar and ash fill the air. Inching upright, I stare through the window just as a blast of fire erupts outside the train.

"What the...we've gotta go!" I cry as the alarm lights kick on. The door's safety lock clicks before I can leave to find help.

I glance at the old man, who sits stone-still.

"Sir, sir!" I shout. "Are you all right?"

He looks at me, then points at the fire beyond the window. "You know, this reminds me of a sad story," he said, his voice emotionless. "I don't suppose you'd humor an old man?"

I glance out the window, then nod at him. I've lived like a pathetic nobody. Maybe I can die doing the only thing I'm good for, listening to whatever this old man has to say in his last moments. Rubbing the sting of exhaust fumes from my eyes, I join him in the green booth, as if we're hanging out.

"There was this man," he says. "We weren't friends, but we were close. Knew him my whole life, matter o' fact. He was a nice man, but his head was never where it should've been. Got a degree, married a lovely woman, and had a daughter, all to feed his own displeasure in life, because he always let the world decide his success."

As the flames outside engulf our car, the elderly man waves the smog away with his yellow hat. I sit stiff as a board without care. Famous artists have depicted death in various ways: a person in white peacefully drifting into a bright light, the devil in black dragging someone into the shadows. I doubt anyone's ever painted death as two men who are so isolated, they're on the brink of burning alive in a train, but no one's going to call asking why they didn't come home.

"Well...one day...this fellow gets everything he wants," the old man says between wheezing breaths. "His boss promotes him...to senior manager...and he finally feels full. He calls Margaret, his wife, to tell her...but she doesn't answer. He doesn't think...anything of it, till he sees the pillar of smoke...filling the air over their neighborhood." The old man swipes at our own cloud of smoke. "While he was working late, poor tired Margaret...forgot to turn off the...boiling pot before putting the baby to bed. She also forgot...the towel on the propane tank...next to the stovetop, and just like that..."

Snapping his fingers, the old man turns to me, tears beneath his baggy lids. "Drank so much...he stopped showing up to work." The old man's voice loses its choked rasp, and his words ring out clear.

"Everything he'd accumulated over the last thirty-seven years burned up in a matter of seconds. Even worse, he never got any joy or peace out of it."

An ear-piercing noise blasts through the train car. *Ding*!

I scour every corner of the ceiling for a loudspeaker or intercom. Where's that noise coming from?

Ding, ding!

What the heck is...wait...

Ding, ding, ding, ding...ding!

I gasp as my eyes shoot open. Clutching the cold blue sheets, I turn my head toward my nightstand. I slept through the first two alarms, so the snooze alert is running like a smoke detector. Taking a heavy breath, I push the sheets aside. Well, time to rush into the day.

DESTINY'S DETOUR

LAURA SHRAKE

LUCINDA GLANCED up from her phone. Romania! Costa Rica! Even Jamaica would have been better than where she was going.

She straightened, and her neck cracked as she stared at the pictures from her childhood that sat atop mismatched, garage sale coffee tables beside her sofa. How could this be God's plan? She slumped into the overstuffed, gray chair her mom had insisted on buying to spruce up her apartment.

Their mission trip destination wasn't a third world country. It was in the middle of the Bible Belt.

Sighing, Lucinda picked up her iPhone, scrolled, then clicked on the one number she could have dialed by heart.

"Hello, this is Jodi Singer," the voice on the other end said. "You know what to do."

Lucinda frowned, holding her finger poised over the disconnect button.

"Hello, hello, are you there?" Aunt Jodi asked.

"I thought I'd reached your voicemail."

"No, you didn't. I don't believe in it, remember?"

"Yeah, that's right." Lucinda nodded, then glanced at the picture of her and Aunt Jodi, chasing after a couple of wandering baby chicks. A moment from ten years ago. "So, what were you doing?"

"Trying to prank you."

"Why would you do that?"

"Yes, my thought exactly." After a short pause, Aunt Jodi asked, "What can I do for you, Junebug?"

Lucinda snorted. "I hate it when you call me that. It makes me feel like I'm ten years old."

"What's wrong with that?"

"I'm not a kid anymore."

Aunt Jodi half laughed. "If you were, maybe I'd have seen you last summer."

Lucinda frowned, untying and retying the tails of her button-down blouse. "I'm sorry. I was busy getting ready for my last year of Bible college and..."

Why hadn't she carved out a week or so to visit the farm?

"It's all right, Lulu," Aunt Jodi said, her voice softening. "You're a grown woman now. You can make your own choices, like you wanted to when you were younger."

"I'll do a better job planning this summer."

"Okay. Did you get your mission trip assignment?"

Lucinda sighed. "Yes, I'm going to Fayetteville, Arkansas."

"Oh, good."

Lucinda jerked her head back. "How can you say that? I wanted to go somewhere I could introduce people to Jesus."

"Don't you think some people there might need to get to know Him?"

"I don't know." Lucinda pinched the bridge of her nose, then rubbed it in a circular motion. "It's just so...rural and Americana. It doesn't seem like much of a mission field."

"I've been praying the Lord would send you and your team where He's prepared people's hearts," Aunt Jodi said. "And that He'd bring the right people across each of your paths."

"I suppose that would be a good thing."

"Jesus can use you to plant seeds of love in those hearts. Like you helped me to plant the garden when you visited me at the farm."

"Okay, but I'm graduating soon." Lucinda bit the inside of her cheek. "After two years of studying and preparing, I'm ready. I thought God had great things for me to do on this trip."

"Think of it this way, if you accept this detour, when it doesn't look how you expected, Jesus can still minister to and through you."

"I s'pose."

"Don't backtalk me, Miss Sassy-pants. You think you know plenty, but I've lived twice as long as you," Aunt Jodi said. "And I've known Jesus since I was nine."

"You told me you got to know him during vacation Bible school."

"That's right. Just because I didn't go to Bible College, don't think I don't know the Word and Holy Spirit like you do."

"Okay. Well, I should let you go," Lucinda said. "You probably need to—"

"Remember to call your mom. Tell her where you're going and when."

Lucinda sucked in a breath and let it out.

"You still there?"

"Yes," Lucinda said.

"Promise me you'll call her. If she doesn't hear from you, she'll worry."

The last thing Mom would do was worry, but Aunt Jodi wouldn't back down until she got her way. "Fine, I'll call her."

"Good." Aunt Jodi paused. "And smile when you talk to her, Lulu."

"Why do you have to call me that? My name is Lucinda."

A long silence filled the phone.

"One more thing," Aunt Jodi said. "It would be thoughtful if you called your dad, too."

Lucinda groaned. "Why should I? What has he done for me?"

"Without him, you wouldn't be here. I'm grateful to both your parents for that."

"Eww, Aunt Jodi! Don't go there. I'll consider it, but no promises."

Lucinda glanced at the clock: 6:12 p.m.

"I'm sorry. I've got to go. Barbara will be here to pick me up in less than ten minutes, and I haven't even started getting ready."

"Okay. I love you, Lulu. I'm praying for you and for your mission trip."

"I love you too, Aunt Jodi. Bye."

"Bye."

Lucinda ended the call and dropped her phone into her purse. Maybe it would be better if her aunt didn't pray quite so much. God seemed to answer so many of them and not always in Lucinda's favor. Most of the time, she wasn't sure He even heard hers.

THE NEXT EVENING

Lucinda tossed her handbag on the coffee table, then removed her backpack and set it against the wall inside her bedroom. Then, she walked back into the living room and sat on the couch.

Her phone buzzed. She pulled it out of her handbag to check her reminders.

Top of today's list: call Mom. An obligation she'd rather forget.

Before she could change her mind, she scrolled through her contacts and clicked on Mom's.

The phone trilled three times.

Lucinda held her finger over the disconnect button, waiting for the fourth ring. Should she hang up?

"Hello, Lucinda."

"Hi, Mom." She smiled, although it felt more like a grimace. "How are you?"

"I'm fine, dear. How are you?"

"I'm doing well. I'm leaving for my mission trip on March 3rd. I'll be gone for seven days."

"Does that mean you'll be done with your Bible College thingy soon, then?"

"Yes, graduation is this spring." Lucinda grinned. "Then, I can start—"

"So, have you started applying to any real colleges yet? For something practical like business or accounting?"

Lucinda gasped. "What do you mean?"

"Do you have a bad connection? Hello? Hello?"

"I can hear you." Lucinda lowered her chin, and her bottom lip trembled. "I suppose you think Bible College has been a vacation between High School and a *real* College?"

"You said it, dear. It's hardly practical. What can you do with it?"

Lucinda shook her head. The last thing she'd tell Mom was that she felt like the Lord had called her into ministry. Maybe after the mission trip or at least by graduation, she'd know what that meant.

She was ready—for something.

"Maybe we can talk about it after graduation." She bit her lip. "You are coming, right?"

"When is it again?"

"Saturday, May 13th at 2:00 p.m."

Mom sighed. "Phil and I are leaving for Spain on May 16th."

"So, you're not coming?" Lucinda asked, her chest tightening.

"I'll have to check with Phil."

"Okay." She blinked a few times and rolled her eyes. "I'd appreciate it if you could let me know by early May."

"I will. Have a good time on your trip."

"Don't you want to know where I'm going?" Lucinda asked.

"Of course, dear." The sound of nails clicking against marble echoed through the speaker. "Where are you headed?"

"I'm going to Fayetteville." When only a long pause answered, Lucinda said, "Arkansas. Right here in the United States."

"Well, that's good, then. Right?"

As Lucinda rotated her neck, her vertebrae cracked. At this rate, she'd need another adjustment before she left. "I guess that's all I called to tell you."

"Okay, well, enjoy your trip."

"Sure. Love you, Mom."

"Yes, me too."

"Bye, then," Lucinda said.

"Goodbye."

Lucinda punched the button to end their call. Well, that had gone about like she'd expected. But at least she'd kept her promise.

One down, one to go.

THE FOLLOWING EVENING

Salad greens, cooked pasta, and an open can of salmon sat strewn across Lucinda's olive green, Formica countertop. Mom's jaw had dropped when she'd first seen that counter. But it was one thing Lucinda couldn't do anything about. Renters weren't allowed to make permanent changes to any of the fixtures without permission. Since it was functional, she didn't care.

She rinsed, chopped, and prepared her dinner for one. Green salad with tomatoes and fresh raspberries, drizzled with olive oil and vinegar, and a cold pasta salad with salmon and mayo. She chewed each bite the recommended thirty times, then swallowed. Next, she washed the dishes, cleaned the kitchen counter, and put each item in its proper place.

When she couldn't think of one more thing she had to do, she pulled out her phone.

Dad—could that title be more misleading? But he was the only one she had.

Mom's third husband, Phil, wasn't exactly prime stepdad material. Mom and Phil had started dating after Lucinda moved into her own place. They'd eloped in Vegas a month after she'd started Bible College. About eighteen months ago, Mom had told her they were married before she came home at Thanksgiving.

Lucinda clicked the call icon, and the phone rang three times.

"Hello," a deep voice said. "Who is this?"

"It's your daughter, Lucinda."

"Oh. Well, it's, um...good to hear from you."

Her name must be missing from his contact list. Which was strange, since he'd called her at Christmas.

She swallowed hard. "I'm going on a mission trip in a few days."

"I meant to call you about that," he said. "Did you need some money?"

Why did he think all she wanted was his money? Her jaw clenched. She'd rather have a smile or a shared meal across a table. That would tell her louder than words that he loved her.

"No, that's okay. The money I needed for my trip came through a few months ago."

"Oh, good. You got it. I mean..."

Lucinda's mouth fell open. "Were you, um, the anonymous donor?"

He sighed. "Sorry. I meant to keep it that way. I just wanted to make sure you had everything you needed. I talked to your aunt Jodi, and—"

"Not Mom?"

"No. I figured Jodi would have a better idea about your plans."

"Really?" Lucinda's brows rose.

"You always seemed to enjoy your trips to visit her each summer."

"Of course, I did." After all, Aunt Jodi had *wanted* her to come visit.

Dad cleared his throat. "I just wanted whatever made you happy."

"What do you mean?"

"Well, I told your mom I'd like to have you come and stay with me for six weeks or so over the summers."

"When...when was that?" After she choked out the words, her throat constricted.

"About ten years ago. The summer after your mom and I divorced."

She frowned. Dad had wanted to see her then? Why hadn't Mom told her?

"Your mother said you didn't want to see me."

"But why..." She blinked back tears and coughed. "Why didn't you ask me?"

Dad sighed. "When I called you on your birthdays, you were always so excited about the time you'd be spending at Jodi's farm." He took a breath, then continued, "I didn't want to pull you away from that, so—"

"So, you didn't think about even asking?"

"I thought you knew I wanted to spend time with you, but you preferred not to. So, I just—"

"Stopped trying?" Lucinda asked.

"No, I just didn't think your answer would change."

She sucked in a breath, then exhaled. "I didn't know you wanted to see me that summer."

"You didn't?"

"No."

"So, Elise never told you."

"No, she didn't. She answered for me. I think you remember what that was like."

He huffed. "Yes, yes, I do." He went silent for a long time.

"You still there?"

"Yes, I'm here. So, would you...well, I guess it doesn't matter. It's probably too late."

"What's too late?" Lucinda asked.

"For us to spend some quality time together as a father and daughter, to get to know each other again."

"We've lost ten years."

"I know." He heaved a sigh. "We can't go back—not that I wouldn't like to—but we could try to move forward."

"When did you get so...philosophical?"

"Maybe I'll tell you about that over dinner, after your mission trip."

"Were you planning to come to Minneapolis?" Lucinda asked.

"I was thinking I would, if you'd like to do something together."

Her stomach fluttered. "Yes, I'd like that."

"Should we pick a date now?"

"Sure." She switched the phone to speaker and pulled up her calendar app. "How does the weekend of April 7th look for you?"

"Yes, that would work. Does Saturday night sound good for dinner?"

She grinned. "Yes, it's a date. A father-daughter date."

"You pick the place."

"Okay," she said, adding an event to the calendar.

"I should let you go."

"Okay. Love you, Dad."

"I love you too, Lulu."

TWO WEEKS LATER—EVENING

Lucinda leaned back into her gray sofa, then her phone buzzed. She plucked it off the coffee table, clicked the button and said, "Hi."

"Hello. How was your mission trip?" Aunt Jodi asked.

"You were right. It wasn't about me," Lucinda tipped her head to the side, then looked up, thinking about the last week. "It was about helping my teammates and receiving ministry from them."

"Tell me about that."

"The director had me room with Tami. I barely knew her before the trip. She was a part-time student, so we didn't have many classes together."

"How did that work out?" Aunt Jodi asked.

"Well, we talked about our lives and families. We got to know each other."

"So, you made a new friend?"

"More like a sister. She prayed for healing in the broken places in our family. That tears would be mended. And that unity in love and peace would be birthed between us." Lucinda clicked the speaker, set her phone on her lap, clasped her hands, and rested her chin on them. "And when she prayed, I felt Jesus right there with us."

Aunt Jodi paused and sniffled. "That's wonderful, Lulu."

"It was such a relief to share my challenges with my parents with someone." Lucinda paused. "Oh, I didn't mean that I can't—"

"I know what you mean," Aunt Jodi said, her voice gentle. "I'm sure it's hard for you to talk to me about your parents. Elise is my sister, so you've tried not to hurt my feelings by saying too much about her. And since your parents are divorced, I'm sure it's even harder to talk to me about Daniel."

"Did you know about, well, about...oh, never mind."

"What is it?"

Lucinda cleared her throat. "When I talked to my dad before the trip—"

"Oh, I'm glad you called Daniel."

"He told me he'd asked Mom if I'd like to spend some time with him over the summer the year they divorced."

"Oh, you mean the first summer you stayed with me at the farm?"

"Yes. Did you know about it?"

"I did, but Elise told me you didn't want to visit him. It was one of the reasons I invited you to come out here. I thought it might take your mind off your parents' divorce."

"Oh."

"You didn't know about that?"

"No."

After a short silence, Aunt Jodi said, "Well, pray about it before you talk to your mom."

Lucinda sighed. "I have been—praying, since I talked to Dad. And I've been thinking about my conversation with Mom."

"That's good. What has Jesus shown you?"

"I've seen that it's no good looking backwards with regret and recrimination. But it's hard." Lucinda pressed her fist against her lips. "I spent ten years thinking Dad didn't love me."

"What else did He show you, Junebug?"

She blinked back tears. "That if Jesus can forgive me, then I can forgive them. And He's given me the grace to do it." Her voice cracked. "But it's up to me."

"I'm glad to hear it."

Leaning forward, Lucinda said, "I'm going to invite Dad to my graduation."

"Your mom won't like that."

Lucinda's head drooped. "I don't even know if she's coming."

"This is a once-in-a-lifetime milestone for you. Give her a little time." Aunt Jodi hummed a few bars of "Amazing Grace," then said, "Just remember, I've known her my whole life, and I've talked to her about it."

"You have?"

"Yes."

"Well, you're still coming, aren't you?" Lucinda asked, twirling the ring on her middle finger.

"Of course. I wouldn't miss it."

Lucinda smiled. "I knew I could count on you."

"You can count on your parents, too, Lulu. Just give them a chance."

"You know, I really do like it when you call me that."

"Call you what?"

"Lulu."

Aunt Jodi laughed. "I knew you'd admit that, someday."

"I even like it when you call me Junebug."

Aunt Jodi hooted. "I wasn't sure you'd ever admit that."

"Everything about the mission trip was so different than what I expected."

"Well, I'm planning to stay a couple of days after your graduation, so maybe we can talk more about it then."

"I'd love that." Lucinda grinned.

"Okay. Well, I've got to go. Cows to milk and chickens to feed. You know the drill."

"I sure do. Love you."

"I love you, too, *Junebug.*"

Lucinda laughed, and they disconnected.

MARCH 15TH—EVENING

Lucinda stared into her bedroom mirror, then stuck out her tongue and waggled her head. Okay, maybe she was being kind of adolescent. She smiled and took a deep breath.

After picking up her phone, she scrolled and clicked.

It rang once, then connected. A male voice said, "Hi, Lucinda."

"Hi, Dad."

"I was hoping you'd call," he said. "How was your mission trip?"

"Better than I expected." She walked to the dresser and stroked the top of her favorite jewelry box, the one with pink daisies on top and a dancing ballerina painted inside. Dad had mailed it to her on her twelfth birthday. "Actually, it was life-changing."

"I'm glad to hear that, I think."

"Dad, I was wondering, that is…" She paused and took a breath. "I'd really like it if you'd…come to my Bible College graduation. Would you?"

"When is it?" he asked.

"May 13th, at 2:00 p.m. It's a Saturday."

After a long silence, he said, "Of course. I'd love to come."

"I have to warn you. I invited mom." Her shoulders tightened, and her stomach clenched. "I don't know if she's coming, but if she does, she'll probably bring Phil."

"That doesn't matter." He laughed. "I said I would come, and I'll be there. Could you text me the details?"

"Sure." Lucinda toggled her phone to text mode, typed in the details, and hit *send*. "Aunt Jodi will be there, too."

Dad chuckled. "Of course. It'll be great to see her. It's been a long time."

"There's something else."

"Oh, what is it?" he asked.

"I'm sorry we didn't have a chance to spend time together when I was growing up, after Mom and I left."

"It's not your fault, honey," he said in a gentle tone. "You didn't know I wanted to see you."

"But you didn't know that I wasn't the one who said *no* to your invitation."

The line went silent for a long moment. "I could have brought it up again when we talked on the phone."

"But why would you?" She sighed. "You thought I didn't want to spend time with you."

"Thinking about the years we've lost makes me sad," he said in a monotone.

"Well, we can't go back, but we can go forward." She stood up straight, squared her shoulders, and took a deep breath. "I was thinking, maybe I could come out to Nebraska and spend a week with you this summer. What do you think?"

Dad coughed and cleared his throat.

Lucinda waited, but he still didn't say anything. Her shoulders fell. "I suppose it's a dumb idea. I'm not a kid anymore, and—"

"No, it's a great idea." He laughed. "I'm just surprised that you'd want to come."

"Well, I will if we can find a time that works for both of us. I'll look for an Airbnb in the area."

"No, you won't." He took a breath. "I want you to stay with me at the house. I have plenty of room."

"Well, okay, then." She smiled. "We'll talk more about it later."

"Okay."

"I love you, Dad."

"I love you, too, Lulu."

MARCH 18TH—EVENING

Lucinda sat on one of a pair of oak swivel barstools at her kitchen counter. She needed the support and stability of something solid beneath her.

Then, she reminded herself that compassion lived in her heart. Christ, the hope of glory, radiated in and through her. She could do this, but she'd need a lot of help from Holy Spirit. It was a good thing He was her friend, like Jesus.

Lucinda took a deep breath, then counted to ten and exhaled slowly. She repeated the process three times, then clicked the phone icon, and it rang.

"Hello, dear."

"Hi, Mom."

"How was your vacation?"

Lucinda gritted her teeth. "My *mission trip* was awesome. We talked to people on the streets—"

"Really, Lucinda? You were talking to a bunch of what— homeless people and vagrants?" Mom let out a heavy sigh. "I thought I raised you better than that."

"We were there to share Jesus with lost and hurting people." Lucinda cocked her head and raked a hand through her hair. "We weren't chatting with the kind of people who hang out at the country club."

"Well, I suppose, if you have to do that sort of thing."

"We went where the director took us and did what she told us to do."

"Oh, I didn't know there was music involved." Mom paused, then asked, "Did you bring your violin? You didn't tell me you'd be giving concerts."

"We weren't. She's not a *conductor*." Lucinda massaged the back of her neck. "She's the director of the Bible College I'm attending."

"Oh, well, you should have just said so, dear."

Lucinda rolled her eyes. Then, she took a breath and counted to five.

"So, you made it home safely?" Mom asked.

Lucinda looked around her apartment, smiled, and nodded. "Yes, I'm safe at home."

"Good, dear. That's good."

"There's something I wanted to let you know." Lucinda took a breath and braced herself. "I invited Dad to my graduation, and he's planning to come."

"I haven't discussed it with Phil yet, so I don't know if we'll be able to fit it in."

"I told you I'd check in with you in mid-April," Lucinda said, fighting to keep her voice level, "since graduation is in mid-May. I really hope you can come."

"I'll let you know."

"Aunt Jodi's coming."

"Of course, she is, dear. The first time you stayed with her, she dragged you to that church of hers. That's where you got sucked into that group of Jesus freaks she calls friends."

"If you don't like Aunt Jodi's friends, why did you send me to stay with her every summer?" Lucinda asked, raising a brow.

"Well, Jodi is nothing if not reliable. I knew you wouldn't get into any trouble while you were under her care."

Lucinda swiveled back and forth on the barstool, then asked, "After you and Dad divorced, did he ever ask if I wanted to visit him?"

The line went silent. "Why do you ask?"

"I talked to him." Lucinda choked out the words; blinking back tears while considering the years she and dad had lost.

"Well, after he left, you were so silent and tragic, I didn't think you wanted to spend time with him. So, that's what I told him."

Lucinda's breath whooshed out. "What did you say?"

"I told him you were angry with him about the divorce and didn't want to see him."

Spots flashed in Lucinda's field of view. "Mom, that was how *you* felt, not how I felt."

"How was I to know?"

"You could have asked me."

Mom huffed. "I didn't think I needed to. Why are you bringing this up now?"

"Because I lost ten years with Dad. Did you even consider my feelings?"

"I assumed you felt the same way I did."

Lucinda reminded herself that Jesus was always with her and she and Dad were working on rebuilding their relationship. "It makes me sad that you didn't see how much it hurt me to think that Daddy didn't want to see me."

"Well, there isn't anything I can do about it now."

Lucinda sighed. "You could say you're sorry."

"I'm sorry you don't understand how I felt," Mom said, the pitch of her voice rising.

Lucinda shook her head. It really was all about Mom—in Mom's mind. "I always tried to see your side, Mom. I was there with you, but I was only ten years old. I needed my mom and my dad."

"He called you on your birthdays, didn't he?" Mom asked.

"Yes."

"And at Christmas?"

"Yes, but when we talked, it was awkward. I didn't know what to say. I thought he'd abandoned me." Lucinda squeezed her eyes shut and scrubbed at her furrowed brow.

"He did, dear."

"How can you say that?" She shook her head. "You were the one who left him."

"Because he made my life unbearable." Mom harrumphed.

"How did he do that?"

"He dragged us out to that forsaken cabin of his."

"You mean the ranch he inherited from his grandfather in Nebraska?" Lucinda asked.

"It was out in the middle of nowhere." Mom's voice became shrill. "We had no neighbors and no life."

"Why did that matter? You had Daddy and me, didn't you?"

Mom gasped. "Really, Lucinda? There was nothing for me to do out there in Hicksville. I had to leave to keep my sanity."

Lucinda rolled her eyes. "Once you had a child, was it really still supposed to be all about you?"

"I always put you first. There were no opportunities for you out there either."

"Daddy was there."

"Well, you had me," Mom said.

Lucinda paused, counted to ten, and gripped the edge of the counter. "I know, and I'm thankful."

"You don't sound like it."

"I'm sorry." Lucinda wanted to be grateful for her mom. She'd prayed about it more than once. But when she thought about who she wanted to confide in, or to have pray for her, it wasn't Mom.

Mom huffed. "Are you?"

"This is hard for me. I'm trying not to blame you. I'm trying to understand how these misunderstandings happened. I've been praying about it, and the Lord is helping me, showing me—"

Mom sniffed. "Well, it doesn't seem like He's shown you how to be kind."

"I'm grateful that you and Dad had me." Lucinda tipped her head and glanced up. "Because you could have chosen not to."

"Lucinda Grace, you should know we never thought of such a thing. We wanted you."

"I'm grateful for that."

"I would hope so," Mom said.

Lucinda smiled. "And I'm thankful that you both love me in your own unique ways."

"I'm glad you didn't lump me in with your father."

"You're both different. And I'm thankful because I've got strengths from each of you that make me who I am."

"Thank you, dear," Mom said.

"Let's talk again soon, okay?"

"Of course."

"Love you," Lucinda said.

"Me too."

APRIL 7TH—FATHER-DAUGHTER DATE

Lucinda stared into the bathroom mirror. Was that a zit? Leaning over the sink and shaking her head, she grabbed her foundation. She shook the bottle, coaxed a drop onto her finger, and dabbed it onto and around the pimple.

After she tapped a hint of blush across her cheekbones and applied bubblegum pink gloss, she spritzed perfume behind her ears.

Her black skirt flowed as she turned, just loose enough to fit over her black leggings. The hem of her fuchsia, raglan, cable-knit sweater skimmed its waistband. Running her hands over the skirt and twisting it a bit to the left, she nodded.

After stepping into the living room and grabbing her purse off the coffee table, she sat on the couch. She pulled out her phone: 5:56 p.m.

Daddy was supposed to pick her up soon.

After fidgeting with her phone for a minute, she dropped it in her purse and glanced toward the door.

The intercom buzzed.

She jumped up, ran to the door, and clicked the button. "Who is it?"

"It's Dad."

"I'll let you in." She pressed the button to unlock the main door.

A couple of minutes later, a knock at the door made her lurch back a step.

She walked forward, peeked through the peephole and grinned, then swung the door open. "Hi, Daddy."

"You look beautiful, Lucinda."

"Thank you." She gestured. "Please come in."

He stepped inside, and she closed the door, taking a moment to compose herself before she turned.

"Would you like to see my place?" she asked.

"Of course."

The tour took a few minutes: living room, kitchen, bedroom, and bathroom.

"It looks nice," he said. "I like your furniture."

"Mom helped me put together the bedroom and living room. The side tables, bookcases, and pictures are garage sale and flea market finds."

He nodded.

"Please have a seat," Lucinda motioned toward the living room.

He took a few steps and sat on the couch.

Lucinda perched on the edge of the gray, overstuffed chair opposite him and twisted a lock of hair around her index finger.

He tilted his head. "You used to do that when you were worried."

"What?"

"Your hair. Are you anxious about our father-daughter date?"

She released the hair, giving him a lop-sided smile. "Maybe, a little. It's been a long time since we did anything together."

"I know. Too long. And it's mostly my fault."

"But we're making up for it now." She glanced down and scuffed her shoe on the carpet.

"Yes, we are." He beamed. "Did you make a dinner reservation?"

"Where we're going, we don't need one."

"I'm intrigued."

"Pizza Deloria. It's around the corner. We can walk there if you'd like."

"Sure. That sounds great."

Lucinda's shoulders relaxed a fraction. With Mom, her suggestion would have thudded to the ground like a hummingbird with clipped wings. But Dad had always liked walking at the ranch, unless he was riding.

"Ready?" he asked, as he rose from the couch.

She nodded, stood, grabbed her things, and followed him out the door.

In less than five minutes, they were seated at one of six booths with red vinyl seat cushions and black Formica tabletops at Pizza Deloria, a tiny restaurant, mostly frequented by locals.

Their waitress, Kelley, placed two waters on the table.

"Hi, Kelley," Lucinda said. "It's good to see you tonight. I didn't know you'd be working,"

"I don't usually on Saturday, but Rodrigo was sick, so I agreed to fill in." Kelley glanced at Lucinda's companion and asked, "Who's this?"

"My Dad." Lucinda gestured at the waitress. "Dad, this is my friend Kelley."

Dad shook Kelley's outstretched hand. "It's great to meet one of my daughter's friends."

"It's nice to meet you, too," Kelley said. "Did you want anything else to drink?"

Dad looked at Lucinda.

She shook her head.

"We're both fine with water for now," Dad said.

Kelley nodded. "I'll give you a few minutes to look at the menu."

Lucinda smiled. "That would be great."

Daddy glanced around the room, then returned his gaze to her. "So, what do you recommend?"

"The thin crust pizza is out of this world. But if you're really hungry, their calzones are big enough to feed two people."

"As I recall, pizza was usually your top pick." Dad smiled.

Lucinda grinned back at him. "When I was ten."

"Why don't we get a pizza and a calzone. That way, I can try both of your favorites?"

"How about a large pepperoni, sausage, and onion pizza?" she said. "And a triple cheese and sausage calzone?"

He chuckled. "Sounds delicious."

Kelley walked over to their table and asked, "Did you decide what you'd like, or do you need more time?"

"We're going to share a large pepperoni, sausage, and onion pizza and a triple cheese and sausage calzone," Lucinda said.

"Okay, I've got it." Kelley wrote on her order pad, then said, "I'll get that going for you." She turned and walked into the kitchen.

"So, tell me about this philosophical change in your life," Lucinda said.

Dad cleared his throat. "Well, in some ways it's not too different from what you're doing."

"Really? You're going to college?"

He laughed. "No, I'm not going to college. But I am...following Christ. I joined the Faithful Church of Christ in Lynch. And I'm going to their Tuesday night Bible study."

Lucinda blinked a few times and grabbed a couple of napkins from the holder in the center of the table. "Oh, Daddy, I'm so glad. When did you? What made..." she dabbed at her eyes, as she tried to form a coherent question.

He smiled. "Well, to answer your first question, it was a little less than six months ago. A friend invited me to church, and after meeting her there for about a month, I found what I've been missing for a long time."

Lucinda cocked a brow, grinned, and asked, "So, was it a romantic interest?"

"I thought so, but then after I met Jesus, I realized that He used my attraction to get my attention." He chuckled, then grinned. "God's got a great sense of humor, doesn't He? Now, I'm concentrating on getting to know Him."

"Wow. I mean, wow!" Lucinda plucked another napkin from the holder and dabbed her tear-filled eyes. "That's amazing. I'm so happy for you."

"Me too." He took a sip of his water. "I'm glad we're taking time to get to know each other. And to reconnect as family."

"So am I." She smiled. "What's the Bible Study topic?"

"The book of John. It's a study on God's love."

"How perfect."

"You know, it really is."

Kelley brought their pizza and calzone on a tray, set the pizza on a stand in the center of the table, and placed the calzone's plate on the tabletop next to it. She stepped to the sidebar and grabbed two plates and silverware, before returning to distribute them. "Enjoy. I'll be back to see if you need anything else."

Dad caught Lucinda's eye and asked, "Would you like to pray?"

Lucinda nodded and bowed her head. "Lord, thank you for this time that Dad and I have together. We bless this food and water, calling it life and healing to our bodies."

They each grabbed a piece of pizza, cut off a section of calzone, and dug in.

"You were right," Dad said, wiping his mouth with a napkin after he'd finished several slices of each. "Those were both delicious. I can see why you like this place."

"I'm glad you were able to come." Lucinda pushed her plate back and set her napkin down beside it.

"I wouldn't have missed this. And I'm looking forward to having you visit this summer."

"Maybe we can go to your church, and your Bible study, together."

"I'd like that."

MAY 13TH—GRADUATION DAY

Lucinda paced back and forth in the church lobby, then pulled out her phone: 1:48 p.m.

She frowned. If Mom didn't arrive soon, she'd miss the ceremony. Glancing inside the sanctuary, Lucinda forced a smile.

Aunt Jodi waved from her seat in the middle of the fourth row. The two aisle seats beside her remained open.

Dad turned and winked from his center tenth row seat.

Lucinda giggled.

This brought back memories of her third-grade orchestra performance. In the middle of the first piece, her bow had glanced off the strings with a screech.

Mom had winced, but Daddy had grinned and winked, just like today.

She pulled out her phone: 1:57 p.m.

Unless they were in the parking lot—and Lucinda didn't dare leave the line to check—Mom and Phil were going to miss her graduation.

She glanced into the sanctuary again. Today was almost perfect, but if Mom were here, she might pick a fight with Dad and ruin everything.

She turned toward the entrance.

Mom stepped through the door, her arm threaded through Phil's cocked elbow, her hand on his forearm. The cap sleeves of her lemon, petite flower print, knee-length chiffon dress revealed tanned and toned arms. Phil's light blue sport coat, pants a couple shades darker, and yellow button-down shirt were a perfect match for Mom's dress. The country club perfect pair.

They took two more steps toward Lucinda. She shook her head and pointed toward the sanctuary doors, and the greeters ushered them inside.

The music started, and the director and her volunteers walked inside. Lucinda and the other students followed, marching one-by-one down the center aisle.

Dad grinned and took pictures as she approached.

Phil and Mom stood next to him. Mom puckered her lips so tight, it looked like she'd swallowed a glass of straight lime juice.

Lucinda directed a hesitant smile her way.

Mom gave her a half-smile in return.

Better than she'd expected.

As she and her fellow graduates filed between their designated seats, Lucinda glanced along her row. At the end, stood Tami Zimri, her mission trip roommate. They exchanged grins.

Lucinda still had no idea what she'd be doing after graduation, but the specifics didn't weigh on her as they had before the trip. Having Dad, Mom, Phil, and Aunt Jodi here filled her heart with awe and gratitude. "Thank you, Jesus," she whispered.

"What?" April, the girl seated next to her, asked.

"I was just thanking Jesus for today."

April smiled. "Me, too."

THE MUSIC BOX

MARY ANN LENARZ

Isabelle looked out on the street as rain slapped the windows in sheets. Thunder rumbled in the distance, and lightning flashed. It was close to sunset, though, as a sliver of silvery pink peeked through the clouds in the west. The gas lights flickered, casting an eerie glow.

She tensed. "My, it's awfully dark this evening."

"Yes," her mother said. "I had to light the lamps to read."

"I haven't seen a single carriage all afternoon." Isabelle said, turning away. "I suppose the storm had something to do with it." She sighed. "Not a single visitor."

"Why don't you play for us," her mother said. "Something cheerful."

"All right." Isabelle took a deep breath and gulped down the last of her tea. Plastering a smile on her face, she went to the piano and lifted the keyboard cover.

She loved playing. Soon, her fingers danced over the keys, and "The Blue Danube" filled the house with Strauss.

Her mother hummed along, her pleasant alto voice still as lovely as when she used to sing in the church choir. "You have a beautiful touch. You should play more often."

"Thank you, Mother." She kept playing. It soothed her heavy heart, and sadness melted away. She couldn't talk to her parents about that sadness. They had already made their wishes known.

"You know, dear," her mother said, "several young men have been by to ask your father's permission to court you. It's been two years since you graduated from high school, and a year since your coming-out party."

Isabelle sighed. Why did Mother have to nag about that? Instead of responding, she kept on playing.

"You can't continue to be so picky," Mother said. "You're almost twenty, and if you keep on, you'll be an old spinster."

"Mother, I'm not yet twenty, and if, as you say, there are several young men, I should be able to get the pick of the litter." She moved from Strauss to Chopin without pause. No need to see her mother's face. She'd intended to shock. Smiling, she played on.

"Isabelle, don't mock me," her mother snapped. "They are all very suitable young men."

By *suitable*, her mother meant rich, titled, the upper crust of society, and spoiled. Isabelle wanted more than to be a showpiece on her husband's arm. She already knew who she wanted, but for their parents...impossible! Never!

No one knew about David and Isabelle...yet.

Mother and Father thought they had the situation under control. That David was no longer in her future.

As she played, her mind wandered to the biblical story of King David as a boy. After he'd been anointed to be king, he was called to the palace to play his lyre. King Saul was plagued with terrors and evil spirits. When David played, the evil spirits left, and Saul had peace. The piano gave her that same peace.

The front door slammed open, and running feet pounded through the entry and echoed in the hall.

"Louisa, Louisa!" Father called.

Goodness, he never got excited.

Her mother jumped up from her chair. "Charles, what on earth is the matter?"

He rushed in, breathless and red-faced, waving the newspaper. "It's official! President Wilson has declared war on the Kaiser." He sank into his chair. "We're going to war."

Her mother gasped. Her hands flew to her chest.

All the heat drained from Isabelle's face, and she stood, refusing to faint. "What about Jackson?"

"Your brother will be all right," Father said. "He's in college. He's levelheaded. I'm sure he'll finish school before running off to join the fray."

Isabelle's thoughts went immediately to David, who had already gone over to France through Canada to join the American Ambulance Field Service.

$\int$

"Isabelle, I must go," he had said on their last evening together. "Who knows if or when we will enter the war. I'll be driving an ambulance, nothing dangerous."

She had trembled. "You are a medical student! Please don't go. You don't have to. What will your parents say? Can't you stay and finish school?"

He had shaken his head. "I've already made arrangements. There's quite a lot of us, you know. I haven't told my parents yet. I will the day before I leave. I'll write to you."

She'd grasped his hands, willing him to stay.

"Isabelle," he'd said, stroking her fingers, "I must do this. I love you. Wait for me." He'd waved as he walked down the street.

$\int$

She pressed a hand to her cheek, as if the touch of his lips still lingered from his goodbye kiss. She stepped away from the piano. "Excuse me. I'm going upstairs to rest."

As she climbed the stairs, her thoughts turned to Jackson. If her brother had his way, he, too, would enlist. Mother would have the vapors, and Father would go red in the face. Jackson would be calm and wait for the storm to pass, giving every reason why it was the right thing to do.

Isabelle sat at the little writing desk in her room and pulled the music box David had given her from its shelf. She ran her fingers over the blue cover and opened it. The notes of "The Blue Danube" filled her room. She closed her eyes, and David stood before her in memory.

"You have to meet my parents," he'd said. "They will love you."

"But I'm not Jewish."

He had taken her hands. "That shouldn't matter. This is 1916. Think more modern. You must."

"I don't know. I'd like you to meet my parents as well. You're a medical student; Father should be impressed."

When Isabella had finally given in, his mother had shouted at her, then said, "David, get her out of here. How could you do this to your mother!" Then, she'd proceeded to call Isabella names in a language she didn't understand. "Are there no pretty Jewish girls, that you have to spend your time with one like that?"

David had grabbed her hand and pulled her out of the house. "I'm so sorry," he'd said, holding her as she shook all over. "I didn't want to believe they would do that." He'd brushed a loose strand of her hair back, and wiped at her tears.

His meeting with her parents had gone just as badly.

"Isabelle, why do you want to spend your time with a Jew?" Her mother had asked, spitting *Jew* out as if it were a dirty word.

Father had told David, "I don't want your kind around my daughter. It's not suitable. I don't expect to see you here again, young man, not in my house."

After that, they'd met in secret. Then, just before Christmas, David had given her the music box.

"We'll elope and head west to Montana," he'd said. "No one will know us. They need doctors out there in some of those small towns. I'll finish school out there after I come home from the war." He'd looked deep into her eyes. "Please wait for me, Isabelle."

"I will. I'll wait for you."

Isabelle shuddered at the memories, forcing her thoughts back to the present—April 1917, and President Wilson had just declared war. What would this mean for all of them?

David had wanted to court her, and that usually led to marriage. If he survived the war, they would still be fighting for their right to be together, unless they went to Montana. Isabelle sighed and closed the lid to the music box, stopping its song, then placed it back on the shelf.

The sun peeked through the window, letting in a pale glow of light in the evening sky. She went back downstairs to find her mother pacing and fanning herself with her handkerchief.

"Oh, Charles," Mother whined. "You can't let him do this!"

"There's nothing I can do. The boy is twenty-two years old," her father said. "If he is determined, you can't stop him."

"But Charles—"

"Be still, Louisa. There's nothing to be done." Father picked up his newspaper and walked into the parlor.

As Isabelle descended the last of the stairs, her mother looked toward her, wringing her hands. "Jackson just called. He's going to enlist. What can I do? How will I do?"

She sounded so pitiful. Isabelle looked at her mother—pale, lost, dependent in all ways on others—and made a silent vow. *Never* would she let herself become so helpless. "Mother, I..." She paused. What could she say?

"Isabelle?"

"Jackson is fine right now," she said. "There's always hope in prayer. That's what you can do." She took a deep breath. "He'll come home before he does anything." She turned and fled back upstairs.

The months flashed by. Suddenly, it was January, cold and harsh. 1918 came in with a blast of frigid air, frost on the window in elaborate designs, and a wild, whipping arctic blast every time the door opened.

Isabelle shivered. She hadn't heard from David in all the time he'd been gone. He'd promised to write. Maybe the mail wasn't getting through because of the war in France and Belgium. They didn't get much news until it was days old.

Father usually grumbled as he read the paper, and then he took it to work with him. He wouldn't discuss the war with her or her mother, to prevent Mother from becoming upset, especially where Jackson was concerned.

Funny, they did get letters from him. Why didn't Isabelle hear from David?

She did everything she could to keep busy, contributing to the war effort the best way she knew how, but it didn't help. Rolling bandages, sending packages of necessities, knitting socks—none of it was enough. Father always picked up the mail, so it had to be all there, but nothing ever came for her.

She spent time checking the hospitals, hoping to receive some word about David. She and Mother brought sweets and reading material for the wounded, but no one had news about him. It was as if he didn't exist.

Isabelle kept busy, prayed for him, and never mentioned him to her parents. Jackson was a subject dear to her mother's heart, and always on her mind and lips. He had learned to fly and joined the Air Corps. If only Isabelle could fly away to find her beloved.

While the war raged in Europe, May bloomed bright around Isabelle's home, the gardens bursting with color. On her way to the parlor one afternoon, she stopped at the pounding of the brass door knocker. She reached the door just as Father walked in from work, followed by a man in uniform.

"Come in, young man," Father said, walking ahead and beckoning the officer past the door. "Come in, come in." He showed the man to the parlor and offered him a drink. "My dear," he said to Isabelle, "this gentleman has a message for you from someone you both know. This is Lt. Peter Danforth III."

Peter took off his hat and clasped her hand. "Nice to meet you in person. I've heard so much about you, I feel like I know you."

Isabelle's face heated. "Thank you. I hope it was good."

He grinned, but his eyes held sadness. He placed an envelope in her hand. "I was told to deliver this to you personally." Turning to Father, he said, "I can't stay, sir. I need to report back. Very nice to meet both of you."

"Come back anytime, Peter," Father said.

"Thank you, sir." He turned to Isabelle. "Ma'am." He repositioned his hat and left.

"I think I'll take this to my room, Father," Isabelle said, "if you don't mind."

"No, no, that's fine." He waved toward the door. "Now, that's the kind of young man you should set your cap for, my dear." He let out a huff and slapped the newspaper in his hand as he sank into his chair.

On her way to the stairs, Isabelle ducked into her father's study for a letter opener. In her haste, she overturned a wastebasket near the desk. As she picked it up, she found a crumpled envelope at the bottom with her name on it. Stunned, she stared at the sender's name. David! She compared it with the one Peter had brought.

"Oh, Father, really?" Tears formed. Had he been keeping back her mail?

Using the letter opener, she slashed both letters, then ran up to her room. She set the music box on her little desk and let it play. Her hands shook as she opened the first letter.

My dearest Isabelle,

I write this to let you know I am well and think of you daily, moment by moment. I am quite close to the front, but God is good. I have been safe, and my every thought is to get home to you. I understand America is now officially at war with Germany, and I am glad to do my part.

I can't say much. What we do is mostly classified. I have been waiting for word from you, as there has been nothing. I know mail is slow going out, but it has been many months. I pray you have not changed your mind or found someone else. I will always love you.

All my love forever,
David

She opened the second letter, and as she read, all the blood drained from her face. Surely her heart had quit beating, leaving her numb and unable to move. "Oh, no, no! Not David! No, no, no!"

She continued reading through blinding tears. This was a mistake. It had to be.

Darling Isabelle,

If you are reading this, it is because I am no longer here. Peter is my good friend, and he promised to deliver this for me if the worst occurred. Since we weren't married, you would never know what happened to me. My parents wouldn't tell you.

I am now with our heavenly Father. With all my heart, I have loved you. I wrote to you and wondered why I never heard from you.

I converted to your Jesus, so I have every hope we will be united in eternity.

Forever and always,
David

Isabelle couldn't move. She had frozen in time and space. Burning tears she couldn't hold back dotted the letter as it floated from her hand to the floor.

"Isabelle," her mother called, "please come here. I need you."

She sat up and took a deep breath. "Yes, Mother, I'm coming." Wiping away the tears, she tried to be brave. She stood on unsteady legs, head held high, and walked out of the room as the last notes of "The Blue Danube" faded away.

FEATHERED FRIENDS

PAMELA AUSTIN

Once upon a time, there was a big, black bird. This crow decided that, instead of singing, he would fly around complaining and gossiping all day long. He was a selfish, greedy bird who collected shiny, interesting objects to keep. He lived in the tall pine trees in the middle of a small town in the country. He was always too busy talking and adding to his collection of treasures to be a real friend and help the other birds.

While flying and searching for treasures, the crow glanced off to the north, where a bluebird made her home in a little house on a fencepost beside a country road. The bluebird was a loner by nature. She was shy, quiet, and very protective of her young. She'd often said she enjoyed peace and calm in her surroundings.

As she often did, the bluebird was softly humming to her children when the crow barged in and said, "I need another doo-ditty to add to my collection. Did you notice how my nest shines with my treasures? I can't believe the garbage our neighbors put in their nests! No class at all."

The bluebird said, "I am humming my children to sleep for their nap right now."

"Really," the crow said, "you should take notice of the messy houses those other birds around here are keeping." On and on, droned the crow, loudly saying, "Caw, caw, caw."

Next, the crow flew on, fixing his sharp eyes to the south, where he spied out the hummingbird, green in color with a ruby-red throat.

The hummingbird was the fastest and most beautiful of the birds. Her small wings were filled with goodwill and harmony. She spread joy and caused delight everywhere she went.

The black crow arrived on her doorstep, demanding, "Hummingbird, come help me find a whatchamacallit!"

"Have you noticed the beautiful colors in the sky this morning?" asked the hummingbird.

"What? The sunrise? You can't put that in your nest. You dart around here and let me know when you see something shiny."

"Crow, isn't the weather wonderful today?" asked the hummingbird.

"Quit wasting time and find me my whatchamacallit!" the crow shouted. "Caw, caw, caw."

Flying fast and furious, the crow nearly knocked the Cardinals' nest down.

The Cardinals, living on the east side of this small town, were a young, loving couple of redbirds who had only recently moved into the neighborhood. These hard workers sang while they built and cared for their nest in the shrubs among the houses.

Having found some shiny tinsel, the Cardinals were using it to repair their nest when the crow zoomed in and rudely interrupted, shouting, "Mine, mine! I seen it first. Give me that thingamajig!'

"Excuse us, Crow," Mr. Cardinal said, "but we are fixing our nest right now. Perhaps we can visit later."

"Finders, keepers," the crow said, "and I found it."

Mrs. Cardinal stared at him. "But we—"

"Caw, caw, caw," the crow said, not listening, and took the tinsel away.

Day after day, the crow cawed and cawed, flying around.

"You are all lazy," he said to the others. "Not to mention, you sing off-key, in my opinion. Quit wasting precious time with all that noise you call singing. I demand a new fandangled, shiny something today. Quit sitting around. Go get me one. You will never be any good to anyone. I expect some help right this minute! I am important...caw, caw, caw."

Soon after, the other birds met in the north while the crow was chasing after something that glittered in the south. The birds wanted to help the crow see the trouble he caused and change his unpleasant ways. They were convinced that the crow was in desperate need of help. The Cardinals agreed to be part of the plan because of the crow's rudeness to them. After thinking about it, the bluebird joined in to restore serenity for her children. The hummingbird quickly outlined a detailed but simple plan, which they all admired and agreed upon.

When the crow returned with a shiny, silver button to show off to the others, they put the plan into action.

Every time the black crow started to say, "Caw, caw, caw," the bird next to him began to sing. The Crow cawed on and on, but the birds refused to pay attention to all his negative talk. The crow flew from bird to bird, refusing to stop. He took turns pointing at each of them and finding fault. However, one by one, each bird in turn hummed or sang instead of listening. He grew confused and, trying to caw louder, choked on his shiny silver button.

After that day, the birds met in the morning and sang their songs to remind the fault-finding crow that life is pleasant. Each bird sang its own song, hoping to help the crow find beauty and value in the goodness of life.

Instead, the crow continued to search for shiny treasures to keep, such as tinsel and little metal objects. His life changed the day he accidently swallowed that shiny silver button, because now, he can no longer sing.

Even today, he sometimes caws, trying to spit out the button stuck in his throat.

The other birds always knew the real values to be treasured. They continue to fly and sing praises in the morning, reminding themselves and all who will listen to be thankful. For they understand the joyous melody of friendship and cheerful rhythm of celebrating life.

After all, where feathered friends gather, a delightful song orchestrated from heaven above breaks forth, just as the sun rises.

CHICKEN SPOTS

PAMELA AUSTIN

I woke up one sunny morning and stared at myself.

"Why me? Why do I have spots all over?" I ran through the house to find my mom.

"It's Chicken Spots," Mom said.

So, I asked her a few questions. "Did a chicken do this to me? Just what kind of chicken was this? Was it a lot of chickens leaving bumps all over me while I slept or something? Did the chickens do a dance or what?"

Mom smiled and said again, "It's Chicken Spots."

I gave these chicken spots a little thought. If I'd had a nightmare, I would remember, I am sure. At that point, Mom took my temperature.

"Will my spots turn colors?" I asked her. "Will I need to join the circus as The Amazing Spot Boy? Will the spots be red, white, and blue for the Fourth of July? Do these Chicken Spots turn into freckles for life?"

Mom raised an eyebrow and said loudly, "Chicken *Spots!*"

"How long will these Chicken Spots itch?"

"Mittens will help," Mom said.

"Oh, why must I wear mittens in July? Will I need to wear a hat and boots as well?"

Mom sighed and took my temperature again, then said, "Oatmeal baths will help."

"Bathing in breakfast?" I backed away. "Just what strange kind of disease do I have? Will I need to eat soap and drink shampoo as well? Or will I soon be scrubbing myself with pizza and washing between my toes with carrots?"

Mom took my temperature again and mumbled something I couldn't understand.

"Where, oh where did this come from?" I asked. "Do I have spots inside me, too? Will my insides need scratching?" I turned in a circle and sang, "Chicken Spots, bumpy spots, itchy spots," then plopped into a chair, too dizzy to stand. "How long do Chicken Spots last?"

Mom said, "Two weeks."

"Fourteen days of my life upside down. Will I return to myself?"

Mom came at me with the thermometer.

I had never caught a chicken before, but if I could, what would it take to make one talk and take this awful, itchy, spotty spell off me? I'd always liked Mom's chicken and mashed potatoes with gravy, but I made a decision right then and there.

I shouted, "I will never eat chicken again!"

Mom said, "You are having your hearing checked as soon as this ends!" She kept yelling, "Chicken Spots" at me.

I was sure it must be part of the cure, along with a thermometer in the ear.

Mom said she's worried now that I am catching Beaver. I simply cannot imagine what that could be! Does having Beaver come from swimming in the river? And how long does that last? Will I grow a tail? Can you have Chicken Spots and Beaver at the same time?

Oh...why me?

WOMAN CAUGHT IN ADULTERY

KAHREN HULL

Author's note: The following is fiction based on the biblical story of the woman caught in adultery (John 8:1–11). It is speculation on how she could have been set up and used, plus what went through the scribes' and Pharisees' minds when they brought her to Jesus. If you think you've been used beyond hope, please read this story of forgiveness and redemption.

SHMUEL PARTED the curtains and inhaled deep as he walked to the cooking area to greet his wife.

"Good morning, dear," Hadassah said, then slid a loaf of flatbread into the stone oven before straightening. "The food is on the table. I would hug you, but my apron is covered in grime."

Shmuel gave her a shoulder hug. "That smells delicious. I married the best." He took his place at the table. As Hadassah turned back to her work and finished mixing the dough for another batch of bread, Shmuel poured his tea, but the jar shook, splattering droplets onto the table. Keeping his gaze glued to Hadassah's back, he made two quick swipes at the table with the sleeves of his garb, then plated his food.

The moment he began breaking his flatbread, Hadassah turned and removed her apron to wipe her hands and brow, then set the cloth at the end of the table.

"There. Time to eat now." She took her place across from him and reached for the jar to pour her tea. "This is the last batch to bake before the noon heat." As she was setting the jar down, she eyed him. "You're fidgeting, dear. Not hungry this morning?"

"I'm...I'm fine. Your food is excellent as usual. I...I need to be on my way." He got up and walked to the front door, then turned and gave her a tight smile.

"All right." Hadassah took a quick sip of tea, then stood. "You remember we need the tent set up? The roof is swept."

Shmuel nodded, "Yes, yes, I remember. It should be up this evening."

"Thank you, dear. You're the best."

He gave her a slight bow and opened the door.

"Uh, Shmuel?"

He stopped and met her gaze, his hand still on the latch.

"Are you sure you're all right? You seem...nervous."

"I'm fine, dear. I have a full day. I'll see you later." He stepped outside and shut the door faster than usual.

Shmuel took a couple of steps, paused for a brief exhale through firm lips, and began his walk to the synagogue.

As if he were invisible, a steady stream of people brushed past him without so much as an "excuse me." The more villagers who passed, the more tense his neck and mouth became. At the top of the village hill, he surveyed the crowds bustling onto the main path from every direction. All headed to one place: the town square in front of the synagogue.

After today, these crowds won't be running after Him *anymore.*

Shmuel walked down the hill and turned onto the main path. Up ahead, a large boulder sat just off the path between two trees. "What perfect timing," he muttered, then strode over and perched on the rock.

He lifted his head into the morning breeze and shut his eyes, whispering, "Stay calm...stay calm. This plan will work," his words exhaling in rhythm with each breath.

"Shmuel?"

He jerked to his feet. "Oh, Baruch. It's you." Shmuel relaxed and returned to the boulder.

Baruch smirked. "You were in some deep thought there. What planet were you on?"

"Very funny. Please, have a seat. There's room for both of us. I need to ask you a favor."

"Oh?"

"My son's bar mitzvah is next week."

"That's coming fast."

"Yes, I know. And the following week we announce my daughter's engagement. Relatives from both sides will be coming and going, some spending the night."

"You need some of them to stay at my place?"

"No," Shmuel said, fighting the urge to wipe his hands on his clothes. "I need you to help me load the tent the synagogue owns onto a cart for transport to my house. The cart belongs to a merchant; he's coming by this morning. After it's loaded, he'll transport it to my place."

"Sure, I can help. I've used that tent—those bundles are cumbersome. It's my morning to fill in where needed, and we're on our way to the synagogue, anyway."

"It's not at the synagogue. It's at Gershon's house, just past the town square."

Baruch straightened his back like a board, his eyes widening. "Gershon's?"

Shmuel fidgeted with the ends of his waist tie. "Well...yes. Gershon's. Did...did you forget he was betrothed last week?"

Baruch leaned forward, resting one elbow on his leg, rubbing his forehead, the other arm falling across his knees. "No, no. I didn't forget."

Shmuel swallowed. "Is there a problem?"

Baruch clasped, then unclasped his hands. "Have you noticed Gershon acting...different lately? Something's not right, even for a newly betrothed man."

Shmuel wrapped, then unwrapped the ends of his waist tie around his fingers. "Wh-what do you mean?"

Baruch sat up and made a quick side-glance to Shmuel, then lowered his gaze. "Last week, I met with him to coordinate the subjects we would teach. He left before we were done, saying he needed to get parchment, and never came back. His manner was odd, even abrupt. After he left, I checked the supply room. There was *plenty* of parchment."

"Well...may-maybe he was preoccu—"

"No...no, Shmuel." Baruch stood and paced in front of him, one hand on his hip, the other rubbing his forehead. "There's no *maybe* here. Something is off. Twice last week, he missed his scheduled teaching, and I had to fill in."

Shmuel stopped fidgeting with his waist tie and steadied his hands and his breathing.

Baruch paced a few more steps, then sat on the boulder. He pressed his palms to the rock, straightened both arms at his sides, and leaned all his weight on his hands. "There's more."

"More?"

Baruch studied Shmuel for a moment, before resting both hands in his lap. "All right, I'll come out and say it. Yesterday, I saw him from a distance...in public...without his garb. I know it was him."

Shmuel rested one elbow on his leg, rubbed his chin, and wiped the sweat from his forehead with his other sleeve.

Baruch stood and leaned against the tree. "You know what's odd here?"

Shmuel opened his mouth, but that was as far as he got.

"I went to the High Priest," Baruch said, "and all he did was shrug. Said it was probably nothing. What's going on, Shmuel?"

More sweat trickled down Shmuel's back, making him grateful

the covering of his garb made him appear normal. "I...I agree with the High Priest. It...It's probably nothing."

Baruch stared at him, his body frozen like a statue, his mouth gaping. Then, he shook his head and returned to the boulder. "Preposterous! You have to see none of this makes sense. Besides, you're also acting...odd. Are your family events too much at one time?"

Shmuel rubbed his palms back and forth from mid-thigh to his knees. "How...How am I acting odd?"

Baruch tilted his head and raised an eyebrow. "For starters, when I first passed, you were muttering. And since when did you become lax towards proper public appearance, not to mention missed teaching sessions for no reason?"

Shmuel stared into the distance.

"And look at your right knee—it's bouncing nonstop."

Shmuel looked at his leg and grabbed his knee as if it had a life of its own. "Can...can we forget about Gershon for now and get the tent?"

Baruch nodded, stood, and offered his hand. "All right, but your anxiety is obvious. I wish I knew what was going on."

Shmuel pulled himself up and stretched his back. "Before I forget, Scribe James and Scribe Nati will be helping us load the tent. They're meeting us at the edge of the square in front of the synagogue, where the steps begin."

"Don't they usually scribe—"

"It's fine!" Shmuel snapped, then softened his tone. "They'll be able to help."

✒

Shmuel maneuvered through the crowds at almost a running pace, his back arched, his expression set in stone.

"Wait," Baruch said, panting. "I need to catch my breath!"

Shmuel stepped off the path, near a rundown brick ledge, and waited for Baruch.

"*What* is going on!?" Baruch asked, hands on knees. "You're walking so angry. Why?"

Shmuel squared himself in front of Baruch, both fists on his hips. "Yes, I'm angry! You want to know why? I'll tell you why. I've spent my adult life studying the Torah *and* the Talmud," he said, glaring. "I know *every* category of all the laws. When someone wants advice, I know *exactly* which section to use."

He caught his breath and allowed his stiffened body to relax, then kicked chunks of dirt toward the ledge. "In my position, I'm obligated as both teacher *and* scholar to follow the law to the letter. And I make sure *everything* is done to the letter, so my household and everyone I teach is above reproach." He kicked a few more chunks of dirt.

Baruch stepped back, sat down on the ledge, then reached for Shmuel's arm. "Please, sit. This old ledge is still solid."

Shmuel chose a spot on the ledge and took another breath. "This guy shows up, claims He is the Messiah, and breaks our sabbath laws with lame excuses. And *throngs* follow Him, nearly mobbing Him at times." Shmuel waved his arms in mad gestures with every word. "Some even *beg* Him to return to their synagogue."[1]

Baruch watched him in silence.

"I'm the one chosen to give counsel to civic leaders and write legal opinions," Shmuel said, pointing to his chest with every word. "I'm the one chosen to be the orator *and* debater at public *and* private hearings. Do people run after any of *us* at the mere whisper of our whereabouts, as hard as we study and work? *No...*" He dropped his hands to his lap.

Baruch just stared at him with understanding eyes.

Shmuel looked square at Baruch. "In case you didn't know,

---

1. Verses that describe not just crowds, but throngs, that followed Him: Matthew 4:25, Matthew 8:1 (AMP), Matthew 13:2 (AMP), Matthew 19:2 (AMP).

claiming the rights of the Messiah is blasphemy against the Most High," he said, his voice dry.

Baruch placed a hand on his shoulder. "Yes, I know what blasphemy is. But take some deep breaths, my friend, and exhale out this anger. You have family milestones happening that are blessed by the Most High. Your focus needs to be on them. You can't remain in this state, even during preparations."

Shmuel let his shoulders relax and sighed out at least a smidgen of his anger.

Baruch patted his shoulder. "Come on. Let's get your tent. Except now, we walk—at a normal pace."

"Fine. We're almost to the square, anyway."

Scribe James sat waiting with Scribe Nati on the steps when Shmuel and Baruch approached.

James elbowed Nati, leaned toward him, and murmured, "Why is Baruch with Shmuel?"

Nati shrugged, then they stood to greet the other men.

"Uh, Shmuel?" James said. "Can we see you, please?"

Right then, Baruch caught the attention of several friends and stepped away to greet them.

With one eye on Baruch, Shmuel pressed his index finger to his lips for an instant.

James and Nati nodded, and James whispered, "Baruch?"

Shmuel nodded, then gestured to Baruch, signaling for him to return to the group.

As Baruch joined them, Shmuel said, "We have no time for pleasantries. Here's the plan. Gershon gave us permission to enter his house, but we must be quiet and quick. When we enter the gate, walk straight through the courtyard, into the house. The tent is in the room toward the back, with the linen curtain across the doorway. You can't miss the tent. There are two long bundles of the tarp and several bundles of poles. It will be easier if one of us removes the curtain. Set everything right outside the gate. If the merchant isn't already waiting for us, he'll be along any time now."

Shmuel started walking, motioning for the others to follow. "If there are no questions, let's go. We can't waste time."

James exchanged a knowing grin with Nati and Baruch, then they followed Shmuel.

The group arrived at Gershon's house as planned and proceeded to the assigned room. Baruch stood back as Shmuel stretched to reach the curtain rod and lifted it from its holder. Then, he gathered the curtain, moved away from the entrance, and started wrapping the curtain around the rod. Baruch allowed the scribes to enter the room first, then followed.

Baruch took one step past the entrance and gasped deep enough to lose his breath at the sight before him. He grabbed the door frame with one hand, clutched his chest with the other, and slid down the frame until he was sitting on the floor.

"Gershon!" He expelled the name with his exhalation. "Wh-what have you done? You're betrothed!" He stared at the younger man, still abed and not alone. "This isn't happening. I've witnessed this now. There's no choice...it's the law. You have to know this is death! Gershon, why?"

Scribes James and Nati had already pulled parchment, reeds, and small ink jars from their robe pockets and were sitting on the floor, doubtless recording everything as it unfolded.

Gershon jumped out of bed, ran to the other side, and grabbed the arm of the woman attempting to hide under the covers. With her free hand, she wrestled Gershon's hand, but he grabbed that arm just above her wrist, pulling her out of bed, her night tunic untwisting as he forced her up. With both feet squarely planted and immovable, Gershon kept his grip on her struggling arms, his shoulders rigid, his lips pressed in a straight line, avoiding all eye contact.

The scribes cringed at the woman's every sob and plea, but they wrote on, documenting every detail.

Baruch leaned his head on his forearm against the doorframe. "Gershon, I know her husband. Why...why didn't you come to us? We could have helped you."

Shmuel dropped the curtain rod, ran to Gershon, and took one of the woman's arms. "Baruch, get up! Help me get her to the square before *He* leaves."

Scribe James took one look at Baruch and ran to take the woman's other arm from Gershon. As the men pulled her outside, she struggled but was unable to break free. Scribe Nati gathered up the parchment, reeds, and ink jars and followed.

Baruch fought for breath. How long had he been sitting here? *I have to get up. This heaviness...I can't move...I have to move...I'll make myself move.* He placed his left hand on the door frame, then his right above the left, each movement sluggish, as though a plumb line to a heavy stone was tied to each wrist. Alternating his hands up the door frame, he pulled himself up. All the while, he struggled to calm his irregular heartbeat with steady breaths.

Standing at last, he leaned his head against both hands, still clutching the door frame. *Now, face the courtyard and start walking... Lift your foot. I can lift my foot...one after the other...and walk...one step at a time...it's not far.* Each step fought him as if he were lifting his entire body weight.

When Baruch arrived at the square, the woman had already been placed in front of Jesus. Before climbing the steps, Baruch pulled one end of his head shawl across his mustache and beard, then rested it on the opposite shoulder. Once he reached the crowd, he wove within it and positioned himself in its center.

After Jesus stood and gave instructions on who could throw the first stone, two Pharisees standing near Baruch started leaving. He followed with his head down, leaving a distance between them, checking that the end of his shawl remained secure over his shoulder. Once he'd left the square, he walked around the building and straightened, allowing his shawl to fall back into place, then entered the synagogue through the back.

As he reached the entrance to his study, a student ran toward him. "Baruch! There you are. The High Priest is looking for you."

Baruch stopped short and looked square at the student. "I'm not available."

"But you're on the sched—"

"I'm *not* available! Do not disturb me—not today."

"Oh, all...all right," the student said, taking a step back. "I will tell him."

Baruch entered his study, closed the curtain, and spent what was left of the morning alone. When quiet descended, signaling that everyone had gone for the afternoon meal, he left unnoticed out the back to return home.

Halfway past the synagogue's plot of land, he spotted something out of the corner of his eye, a movement through an opening in a grove of trees that marked the property line. He stepped back, peeked through tree branches, and stepped back again. Shmuel, sitting in the farthest corner of the plot. Baruch let out a breath. Shmuel hadn't seen him. He started to walk away, but he should at least check on his friend. He could always run if he had to.

Baruch stepped through the trees and, cautious and quiet, wound his way along paths around flower gardens. Low hedges sectioned off the gardens, with a bench inside each. Some sections included trees just tall enough to provide shade.

He stepped up to Shmuel's bench and was about to sit beside him when he spotted his friend's headpiece on the ground. He picked it up, brushed off the dirt, and sat on the other end of the bench, placing the headpiece between them.

Shmuel's tear-filled eyes stared straight ahead into nothing.

Baruch fidgeted with his fingers, making several side glances at Shmuel, trying not to focus on his disheveled hair, the dirt down the front of his robe, his outer shawl hanging from one shoulder, or his scraped knuckles.

"Well...He sure outwitted you," Baruch said at last, his voice just above a whisper.[2]

"Shut up, Baruch!"

"I will," he said in his normal tone. He removed his own headpiece, set it next to Shmuel's, and ran his fingers through the top of his hair. "Have you seen Gershon?"

Shmuel continued staring into nothing. "During all the commotion, he snuck up to the roof and lay flat until everyone was gone. The merchant smuggled him out. I don't know if that was before or after transporting the tent to my place. I only know he won't be back."

Baruch moistened his lower lip. "And his betrothed?"

Shmuel swallowed, shifted his position, and lowered his gaze. "She returned to her village right after their betrothal to wait for him. I don't know what she knew or what will become of them now."

Shmuel brushed the dirt from his robe and attempted to straighten his outer shawl. "You know, I...I also saw Gershon without his garb. I left the house for the synagogue hours earlier that morning. The quietness and stillness at daybreak—I wanted to savor that peacefulness. I was approaching the steps to the square when I

____

2.   This story about the woman caught in adultery is not the first time scribes and Pharisees tried to trick Jesus. Luke 11:54 (AMP) states that scribes and Pharisees would secretly watch and plot and lie in wait for Him, to seize upon something he might say, so they could accuse Him.

Luke 20:19-20, 26 (AMP) describes how the scribes and chief priests tried to find a way to arrest Him, watching for an opportunity to ensnare him, even sending spies, who pretended to be upright, honest, and sincere to lay hold of something He might say, so as to turn Him over to the control and authority of the governor. Verse 26 describes how nobody could use anything He said against Him and instead marveled at what He said and kept quiet.

happened to look to my left. *She* was leaving Gershon's house. A moment later, he followed.

Shmuel looked at Baruch, "I also went to the High Priest. He went so deep into thought, I wondered if he knew I was still in front of him. To my relief, he returned to the present and told me we would hold a secret meeting; only the few of us. He had a general plan, and we all finalized it. Gershon was granted immunity."

Baruch placed both hands on his knees, his back and arms straight. "That was quite a well-laid plan, but why did you pull me into it?"

"You weren't supposed to be. Another Pharisee was to meet me at my house. He didn't show up. You happened by. The plan was in place, and it had to all go down before *He* was done speaking."

Baruch rested one elbow on his knee and rubbed his lips before letting his arm drop across his lap. "Where are the scribes?"

Shmuel shook his head. "I didn't notice where they went when they left the square." His lips quivered, another supply of tears forming. "When I left, I stood to the side of the main entrance, where I could observe. He told her she wasn't condemned."

Shmuel wiped his eyes with the sleeve of his robe and stifled the onset of sobs. "After she left the square, He turned and looked straight at me. His eyes did not search for me. He knew exactly where I was standing."

Baruch rested a hand on his friend's shoulder.

Shmuel jerked away. "Don't. I'm unclean. I held her arm, remember?"

Baruch dropped his arm to his side. "Good thing nobody saw that."

Shmuel crumpled his shawl in both hands, slumped forward, and sobbed into it.

Baruch set both headpieces on the ground and rested his hand on the bench just short of touching Shmuel, every few moments giving him pained looks.

Shmuel at last sat up and wiped his face, then wrapped and

unwrapped his shawl around his knuckles. "His eyes were piercing—like an arrow with a perfect aim—to the very core of my being. His comment was bad enough. I felt so...exposed...with nowhere to hide. I couldn't take that comment *and* His eyes."

Baruch moved his hand back to his own side. "What did you do?"

"Dashed through the synagogue, came out the back, and ran here. I tripped on my way over...fell flat on my face. I don't even know what tripped me." Shmuel uncrumpled his shawl, draped it over one shoulder, and shifted his posture. "Next thing I knew, I was punching the ground, the rock, a tree trunk, a bench. I don't even know what I was punching. I don't recall how I got to this bench. Then, I threw my headpiece."

He stared at the butterflies on the hedges, still fidgeting with the edge of his shawl, remnants of tears in his eyes. "All I wanted to do was prove Him wrong. If someone who claims the rights of the Most High excused this law, it was proof He was blaspheming and a false messiah. Then, we'd have Him. An easy case for the Sanhedrin court."

Baruch nodded a few times, his eyebrows drawing together.

Shmuel let his shawl go and spoke with his hands. "It wasn't just his eyes. It was His comment. How can one comment pierce someone that deep? How?"

He wiped the remaining tears from his eyes. "You should have seen her—she danced on air when she left the square, acting like every disgraced mark had been removed from her."[3] He turned to Baruch, his hand motions intense. "How can a woman like her be restored after she has been caught? How? And He tells her *He* doesn't

---

3. In the Biblical account of the woman caught in adultery, she did not deny her actions. I John 1:9 (NKJV): "If we confess our sins, He is faithful and just to forgive us our sins and to cleanse us from all unrighteousness." The Greek word for *cleanse* also means *to purify*. Jesus *purifies* us from all the unrighteousness of our sins. Also, Luke 5:24 (AMP): "But that you may know that the Son of Man has the [power of] authority and right on earth to forgive sins,..."

find her guilty. Who can do that? And how is that even possible when the law clearly requires her death!"[4]

Baruch studied Shmuel, raising an eyebrow. "Well...maybe He...is the Mess—"

Shmuel held both sides of his head, shaking it back and forth. "I... I can't take this anymore." He stood, his shawl falling to the ground, and strode toward the garden's exit at his usual brisk pace.

"Shmuel, wait...here." Baruch stood and picked up the shawl and headpiece. "You need your—"

"No!" Shmuel stopped short and faced him. "I don't *want* them!"

Baruch's eyes widened. "Wh-where are you going, then?"

"I don't know...somewhere...anywhere. Read my own writings to find out how many sacrifices I make, how many trespass offerings I give, how many times I immerse in a mikva. I don't know. Somewhere in all this..." He shook his head. "I go to Hadassah." Then, he turned on his heel and left the garden.[5]

Baruch returned to the bench, holding Shmuel's headpiece and shawl, watching him leave with an aching heart. He lowered his head and whispered, "YHWH, only you can confirm that *He* is the Messiah."[6]

---

4. Acts 13:38-39 (NKJV): "Therefore, let it be known to you, brethren, that through this Man is preached to you the forgiveness of sins; and by Him everyone who believes is justified from all things from which you could not be justified by the Law of Moses."
5. Shmuel was a Pharisee who lived by works and the law, striving to be perfect to earn God's favor. But the woman who was caught, who was far from perfect, encountered the Messiah's grace and mercy. There is no religious system that can save anyone. No number of laws you follow can save you. Only the Messiah come in human flesh.
6. There were Pharisees, besides Nicodemus, who believed that Jesus is the Messiah. Acts 15:5 (AMP): "But some who believed [who acknowledged Jesus as their Savior and devoted themselves to Him] belonged to the sect of the Pharisees..." Also, in Luke 13:31, the Pharisees went to Jesus to warn him of Herod's plot to kill him. There were also leaders. John 12:42 gives an account of leading men, the authorities, and the nobles who also believed but did not confess it because of fear of the Pharisees.

SCIENCE FICTION & FANTASY

TRUE TO FORM

SHARON ROSE

Tingles shot along Timon's skin. No matter how many times he heard Philip tell this story, it always thrilled. Always filled him with longing.

Philip's face glowed more from excitement than the sheen of sweat under the blazing sun. "One minute, I'm beside the Ethiopian in the oasis pool. The next, I'm on the outskirts of Azotus, with water still running down my legs. There was not a single moment in between. I was just *there*."

Luke's pen no longer scratched across the parchment in his lap. No one could hear Philip recount this miracle without being transfixed. Some peppered him with questions. Others mocked. But after a long gaze into Philip's eyes, Luke dipped his pen and continued writing.

Timon wasn't surprised. When Luke had something important to say, it came from his pen, not his tongue.

Luke finished and placed the parchment within the stiff leather case he carried everywhere. "Thank you, Philip. I've heard this story second-hand, but I needed to hear it from your own lips."

"Do you believe me?"

Timon held his breath. He'd known Philip for years, ever since they'd waited on the widows back in Jerusalem. It galled him when people doubted.

"Every word, Philip," Luke said. "Even if I didn't know you, I know the Spirit. He bears witness with you. This miracle will be in the letter I'm writing."

"When will you finish?" Timon asked.

A shadow crossed Luke's face. "I...don't know, Simon—er, *Timon*." He clutched Timon's arm. "I'm so sorry. It's only while talking that I mix up names. I have them all written down, and yours shall be faithfully recorded in the letter."

As though he had done anything for Luke to write about. His mundane life was as forgettable as his name. "It's everyone else's story that I want to read. I know you research carefully and that takes time, but...how about a goal? By year's end, yes?"

Luke snorted, staring at the dust. "Sometimes, I feel like...never."

"But—it's so important!"

"Is it? How many people will read it?"

Timon could hardly believe his ears. "Well, for starters, Theophilus will read it to his household, then to his local assembly. He can certainly afford scribes to make copies, and you know that letters are being carried throughout the church."

The corners of Luke's mouth crept up. "You think highly of me. I thank you."

Philip gripped Luke's shoulder. "So do I, but that's not the point, is it? I'll ask you this, instead. Does it matter how many people read it? God sent me into the desert for one Ethiopian. And didn't our Lord say that a shepherd rejoices over saving only one lost sheep?"

Luke gave him a wry smile. "You're right, of course."

"I am. Don't ever let me hear that you've given up. I'll come looking for you."

A chuckle eased Luke's somber expression. "I don't think I *can* give up. The fervor that comes on me to write is indescribable. These sudden discouragements..." He raised a shoulder. "They prove that the evil one wants to stop me. All the more reason to continue." He shoved himself to his feet. "God bless you, my brothers."

Timon shaded his eyes, watching Luke walk away. Heat waves shimmered around his retreating form. The assembly rooms would be stifling tonight. He'd be drenched in sweat before he finished serving.

The endless serving. Why couldn't he have an important calling like Philip or Luke?

"What troubles you, Timon?" Philip asked.

Was he that obvious? He relaxed his frown. "Oh, it's nothing. I better get moving too."

Philip stood when Timon did and fell into step beside him. "Nothing? I know you better than that. You go from vibrant to empty. What takes you there?"

Timon stared at the dusty road. He hated to sound discontented. Hated even more to admit it was true. "It's not important. It's just..." Words refused to form.

"*Just* is no answer. Spit it out, man."

"What I do doesn't matter." He clenched his fists. "And I know I shouldn't feel this way. The widows and orphans must be fed. I'd never abandon them. But you and Luke change lives." The hidden ember within him flamed, and words rushed out. "Remember the seven of us who were appointed in Jerusalem? Everyone else has gone on to great things. Stephen preached to our highest authorities, and his words still echo long after his death. God works miracles through you and converts whole towns. In Samaria, no less." He splayed his fingers. "But me? Even when I move to different cities, I end up filling empty mouths day after day. What's wrong with me?"

"Have you ever wondered why Stephen and I were chosen to serve widows?"

Timon stared at him. Had he even been listening?

"We were hopelessly inept," Philip said. "Would anyone have been fed without you?"

"Well...uh..."

Philip guffawed. "Go ahead—say it. The answer is *no*. You may even admit that we were more of a trial than a help."

"You were...diligent."

"And you are forgiving. Do you remember the time Stephen had all the fish delivered to one assembly and all the bread to another?"

"Could I ever forget?" Timon produced a dramatic shudder, though he grinned. "Or the look on his face? It was the grace of God that I straightened out that mess before anyone arrived."

"But you did. The point is, the elders had to ensure that the widows were fed. You made it happen. The rest of us were a bunch of colts, bursting with zeal but no sense. They were wise to give us practical work until we matured.

"So, back to your question." Philip gripped Timon's shoulder. "Nothing is wrong with you, but much is right. You are doing the task God assigned you. And admit it..." He stopped and turned Timon to meet his eyes. "You're good at it."

Warmth spread through Timon. He'd gladly perform any task for his Lord, no matter how insignificant. If only he could see a glimmer of lasting value. But Philip was doing his best to cheer him up. It wasn't his fault that his words didn't change anything. How could he end this discussion? "I suppose I should quit wondering what it's like for you. It just makes me discontented." They started walking again, and Timon hoped that was the end of it.

Not for Philip. "What do you wonder?"

This wasn't going to make it better, but Timon couldn't resist. "What did it feel like to be caught away? Was it terribly shocking?"

"Oddly, no. I felt calm—even though I *was* surprised." Philip smirked as if at a memory. "When I wandered into Azotus, I was staring at everything with my mouth hanging open. Someone asked me, 'Haven't you ever seen a town before?'"

Timon chuckled at Philip's imitation. "How do you mimic people so well?"

"That's nothing. I'll tell you what's really amazing! That Ethiopian had an ear-twisting accent. He can read four languages, but he could barely converse with anyone in Jerusalem. Yet I could understand him perfectly, and he understood me. It happens wherever I travel, instant comprehension and clear speech."

Longing surged again, like a bird trying to break free from his chest. Trapped, it would shrivel into disappointment like always, but he couldn't resist imagining.

Tingles surged through his body. He shivered in a cool breeze, and his next footstep hit rock. Smooth rock, set in squares along the roadside.

Timon stared up the paved road. "Philip?" His voice squeaked like he was thirteen.

"Yeah." Shocked awe whispered on Philip's strange syllable.

He must see the same impossible vision Timon did. "Where *are* we?"

"I have no idea. Even Rome doesn't have buildings like this."

The nearest were taller than the temple, but possible. Those beyond—they seemed to scrape the sky!

Someone detoured around them with a contemptuous snort. "Haven't you ever seen a city before?"

They looked at each other and burst into laughter. Philip collapsed onto a low wall, clutching his sides, and Timon sat next to him. People hurried by, pointedly ignoring them.

Timon caught snatches of conversation. "It's just like you said, Philip. I understand them. But where...when...?"

"You sense it, too?"

"What do you mean?"

Philip's voice dropped. "We aren't just in a different place. We're in a different time."

"Yes," Timon said slowly, trying to get a better look at one of the wheeled things that whooshed past them. "It feels like centuries have passed. Is that possible?"

"Once when I heard brother Peter preach, he said the strangest thing. 'A day with the Lord is like a thousand years, and a thousand years is like a day.' I didn't understand at all, but now? A day did not pass for us." He spread his hands in broad gestures. "Yet these wheeled things speed by with nothing to pull them, buildings rise too high to be built, and..." He plucked at the bluish fabric covering his leg. "What are we wearing?"

Strange garments, but words came to Timon. "Trousers. Although this blue kind are called jeans."

"You're catching onto the language better than I am." Philip felt around the top of his jeans and slid his hand into a gap. "I kind of like these concealed pouches."

"Pockets."

"Oh. Yeah, right."

Timon shoved his hands deep into his own pockets, marveling at how natural they felt. There was something inside one. He wrapped his fingers around it and drew it out. Folded parchment. He pulled it straight. Centered on it was a drawing of a high-browed, dignified man with tiny letters underneath. Wonder spiked chills. He could read them! *Franklin.* Like Caesar on a coin. "This is money."

Philip scoffed. "How can parchment be money?"

"I don't know, but it says it right here." He pointed at the lower corner. "*One hundred dollars,* and this shiny green is the number *100.*"

Philip frowned at it. "I think you're right. Do you suppose that's a lot or a little?"

Timon got the uncomfortable feeling of being watched and glanced up. Sure enough. He pushed the money back into his pocket. "I don't know, but God provided, so it is sufficient."

"Good point." Philip's eyes tracked one of the speeding—ah, *cars.* "Such an unnatural scent. I almost prefer dung."

The cars darted along the street, only to stop quickly at

intersections and wait their turn to cross. Were those colored lights controlling it all? Mindlessly ordering both cars and people, telling them when and where to go, holding them back in little herds, even when the way was clear. Incredible! And skeptics claimed that the message of Christ was hard to believe.

The lights changed, and a herd strolled past, breaking into smaller groups. They chattered in this language that Timon had never heard until he and Philip spoke it. He wanted to jump up and shout. At last, his chance had come. This was his time to make a life-changing impact.

Philip, of course, had to make it sound like status quo. "You can understand them, right?"

Timon forced his voice to matter-of-fact. "Every word."

Two women strode by, one of them furious. "He has an MBA, so he tells us twice a day, but he can't even calculate an accurate ROI."

Timon blinked hard. "Um, most of it."

"That one was weird," Philip said. "Maybe that's how they curse here." Philip slapped his legs and stood. "Come on. There's got to be a reason we're here. Let's get moving."

Timon jumped up and followed him to the nearest intersection. How like Philip. Just head out with no idea where he was going. "Shouldn't we have a plan, or at least a goal?"

"I've got nothing." Philip spread his hands. "What urge is rising in you?"

Timon's eyes were drawn to one side. A few blocks away, a spire poked above a brick building. "Look."

Philip followed the line of his pointing finger. "At what?"

"The top of that spire. It's shaped like a cross. Maybe we should go there."

"Crucifixion is still a thing?" He twitched his head. "They have the strangest way of turning a phrase in this language. I've gotta say, Timon, an execution hill is not a good place to evangelize."

"Of course not, but it couldn't mean that. This city isn't Roman.

You said so yourself. The cross reminds me of Jesus. Are you coming?"

Philip grinned. "Lead on."

The fitful breeze followed them down the street. The unfamiliar sights took on meaning. Someone placed food on a table between two people. That was a restaurant. Those others were shops, like indoor market stalls. And the brick building with a spire—that was called a church. Why? Church meant the followers of Christ. The dull white building next to it bore the words *Hope Mission*. Equally strange. A mission was what one did, not a building.

Double doors of cracked wood blocked the arched entry of the church. Now that they stood in front of it, Timon caught sight of a small garden wedged between the two structures. A scrawny olive tree draped a branch over a stone bench. Something moved on the bench, and Timon stepped closer to see what the wind ruffled. He drew an awed breath. It was a stack of impossibly thin parchments, all anchored together along one side. A book. Brilliant! He glimpsed a couple words, *Psalms*, then *Isaiah*. Did it hold all the words of many scrolls?

"Good morning," a woman said. Timon startled, for he hadn't seen her from the street. She emptied a watering can over a bed of herbs. "Are you hungry?" The tiny scrunch of her eyes hinted at worry. "I'm afraid we can't open until five o'clock today, but perhaps I can find something for you."

Philip found his tongue first—of course. "Uh, no. That is, no, ma'am, we're not hungry."

"Oh. Sorry. Hope I didn't offend you. It's just that most people come for food." She darted her hand out. "I'm Marty. I manage the mission."

Philip extended his hand in like manner. She grabbed it and gave it a quick pump. Without the least hint of shock in his voice, he replied, "I'm Philip, and this is Timon."

"Simon?" she asked, as he let her pump his hand.

"Timon," he corrected.

"Ah. Unusual name. And yet..." She tucked a gray-brown lock of hair behind her ear. "Somehow, it's familiar." A twinkle lit her hazel eyes, and she gestured toward the bound parchments. "Perhaps you stopped because you're interested in my Bible."

"I, uh, am interested in writings." Timon groaned inside. Why couldn't he come up with anything sensible to say?

But Marty just picked up the Bible and placed it in his hands. "You're welcome to a closer look."

He stared at the page, dumbfounded. *Acts 6* was inscribed across the top, but the text below—he devoured it. Philip could talk to the woman. He was already questioning some detail. "You said something about managing the mission. What do you mean?"

"I run all the practical things that Pastor John tends to forget about," she said. "Getting enough food for the homeless people, cooking, organizing volunteers. Pastor John feeds their souls, and I feed their bodies."

Philip nudged Timon. "Did you hear that? She feeds homeless people." He must have seen shock on Timon's face and asked, "What are you reading?"

Timon pointed at the words and struggled to keep the conversation going while Philip took the Bible. "Oh, uh, poor people?" Her expression told him he wasn't doing well.

"Yes. What do you do?"

"Well, I..." He uttered an uncertain titter. "I feed widows and orphans."

She tilted her head back and laughed. "So, that's what surprised you. There aren't many of us, are there? How long have you been at it?"

"Many years." Timon sighed. "More than I ever expected."

"Is the sense of futility getting to you? Feeding the same hungry mouths day after day?"

He couldn't believe his ears. Another person who actually understood. Far better than Philip did. "Yes. You have those feelings, too?"

"'Course I do."

"Hey, Marty!" a voice shouted from across the street. "Three more last night."

Timon twisted around. A young man with dark skin strode down the sidewalk, triumph shining through his toothy grin.

Marty's smile reflected his joy as she shouted back, "True to your form!"

"What does all that mean?" Timon asked.

"That's Tamru, one of the reasons I carry on. Five years ago, everyone thought he was a lost cause. He's the son of Ethiopian immigrants. They're Christians, but he got rebellious and ran away from home. Started hanging with the wrong crowd. In trouble more often than not. He only came to the mission 'cause he was hungry and too proud to go home. But he finally started to listen." She beamed. "It changed his life. Now, he takes it to the streets. That little bit you heard is our code. He tells me a number, but I know what he means. Last night, he introduced three people to Jesus."

Ah, the Word still spread! "What does 'true to your form' mean?'"

"Oh, that's just the way Pastor John phrased it one day when he was talking about how everyone needs to follow their own calling. Sort of like maintaining good form during a race so you can go the distance. But also remembering that our own *true to form* won't look like someone else's. A wrestler and a runner may both win the prize, but what they are doing looks entirely different."

Marty paused and took in Philip's bemused expression. "What *is* it you two have found in there to make you look so stunned?"

Timon took the Bible from Philip before it could end up on the dirty sidewalk. He'd never seen Philip speechless, but he'd seen him drop plenty. Besides, there was something Timon needed to ask— driving at him like he'd left a task undone. "You said something about not being able to open until five o'clock, and frankly, I've seen enough worry to recognize it."

The tight look returned to her eyes. "We try for three meals a day. Usually works out, but we're a little behind."

Timon reached into his pocket and pulled out the money. "We're new to this city. How many meals will this buy here?"

Marty pushed her lower lip out. "Mm, in a fancy restaurant downtown, two. In my mission, more than a hundred."

That was it. Timon put the strange money between the pages and closed the Bible on it. "I always like to see money in the hands of the best steward. As for what Philip and I are gawking at, we just read our names together." He handed the Bible to her. "May our Lord's grace be upon you, and may His rest lighten the work of your mission."

She blinked her eyes wide, then flipped the Bible open, the pages separating at the money. She pushed it aside, seeking words. Then, her brow rose even higher. "Ah! There's your name, Timon, and Philip, too. Funny coincidence, but I still don't see why—"

In the moment that her gaze met his, the city vanished.

Familiar heat, dust, and sunlight surrounded the men. Their own world. The same, but forever different. At least for them.

Minutes passed before Timon broke the silence with a whisper. "I've known His love all these years, and still have not fathomed it! That He'd send me all that way just to show me..." His voice choked off.

"And me." Philip sounded equally stunned. "I didn't even realize I needed it, but I did. Ethiopian Christians...we're all connected. Like the entwined ropes of a huge net thrown out over centuries. Do you realize what we were reading?"

"Luke's letter. And much more was in that book." Hot, dry air filled Timon's lungs, grounding him to his own time and place. "The end of the age is not in our days. Nor have we found the ends of the earth. Orphans must grow up, become disciples of our Lord, and carry His words *far*. Much farther and many more generations than I ever imagined." His words vibrated the quiet of the dusty road. "We are part of a magnificent plan!"

Author's note: This time-travel story grew from a challenge to write about a Bible character who is rarely mentioned. I chose Timon, whose name appears only once in the Bible (Acts 6:5).

For more information on Sharon Rose's books, visit her website: SharonRoseAuthor.com.

VINESINGER

BRIDGETT POWERS

The day Shara joined the mission to rescue the Wise One, she couldn't stop singing. It was her way. In joy, she sang. In sorrow, she sang. When nervous...she sang.

The brown and green strands of her tail fanned out, longer and wider than her body, as she took a running leap at the vine. She gripped the silken stalk with both hands, her tiny brown fingers barely spanning its girth, then swung up in an arc and flipped through the air. Curling her tail around a branch, she released the vine to hang upside-down, scanning the trees for the others.

Inhaling the thick jungle air, she fought the urge to close her eyes. The slow rhythm of the tree's growth pulsed through her tail. Stirred by her passing, the underbrush swished in a languid dance, giving rise to the honeyed scents of flowers it protected from the heat. Ah, so much life growing around her!

The Wise One claimed humans couldn't sense the pulse of life, as could Ehlief growers and healers. Shara wrinkled her nose. What good was humankind's gift of twice an Ehlief's height if they couldn't even...

A flash of purple cut through the jungle and her musings.

Swallowing the tune building in her throat, Shara flipped upward to catch the nearest branch and follow. She was one of *them* now, a warrior.

"You're doing it again," the captain barked under his breath, his purple and green tail snapping, blade-like, behind him.

"Doing what?" Shara whispered.

"Singing," the captain hissed, his pointy brown ears twitching. "All of Zyungland will know we're coming!"

Oh. Some songs just wouldn't be stifled.

"Stealth, Shara," he whisper-shouted. "No noise. No chattering faster than the birds nesting in your home-tree. And no singing!"

Stealth. She could do stealth. The Wise One's life depended on it.

As she swung after the captain, a new thought dampened her spirits. What would the Zyung tribesmen who had taken the ancient seer do once they discovered that her "magic" would give them no advantage over an enemy tribe? Magic, indeed! The King of All Lands granted each Ehlief specific gifts and a role to play, signified by the two or three colors in his or her tail. Like other humans, the Zyung had no tails. Perhaps that explained everything.

But what explanation was there for Shara's...oddity? She swung to another branch, trying to banish memories of the questions whispered behind fanned tails when no one thought she was listening. With her strands of grower-brown and defender-green, she fit nowhere. Too hyper to be one of the healers, all calming voices and tails of brown and white. Too vivacious to be a warrior, with their purple and green balance of destruction and defense. What *was* she?

Despite the captain's argument that a grower of life could never perform a warrior's duty, their chief had insisted she join this mission. "Her aim's as good as yours, Captain," he'd said. "She's only 150 summers. Her whimsy will fade soon enough."

Whimsy? Ha! As she scanned the ground for tracks, her heart pounded through her ears, leaving room for neither whim nor whisper. The Zyung were close.

"Silence!" the captain hissed.

What? He'd heard...? Oh, she was singing again. She bit her lip and followed him.

Two Zyung sentries strode into view below, their bronze skin glistening. The captain gestured at the sentry on the right, then pointed his bow at the one on the left. His target fell, arrow-pierced.

Shara took aim, but at the thought of ending life, half the strands in her tail stiffened. She glanced about for another way. *Any* way. That was brown in her tail, after all, not purple. There! She aimed at a spot over the Zyung's head. Her arrow flew true, severing a hard-shelled fruit from its stem. The hull struck the sentry's skull, felling him without sound. He would wake, but not until they'd gone.

The captain narrowed his eyes on her, then motioned onward.

They continued to the enemy camp without further incident. At its center stood the Wise One, trussed up like a hunter's meal, tiny flames tickling her wrinkled toes, vines binding even her faded blue and yellow tail. Her wizened face crinkled further as a Zyung stirred the coals and demanded she use her magic.

The green strands of Shara's tail sprang upward like a wall of spears at her back, and a shrill note escaped her lips. The jungle erupted in a chaos of color and sound, ending with the point of a Zyung spear planted in the captain's stomach.

No! The whispers were true. She'd endangered them all!

A lament burst from the pit of Shara's soul. Anguished notes carried her cry to the King of All Lands. *Fix this!*

The brown strands joined the green in her tail, curling up over her head until even she caught sight of them. As they writhed, warmth pulsed through her body, a rhythm that radiated to the tips of her toes, her fingers, and even to the ends of her spiky hair.

Shara's ethereal song multiplied and seemed to vitalize the very forest around her. Vines slithered along the ground, dropped from trees, untied themselves from Zyung bundles. They snaked around the Zyung tribesman as he pressed his spear harder into the captain's gut. Shara lengthened her notes, and the vines tightened, choking the enemy. The sight of the struggling man strangled Shara's song, leaving it weak and wispy as his breath.

Like dry leaves, the Wise One's voice rustled through the now silent clearing, "The Vinesinger has come!"

The Vinesinger, defender of the Ehlief? *Her?* Shara swung around to face the Wise One.

The ancient Ehlief sat beyond the fire, cradled in her former bonds. Vines cocooned every Zyung in sight, pinning, crushing, strangling.

Shara clamped both hands to her mouth, eyes wide.

The captain pinned her with a flinty stare. "Finish the song, Shara," he ordered.

For the first time in her life, the realm required her voice, and she longed to remain silent.

Editor's note: This story is set in the distant past of the Seven Lands, the world of the author's Light-Wielder Chronicles series and its prequel, "Tria," which appears later in this anthology. "Vinesinger" was originally published in Havok *magazine 1.3, in July, 2014. For more stories by Bridgett, visit her website: BridgettPowers.com.*

A WRITING COMPANION

DREW CLAPP

I scratched my golden feathering, and some of it floated to the floor. The doggone bath had dried my skin…again. I glanced at my buddy. Maybe he'd help with a few scratches.

He tapped the table and stared at the square of light shining from the box in front of him. Sighing, he crumpled the thick fur on his head.

I flattened my ears back. *He almost never does this!* When he climbed the stairs to this guest room, he usually pounced on the small box tied to the big one with the light that shows pictures. What could I do? My tail twitched. *Ah, I know.*

I nudged his arm and tucked my snout into his lap. He stroked my head as I turned and moved away. His hand slid from my neck to my back, then to my haunches. I blew out a shivery breath, the unreachable itches relieved. He stopped scratching.

"*Ruff!*" I barked twice, looking up at him, then growled.

My human turned and looked at me. "What is it, Graham? You have been fed and out. I checked your water, and it's fine."

I pinned my ears back, smiled, and latched onto his forearm.

He didn't budge. "I have to finish this scene. What is it? Do you want to play?"

I tugged at his clothes.

"Okay, bud. I'm not getting anything done anyway. Let's go outside." He shut the box.

My buddy skipped down the stairs. I stopped and stared through the posts of the banister and watched. He snapped his fingers and pointed at his feet.

"Come, Graham." My human patted his leg. "I have treats."

Treats! He was committed. My mission was a go! I scampered down the steps.

My buddy walked through the dining room and kitchen. He whistled, and I pranced into the mud room that didn't have any mud in it.

What would we play? Fetch or maybe Keep Away with my favorite stick?"

He lifted a hand and pressed it to my face. "Sit...Stay."

My human slipped on a coat, then grabbed gloves and dropped them on one of my food, treat, and supply bins. He stooped to lace shoes, and I gave him several well-placed kisses across his cheeks and mouth.

He coughed and wrinkled his snout. "Yes, yes. I love you too, Graham."

I wagged and wagged, eager to run loops in the backyard, as my buddy slid the gloves on and opened the door to the car kennel. We stepped inside, then he grabbed the hidden tennis ball and squeezed it. I jumped at it.

"No, down!" He kneed my chest. "Settle...Sit."

I whimpered as my tail thwacked against the wall. He opened the side door and gestured.

I darted to his side, sat, and glanced at him. *Come on, throw it.*

He waited a few moments, then hurled the green sphere.

Quivering, I looked at the ball, then him. *I'm waiting. Say it!*

My human clapped his hands. "Okay!"

I dashed across the snow and dead grass. My jaw trembled as I clamped my teeth onto the squishy, squeaky ball, just hard enough to pick it up. Then, I galloped back and forth on the soft ground, flinging mud and frozen chunks behind me. I returned and pushed the ball into my buddy's hand. He wrapped his palm around it, and I jerked the ball away.

My human signaled. "Drop."

"*Rrr, rrr!*" I prodded and taunted him. *It's mine now.*

"No..." he said. "Drop."

I growled again.

"Drop."

Still growling, I clenched the ball tighter, and we whirled around each other.

He wrenched it out of my mouth. "Sit."

I did but gave him my deepest *Rrruff* to show what I thought of that.

"Patience." He threw the ball again. "Fetch."

I darted off, scooped up the treasure, and rushed up a hill. After sprinting to the other side, I looped some lonely plants. The smooth white stuff crunched beneath my paws as I bolted up a steep slope and along the tree line. I turned, slipped, and ran the same track several more times, then plopped on the ground overlooking the fire pit and dropped the ball. It rolled down and stopped. I looked at my buddy. What would he do?

He walked toward the ball.

Aha, I see you going after my toy. I dipped my head, watching for my human's next move, daring him to get it.

He took a few more steps and crouched.

I licked my nose. *You think you're faster than me? We will see.* I yawned. *Don't think you're fooling me. That was a distraction.*

My buddy walked sideways, sauntered back, then lunged.

I leapt forward, swiped the toy, and bounded to a safer distance.

The squeaky ball announced my victory. I strutted around, tolling the news to the nearby trees and bushes. An invisible blast shook the foliage and joined in my celebration, waving congratulations. I trotted around my buddy in triumph.

He squatted and pulled out a treat. I dropped the ball and sat.

"Good boy." My human broke the biscuit. "Sit...Stay."

I barked and obeyed.

"Nice," he said, then held out the treat.

I snatched the crunchy delight. He tossed the ball to himself, counted down from ten, and lobbed the rounded toy.

I glanced at him, then to where it landed.

He shouted, "Fetch!"

I looked at my buddy and dropped the green ball in front of his feet. *Please don't stop. I want to keep playing.* Soft growls rumbled in my throat as my tail swished the snow.

My human picked up the ball. "Stay." He ran to another spot in the backyard.

I perked my ears. What was he doing?

He squeezed the ball and threw it. "Good stay, Graham." He clapped. "Fetch!"

I charged to the sunken treasure and sprinted a few loops. After circling the firepit and passing a garden, I flumped on the cool ground and released the squeak toy. I panted and licked off the snow-covered ball, then poked at it, nudging it toward my buddy.

You can have it...at least for now. I furrowed my brow and stared at him. *"How can you stand there? I have been doing all the hard play.*

I rested my head on my front paws and crunched on snowy clusters within reach. The refreshing clumps quenched any trace of thirst. I chewed the frozen irritants between my paws and nails.

My human grabbed the ball and dashed from the trees to the flowerbed to the driveway. I watched his silly movements. He huffed, puffed, and sat on the ground.

I popped my head up and grinned. *Ha! Now you know how I feel.*

He rubbed his jaw, stood, then walked over and opened the side door. I followed him in, and he laid the ball behind a black-and-yellow container.

I cocked my head. *What do you want to do now?*

When he walked into the main part of the house, I leaped up the steps and drank some water. Something jingled behind me. I finished my food and turned around.

My buddy held a bag and the leash.

I curled my tail. *Are you going to do what I'm thinking?*

"Yes, Graham. We are going for a walk," my human said, clipping my collar around my neck. He stuffed the bag into his pocket.

Fantastic! A nice walk meant I could meet others like him, and he could talk with them. I would also see others like me. He opened the wide door to the car kennel, pulled out slack in my leash, and locked the lead. I heeled.

We crept down the glazed, hard hill that sloped toward the street from the car kennel. Several long, fluffy patches and dry tracks gave us safe passage to the road. I weaved on and off the hard hill, sniffing along the short banks.

Our road lay beyond two of my favorite marked spots: a big rock and the mailbox. The street had been cleared. I stopped and sniffed its edge. I'd forgotten an important matter while busy playing. I raised my leg.

After a moment, my human asked, "Are you done yet, Graham?" annoyance infusing his voice. "We won't get back in time if you keep this up."

Don't worry. I'm almost finished. I gazed at my buddy, then lowered my leg. *All done.*

We rounded the first curve and walked alongside a thick forest. The broad canopy fluttered as a chilling breeze ruffled my fur. The road turned again, and someone *woofed* ahead. A beige, curly-haired dog darted toward us.

My human waved. "Hi, Lady. It is nice to see you, too."

"*Ruff!*" The golden doodle shouted.

Wanting to greet our four-legged neighbor, I pulled and stretched, but the leash yanked me back. I whined and waggled my tail, widening my eyes up at my buddy. *Why can't I say* hi?

"Let's go." My human stepped forward. "I am glad you could see Lady, Graham, but we need to keep moving. Mom wants an errand done sooner than later."

Errand? "*Rrr-rruff!*" I said, craning my neck to keep Lady in view as we completed the last bend. Oh, well. We got to see her. That was better than nothing.

"You can say *hi* when we return," my human said as we approached an extension of the road.

My buddy and I drew near a hill. The noisy wetland behind the next house croaked and chirped. The tall grass and bushes swayed with the breeze. What caused all the endless loudness? I watched a bird fly overhead and sniffed the air. The nature smells made me want to investigate.

We trudged halfway up the incline. Cracks splayed the border like the webs of my balled hair in our house's corners. We reached the top and spun around. The downhill trip was quicker but treacherous for my buddy. He hopped over shiny spots and splits. I hoped the weather would clear the road for later outings. Several humans exited the trail onto the street.

Ah! I backed up and perked my ears. Who were these people? I pranced toward the group.

The female pushed a cart with tiny wheels that carried two human puppies, and a male walked beside her. Two more little humans each rode a three-wheeled thing with handles. One twirled a bulging frisbee I longed to chase. The littlest of the two in the cart smiled and laughed. The other one reached out toward me.

"Graham has grown up so much," the adult female said. "How is he?"

"He's great," my buddy said, gesturing for me to sit.

I obeyed as the woman asked, "How old is he now?"

"Three in a couple of weeks."

"He is so well-behaved."

My buddy grinned. "Thanks. He's a good boy."

The male asked, "Has he been on any hunting excursions yet?"

"No." My human stroked my head. "He has proven to be a good hunter, though."

"Can we pet him?" the boy and girl on the three-wheeled things asked at the same time.

My buddy signaled the down command. "Of course."

I lay on a dry patch next to him. The little humans climbed off their three-wheels, then scratched behind my ears and rubbed my chest.

I rolled over and arched my paws. *Ooh, I needed this. Thank you so much.*

The grown humans motioned to their little ones, and they continued walking past us.

My buddy and I reached the end of the road and U-turned. A few cars rushed by on the busy street beside us. Someone on a bicycle sped across the entrance. A gust shoved us forward.

We passed the family again, then Lady's house. She trotted closer to us from her perch and barked.

I wagged my tail and *woofed*, fighting the urge to strain my leash again. *It's good to see you, Lady. I would say* hi, *but my human says we need to get back.*

We strolled up a mound to the street's other end and changed direction. A couple cars swerved and parked at a sign. We walked to my buddy's car kennel, and I sat as he tapped a tiny, flat box next to the big door.

As it opened, my buddy hand signaled. "Wait."

He motioned for me to come, and I pranced into the car kennel, then into the house after him. He put away the bag, and I followed him through the kitchen and onto the porch. What would happen next?

My human waved at the female he called *Mom*. "I will be back in a jiffy."

"Okay, honey. Love you," Mom said, hugging my buddy.

He looked at me. "Are you ready to go in the car?"

I tilted my head, then raced into the mud room. *A car ride! Yay! Where are we going?*

My buddy joined me, then led the way into the car's kennel and lowered his hand in a signal. "Down...Wait."

I dropped my rear onto the floor. My human opened the car door. He counted down from five. I dashed out and leaped into the backseat.

I panted as my buddy closed my door and got in the front. The engine started, we moved out into the sunlight, and the car's kennel door shut behind us. I turned and sniffed, unable to find a place to settle. Wind blasted over me. My buddy had opened the windows. How could I resist sticking my head out? *Ahh, that's much better.* The jerky motions and turns made it difficult to lie down, anyway.

We turned again and slowed, then stopped between other cars.

"I'll be right back, bud. Stay," my buddy said, stretching a palm toward me. "Be good."

He got out of the car and passed through the sliding doors into the building in front of us.

I flattened my ears and almost whined. *He'll be back. I know it.* I twitched my nose and climbed over the center to his seat to get a better view of everything. *What are those smells? They're great.*

Something growled outside. A dog peered at me from another car.

I *woofed* back. *Ha! You can't get to me.*

Persons walked in and out of the building, but where was my buddy?

I sniffed and smiled, catching his scent. *There he is.* What did he have in his hands? They looked tasty, whatever they were. A couple bunches of a strange, yellow bone, a bag of orange-skinned balls, and...*What are those small bowls with green lids?*

My buddy opened the car door.

I looked at him, refusing to budge. *I want to drive.*

"Sorry Graham, but I don't think you can legally drive, bud." He laughed. "Come on, *bouger*."

I moved to the rear seat. He placed the bag of colorful human treats on the chair next to him and turned on the car. I grinned out the window during the pretty ride back. The trees and bushes reminded me of the fun walks and runs my buddy and I take.

We pulled into the car kennel, he got out and opened the back door, and we entered the house.

He crouched and massaged my face. "All done now, Graham."

My human put his treats away, then walked upstairs to the guest room.

I pounced up the stairs and curled up under his table. The time had come to rest from the active morning. He had gotten some exercise, both in the yard and during the walk. This gave him the chance to talk with other humans, and maybe so did his time behind those sliding doors. That was important, too. He needed this training.

My buddy sat at his table and tapped on his rectangular box. The rapid clicks increased, and he laughed.

I went all warm beneath my fur the way I do when he smiles, then laid my head on his feet. *Mission: Accomplished.*

THE FABRIC OF SPACETIME

MICHAEL SPENCE

Author's note: The following is a chapter from a novel in progress. A policeman named Crown, from a world where electromechanical technology prevails, has mysteriously appeared in university instructor Stephen's world, where the technology is magical. The presence of the visitor threatens a delicate balance in the cosmos. It doesn't help that the two men are astoundingly similar...

"YOU DON'T THINK it's feasible?" Preceptor Patrick Gaylord, of the University of Albion's mathematics department, said, his face bearing a half-grin.

"Feasible? It's not even possible!" Magister Stephen, of the College of Wizardry, shot back. "We call this a *universe* for a reason. It's *uni*. It's *one*. To say there's more than one universe is...is like saying some unicorns have two horns! The word itself speaks of exclusivity."

It was Friday night, and the crowd at Bryski's Brewskis was taking full advantage. More than a few undergraduates played darts. Various parties of townspeople played bridge, while others gathered around the newspeakers to listen to the game. Stephen and Lord High Wizard Logas, Advisor to the King and chairman of the Thaumaturgy Department, along with this week's guest, were in their regular booth conducting the weekly dissection of Life, the Universe, and Jolly Near Everything. This week, it was the middle term coming under the scalpel.

From his silent corner of the booth, Logas spoke up for the first time. "And that is the sum of your argument? Hmm. Where did that word come from?"

The corner of Stephen's grimace twitched. After a moment's pause, he muttered, "Latin *unus,* 'one,' and *versus,* 'turned.' Everything turned into one."

"Aye. Latin." Logas nodded. "A tongue originating, if I have it right, rather subsequent to the creation of the world. And it sums up all the world, the spheres, the cosmos, everything one can observe, in one tidy package. Totality...because we've observed nothing else. Given that last point, are you still going to hold to your argument?"

Stephen pinched his eyes closed for a moment, his thoughts somewhere between *My honorable master has the truth of it as usual* and *I hate it when he's right.* "No," he conceded. "It wasn't my whole argument—"

"I'm relieved to hear that," Logas said, chuckling. "Otherwise, I would be forced to question the degree I awarded you. And you know how much I dislike second-guessing myself."

"Your point is, of course, sound," Stephen said, gazing into his stein, decorated with the tavern's nested-*B*s logo in relief. "I'm not saying anyone could have applied a Latin label to the created work at its completion, and yes, 'Any language of our own devising both expresses and sometimes even forms the way we see our surroundings.'"

"Good," Patrick said. "Nice to see you haven't forgotten your own dissertation."

"You read it?" Stephen said. "I'm impressed. Also, my sympathies. But what I don't see is how your suggestion of more than one univ— oh, I don't know, can we say more than one reality? Even *that's* problematic, because we're saying two contradictory things can both be real, and that's too chaotic for my comfort."

Patrick smiled. "If you'll bear with me, I want to pursue this a wee bit further. May I take the next round?" At the two wizards' nods, he slid to the edge of the booth and beckoned.

The serving man appeared, gave them all a nod, and headed back to the bar. A third tray of drinks soon graced their table: oolong tea for Lord Logas, a dark ale for Patrick, and Irish whisky plus a dark amber Grestigische beer for Stephen. Mme. Bryski was known both for running a tight ship and for her wide range of beverage offerings.

"All right, first things," Patrick said. "Let's start with the essential question: Can one event have more than one result? And by that, I don't mean possibilities; that's easy. I mean realized consequences."

Stephen pursed his lips. "I can see how two or more things might result from one event. But I would call them separate elements or aspects of a single result. What I gather you're saying is, can one event have both one result and the opposite result. See, that's what I'm objecting to! They contradict. Basic logic rules out an assertion and its contradiction. They cannot both be real."

"I agree." Patrick picked up his mug and took a healthy pull. "Two such things cannot coexist. An irresistible force rules out the possibility of an immovable object, and vice versa. This being the case, I would indeed seem to have a dilemma on my hands. My Lord Wizard," he said to Logas, "would you say there was a way out of the quandary? Because I believe there is."

Lord Logas, who seemed to have been studying the contents of his teacup, raised his eyes toward some invisible horizon. "Considering what you've just said, I'm thinking the one term that offers some flexibility is *coexist*. Take away the less negotiable terms, and our issue becomes, 'Can there be two or more simultaneous existences?' That is, two or more simultaneous frameworks of existence or reality. Of course, that brings us back to Stephen's discomfort with plural realities."

Stephen chuckled. "Oddly enough, it sounds easier to bear when we clothe it in technical language." He raised his whisky glass in a toast. "Academia to the rescue!"

"And what that means is," Patrick said, "that we would have one realm of creation in which it is possible to have plural histories. Or we could call them strings or threads of time."

"But you'll note," Stephen said, "we haven't established why that plurality must be. We've simply worded the issue to sound more acceptable." He shrugged. "All right, I yield provisionally to that one. *Universe* could mean one complex creation that includes plural, erm, threads of existence. And if the two different consequences of the single action are each confined to a different thread, then we satisfy the non-contraction principle. But why should it? What would be the point of having multiple threads?"

Logas *hmphed*. "Go back to basics. What is the point of having even one thread, namely ours?"

"Don't look at me," Patrick said, raising his hands. "I'm just the maths bloke here. I look for the patterns and then build on them. *Why* is what you wizards do."

Two sets of eyes fastened upon Stephen, who squirmed just a bit.

Logas said, "'First step—'" and then Stephen joined in with "'What does the text say?'"

Stephen pursed his lips and took a breath. "World created, formed, made...well, we do have the foundations of the earth laid, 'and all the morning stars sang for joy.' Clearly, someone found it all entertaining. And there's the Hebrew nation, which God said he made so they would 'show forth' his praise, and others would listen to them, so that ultimately you have everyone knowing and praising him."

"Makes sense," Patrick said. "The chief end of man: 'to glorify God and enjoy him forever.' Let's start with that premise—that any thread exists so those in it should know and celebrate God. Well, then. I don't know as much of the text as those in the College do, but there is one I know and love: Job. What's the first thing God says in that book?"

"A pop quiz, now, is it?" Stephen shot back. "Be glad I'm such a nice chap and won't throw a displacement spell on your ale. You could easily be wearing it."

"Now there's a mature response," said Lord Logas. "On the other hand, I've seen far worse in faculty meetings."

"And here I thought," Patrick said, "that the Thaumaturgy Department were the most upright, sober, stiff-upper-lipped in all the University! How the most cherished of illusions shatter." When Stephen picked up a biscuit as if to throw it, Patrick lifted a hand. "All right, all right. *Pax!* Anyhow, there's the question, and I have no doubt you know the answer."

Stephen rested his elbows on the table and steepled his fingers. "Job...all right, angels assembling in heaven. Satan's there. Possibly summoned."

"So, what's the first thing God says to Satan?"

"Mm... 'Where have you been?'"

Patrick smiled. "To which he responds, 'Why, strolling here and there, up and down, checking out my territory.' And God fires back, 'Yours, eh? Have you checked out Job lately?' And then Satan retorts..." Patrick paused, eyeing Stephen.

Stephen said, "Basically, he's saying, 'Well, yeah, he honors you the way you're doing things! But what if you did *this* instead?'"

"And there," Patrick said, "we have it. For each history, someone might propose an alternate course of events. And there may well *be* legitimate alternatives. Not an infinite number, mind you. For one thing, worlds finite, only God infinite. For another, some differences would be so trivial as to be dispensable. But then you have alternatives that are truly alternate. Plural threads allow God to demonstrate conclusively that, however things progress, he is vindicated."

Stephen lifted one brow. "So, there could conceivably be a world in which Job failed the test, but one of his friends didn't?"

"Exactly." Patrick leaned forward. "There could even be worlds in which Adam fell, but under quite different circumstances."

Stephen remained silent a moment. "All right, I'll give you that. The idea of multiple threads within creation does possess some coherence. Now, do we know for certain that they do in fact exist?"

"I don't see how we can truly deny it," Patrick said, swirling his beverage. "Somewhere in this parish, there's a man who looks enough like you that people here think he *is* you. He's not a wizard but appears to be a Guardsman of some kind. He claims no one in his world does wizardry, but he's got things in his kit that we've never seen in this world, nor have we found anything like them in the literature." Patrick wagged a finger at Stephen. "And his name, Crown, might as well be yours, Magister *Stephanos*. I'd say that for someone who's not you, he very easily could be, but so many things about him strongly suggest that he's not from our earth."

They both looked at Logas for confirmation or denial, but he chuckled and held up his hands. "Goodness, don't look to me to referee! I'm rather enjoying this."

"Right, sir," Stephen said, "but do you think all this is holding together?"

"Oh, I'm still listening. Are *you* satisfied with it?"

Stephen sat back. "I might be...wait. Wait one minute. We're not done here, not by a long shot." He held up a forefinger. "I'm going to claim the right of counter-quiz. No, it's not a barrister's term; I just made it up." He pointed his index finger at Patrick. "There's something we consider to be the focal point of history—call it the centerpiece of our world's thread, if you like. Everything led up to it, and everything since then has been affected by it. What would you say it is?"

A grin tugged at Patrick's lip. "Graduation day!" He looked around the table for a reaction. Logas smiled, but Stephen didn't let his stare budge. "All right, all right," Patrick said. "The answer to your riddle is the Crucifixion."

"Just so! The death and resurrection of *Iēsous Christos Theou Hyios*

Sōtēr! The *Ichthys*!" Stephen stabbed the table with a finger at every word. *Poke*. "Jesus, the"—*poke*—"Christ"—*poke*—"God's"—*poke*—"Son, the"—*poke*—"Savior! And death was by crucifixion—which we use not only as a benchmark but a high-water mark for cruelty. No one has come up with anything more barbaric. On top of that, we understand that his death was enough to provide propitiation, redemption, salvation for everyone from the beginning to the end of the world, whether or not they participate in it. 'Once for all,' the Apostle wrote, 'the just for the unjust.'

"Now, what happens when we place this in a multi-threaded universe? Are we saying that our history is the *only* one in which he was crucified? If so, does this mean that Guardsman Crown's world has no redemption, et cetera? Or must we say that the Christ went through this experience in each of these finite but nonetheless many threads? I must say, that seems more than a trifle sadistic. And if so, then was his work in *our* world truly 'once for *all*,' or is the *all* merely relative? I'm sure the Apostle didn't think so."

Patrick looked over at Logas, but the Lord High Wizard remained quiet, giving him only a raised eyebrow as if to say, *Well, now, what will you do with this?*

Patrick took a deep breath. "Hm. Let's see if I have my catechism correct. Jesus: infinite Son in finite flesh. Accordingly, his death was an infinite experience, and so could apply to every human being who ever existed and will exist. If this infinite God-man appeared in each thread, then so would that infinite death."

He looked at Logas again, who smiled and said, "Keep going."

"And you're right. That seems incredibly redundant. God's extravagant—look at the number of stars and galaxies, not to mention the many species of beasties on this earth, overwhelming numbers of frogs, locusts, and such in divine curses—and of course, let's not forget one child's lunch turning into a meal for some twelve thousand people, including the women and children, with plenty of leftovers to boot. Extravagant he may be—but he's not wasteful. I agree that his death in any one world would be sufficient to redeem as many people as are his in all of them. There's no point in multiplying infinity. Multiple sacrifices of this sort do seem wasteful. Therefore…" He looked at Lord Logas once again. "Am I a heretic yet, milord?"

Logas took another sip of his tea. "Not at all. I am curious to hear where you're going with this, though. You seem to have put yourself right back into a conundrum. And," he said, waving to a serving man, "this tea is cold." The server came to their table, and Logas ordered more hot water. "Anyone else need fourths?"

"No," Patrick said, "but could I ask you to bring us a slate?"

The server nodded and headed off.

Patrick straightened his shoulders. "I think there may be a way through this. Consider the fifteenth chapter of 1 Corinthians. The Apostle says that the Christ will deliver all the kingdom to the Father after he has put all enemies under his feet, including death itself. Then, his subjugated enemies, and he himself, will be subjected to the Father, bringing everything together. God the Son gathers it up and presents it to God the Father."

The slate and stylus arrived together with a pot of hot water. While Logas warmed up his tea, Patrick placed a dot near the top of the writing surface.

"Here's our history's endpoint. Everything has been brought together. Show's over. Time for a fresh start, on a new heaven and earth. Judgment executed, sin removed, all need for second-guessing gone. No need for multiple threads. Thereafter, into eternity, it's all a single world. Perhaps with multiple planets.

"But consider the possibility that the Apostle's words embrace not only our history, but all of them. The Son presents *all* his people, *all* his enemies to the Father at this one point. All threads meet up here and end their separate existence. *E pluribus unum.* What's more, I suggest that this is not the only time everything is gathered. There's one other occasion."

"Go on," Stephen said. "I was going to say creation, but I suspect you don't mean that."

"Right. Remember, there could be a separate creation for each kind of Fall." Patrick made another dot near the bottom.

"What we have here is the Crucifixion. Actually, this dot sums up the entire time of Jesus' presence on earth, from Annunciation to Ascension, even to Pentecost if you like—what some have called 'the Christ event.' During those years, the earth was a single entity, its threads all woven together into one undivided cord."

"Hold on," Stephen said. "Are you saying the earth's population increased ten-thousandfold or more? That if we had been there, Crown and I would each have occupied a separate place on that earth?"

Patrick chuckled. "That would be a hideous mess, wouldn't it? I'm going to say no. Instead, I suggest that, in God's sovereignty, all the histories up until then were framed so that at some point they grew more and more similar, and by the time the Christ arrived, they had merged into one—and so had all previously divergent family and personal histories. You and Crown would have been one single person."

Logas cleared his throat. "There would seem to be a physics problem here. Each world-line—each thread—brings with it a humanity with a considerable amount of mass. How might persons merge without becoming many times heavier or larger?"

"Here's where I say, 'I don't know.'" Patrick took a drink from his long-neglected ale. "On the other hand, I could also ask, where did the extra mass come from that expressed itself in twelve-ish thousand meals' worth of bread and fish? And I have even less trouble believing that, since God crafted each of the histories, he can merge them at some point even without an eschatological event such as final judgment. Perhaps properties such as mass were simply suspended for that length of time, to be reinstated afterwards. We've certainly seen other properties manipulated in that land, such as in Joshua's extended day and King Hezekiah's retraced hours.

"So there you are: one Atonement event, sufficient for, and extending to, all the woven threads. Which afterwards go their separate ways." He drew a straight line from the dot at the bottom to the one at the top. "Here's our thread." He then drew another line starting at the bottom dot but jogging to the left of the center line before curving back to the top dot. The enspelled slate refined his line into a gentle arc. "Here's the thread from which Crown comes. This—" he drew an arrow from the arc at its widest point to the center line— "represents Crown's fall from his world to us via his 'Lens,' or whatever it is." Adding two tiny lines to the arrowhead to make an *X*, he said, "And, as various maps tell us, *You Are Here*."

After erasing the *X* and the small bridging line, he drew more arcs between the same two endpoints.

"Ah," Stephen said, "time is a giant banana!"

Patrick said nothing but proceeded to draw arcs on the other side of the central thread.

Logas said, "You're positing a second time dimension, eh?"

"Huh. I guess I am, if we're going to separate one thread from another at any point." Patrick examined his sketch again. "I suppose you could even have a third, a kind of *z*-axis, in which case this figure would be a solid. That doesn't surprise you, though, does it? I know you've not forgotten the events of last May, with Magistrix Judith and Magister Palmer."

Lord Logas shook his head.

Stephen stared at the tabletop. Despite all they had learned, the University had not recovered emotionally from the tragic conclusion of that business, with its reminder that any science that addressed the structure of creation dealt in grave matters, indeed.

"In any event," Patrick went on, "here you are, with the various threads all together in one model."

The resulting ellipsoid shape rather resembled a rugby ball, except that at each end it came to a point, bringing it closer to what people in the transatlantic Colonies called a *football* than to what those in Albion meant by the word.

"And let us not forget the threads gathered into the time of the Incarnation." Patrick did some more sketching, and then turned the diagram ninety degrees.

Stephen's eyes grew wide. Even Lord Logas raised an eyebrow and put his teacup down without looking to see where it landed.

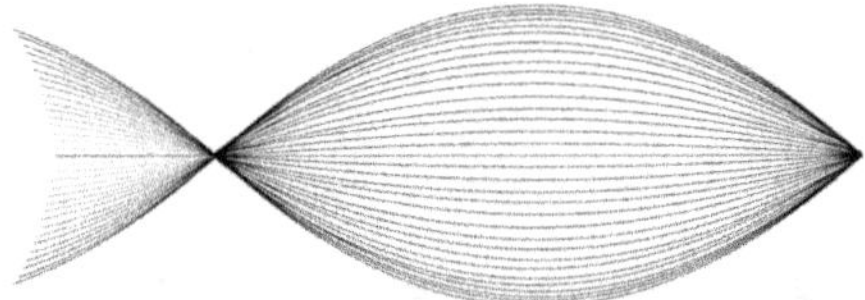

The woven-thread model had become a stylized fish or *ichthys*, the secret sign—based on the initials of the Greek titles Stephen had first cited for the Christ—that early persecuted believers had used to identify themselves to each other.

Patrick smiled. "And you thought it was just a clever acrostic."

THE BIRTH OF THE MORNING STAR
DREW CLAPP

LUCIFER

Michael walked across the glistening marble floor of the outer courtyard, glancing between the brilliant, vine-draped pillars along its edges. He shook his head at his excessive caution. Could anything or anyone dare disturb the serenity of this place? He redirected his gaze to the windows sparkling within the recesses of the thick bulwark. What assignment did the Master have for him this time? Some fracas in the far northwestern region of the universe? Maybe maintaining order on another planet?

Approaching the inner court, Michael smiled. He would never tire of gazing upon the scintillating palace, or the diadem trees lining both sides of its entrance. The musical lapping of the wide river flowing from beneath the entry lulled his senses, even as the fragrances from the hanging gardens bordering its banks invigorated them. As he neared the palace steps, the glistening water rushed past him, down a channel speckled with glimmering stone.

Cherubim saluted when Michael reached the top step. The towering doors, engraved with names, opened on their own and brightness encompassed him. He stepped inside, then walked to the crystal throne room and paused in its doorway. He fixed his gaze on the twelve chairs lining one wall, giving himself a moment to adjust to the tremendous power charging the atmosphere. Seraphim flew around the room, singing praises, as always.

A voice thundered from the throne. "Come, Michael."

At once, Michael walked to the center of the room and knelt. "How may I serve you, Master?"

"I have someone I would like to introduce to you."

As Michael rose, a coruscant entity with blond braids captured his attention.

The being's amethyst cape flowed from a multihued, onyx breastplate and shoulder pads. A turquoise sash crisscrossed his sparkling, beryl figure.

"Who is this, Master?" Michael asked, stretching a hand toward the entity.

"Lucifer." The Master stood and smiled. "He will lead worship here. I can hardly wait to hear what the stars will say."

"Glory to You, Master!"

"He is My most beautiful of all created beings: The Guardian Cherub."

Michael lifted a brow. "Better than Metatron?"

"Yes, even him."

Michael turned to Lucifer and hugged this new creation, then stepped back to admire the Master's handiwork.

Lucifer embodied every kind of precious stone. The carnelian and chrysolite interwoven to form his chest shone through his tight robe. The bright emerald outline of his body radiated behind the garment's stitching and overlapped the pale topaz contours defining his perfect, well-built frame. His burnished jasper legs and arms reflected the intense Glory of the Master.

"Michael, take him on a tour of Heaven," the Master said, nudging Lucifer forward. "Especially My Holy Mount."

Michael nodded. "Yes, Master."

THE HOLY CITY

Lucifer and Michael approached the large pearl gate on the southern border of the outer courtyard. The tall, thick walls flashed with similar gemstones to those adorning him. The entry opened and they walked to the edge of a cliff overlooking a vast city. A majestic mountain range stood in the distance, beyond a brilliant prairie and vivid, diamond-like forest.

Lucifer's eyes widened. "This place is amazing!"

"Yes, it is." Michael said, patting him on the back. "Welcome to the dominion of the Creator."

"Why was this made?"

"The Creator wants all to enjoy His presence and experience this place forever."

Lucifer scratched his golden hair. "Does He care that much about His creation?"

"More than can be comprehended," Michael said, leaping into the air and waving for Lucifer to join him. "Come. Let's explore the Golden City."

Lucifer hesitated. Might surged through his body, but nothing happened. An inner knowing prodded him to continue. He sighed, closed his eyes, and jumped. Appendages sprang open on his back and flapped, then a whirlwind thrust him upward.

"Wow," he said, "I didn't realize I could do that."

Michael smiled. "You will learn of many things by the end of our time together."

Lucifer followed Michael into a dive toward the Golden City. They soared over the gleaming lowlands. Sparkling streams flowed down the cliffside, invigorating the foliage. Some spilled into overflowing ponds, the excess water making flowers with translucent stalks sprout along their banks. The blooms illuminated the ground.

Lucifer's own light caused plants to burst forth with crystalline colors as his aura passed over the terrain. He and Michael plunged through recesses in the land and blasted across the prairie. He stretched out a hand and brushed the tips of the grass. Then, they entered the vicinity of the Golden City.

"What about the Holy Mount?" Lucifer asked as they touched down.

Michael motioned toward an entrance between watchtowers. "That will be our second-to-last stop."

"What's last?"

"That is the most important. It will be your headquarters."

"I have a headquarters?"

"Yes. The Master always gives His servants a domain."

Lucifer followed Michael through the wide gateway. He paused and scanned the endless, sky-high walls. The pure gold streets crisscrossed for miles. The glistening city refracted the bright light from the palace in the distance. Angels with tool belts carved patterns in the walls of mansions and inserted gems into grooves.

Lucifer blinked. A man with a golden sash around his chest approached. The snowy hair covering His shoulders rippled as He walked. His shiny bronze feet glowed, but His eyes blazed even brighter. Michael knelt, so Lucifer did the same.

"Who is this?" The man asked in a voice like many waters.

"This is Lucifer, sir." Michael said, laying a hand on Lucifer's back. "The Master recently created him."

"Rise." When they did so, the shimmering man clasped Lucifer's shoulders. "I am the Prince of Peace. Welcome to the Eternal Realm. You are the Son of the Dawn and I am delighted in you."

Lucifer bowed. *The* Son of the Dawn? That sounded significant. He smiled, then snapped upright and looked around, raising one brow. The Prince had departed.

Michael stretched out a hand. "Let us continue."

Lucifer followed him along the streets. No residence they passed had been the same as another. Grass covered several lawns, lush vegetation and flowers filled others, and still more contained a potpourri of both. They crossed into a division lined with interconnected housing. The stacked, star-shaped homes interlocked with each other.

Lucifer did a double-take as they drew near an imposing building overshadowing the glimmering megalopolis. Angels ascended and descended the steps leading to a colonnade in front of it.

"What is that?" Lucifer pointed at the majestic structure. "It's beautiful."

Michael grinned. "That is the temple of the Master. He will dwell there soon."

"Why not now?"

"It is yet for an appointed time."

"Hmm." Lucifer rubbed his chin. "If I were He, I would want to live there now."

Michael shot him a sharp look. "Son of the Dawn, be careful not to think like that."

"Sorry." Lucifer gritted his teeth.

As he and Michael climbed the ivory stairway, Lucifer waved at a few passing angels. His eyes widened as they reached the top of the outer courtyard and walked through the East Gate. A wall encompassed the temple area. Three guardrooms lined the ramparts on both sides, each lodge with narrow embrasures in its crenelated parapets. Thirty more chambers similar in length and width had been constructed all around the court. The panels of the enclosure had been decorated with palm trees.

Lucifer brushed his fingers along a huge bronze altar. "What are the angels we passed doing?"

"They have all been dispatched to fulfill assignments on planets around the universe."

"Will we be going to one of those soon?"

"Yes. Let's go inside the temple."

Lucifer and Michael walked through the gate into a vestibule. Brilliant gardens covered the archway leading to the portico. Lucifer craned his neck, examining the three levels of side rooms surrounding the interior. They had been built in stages sloping upward, each tier wider than the one beneath it. Ledges supported the entire structure. He swept his gaze up a stairway that climbed the walls from the lowest floor to the top. A lustrous stone hallway branched off from an inner sanctuary.

"Are we allowed to go in there?" Lucifer asked, motioning to the central chamber with paneling carved to depict alternating images of cherubim, pomegranates, and flowers.

Michael shook his head. "No. It is sacred."

"Why is that?"

"The Master desires that place for Himself, in order to dwell among those who believe in Him. Come, we must move on."

THE HOLY MOUNT

Lucifer glided beside Michael over a sparkling sea and glanced behind them. The incandescent palace blended with the Holy City in the background. Something new arrested his attention, an amalgamation of music exuding from the city.

Lucifer grinned. The enrapturing melodies flooded his ears as he scanned the sky. The splendor of the landscape pulsed like the gentle waves lapping the shore below them. Flamboyant colors reverberated throughout the atmosphere, dancing in sync with the clouds.

Lucifer gasped. "Is that what I think it is?"

"Yes." Michael nodded as they drew close to a high, flaming mountain. "The Master's Holy Mount."

Lucifer tensed. "Will we be consumed?"

"No, be at peace."

Lucifer blinked. What caused the mountain to resist being burned up? How did the trees and bushes avoid getting scorched? The foliage remained aflame, but the fire brightened…even purified… the plants.

A glint caught his attention. He looked down and his entire being glowed. His aura erupted with multihued threads of light. As they approached the summit, he spotted fiery stones lining a path, which led to a podium in front of a white throne. Seven golden lampstands surrounded the throne. An altar stood to each side of the glistening, embossed chair. The seat spewed sparks and crystalline energy waves. The mountaintop overlooked a vast gulf and wide valley.

"Why is there a throne on top of the Holy Mount?" Lucifer asked as he touched down.

"The Master has reserved this place for a future time." Michael furrowed his brow. "This is also known as the Mount of Assembly."

"What is meant to occur here?"

"A final judgment."

"Judgment for what?" Lucifer asked, tilting his head. "Everything is perfect."

"The Master is the only One who knows."

Lucifer peered down the ravine. "Where does the gorge lead?"

"An abyss with a lake of fire," Michael said, extending the hilt of his sheathed sword toward Lucifer. "Come. We have one more place to visit."

Lucifer touched the hilt of the sword, and a flash surrounded Michael and himself. A rush enveloped his ears, and he hurtled through space. Stars and galaxies sped past. His aura morphed into a shimmering nebula of sparkles. They drew near a pale blue speck hovering in the dense void.

THE GARDEN OF EDEN

Lucifer and Michael entered the atmosphere. The cloud of sparkles around Lucifer burst into a fiery ball and generated a multicolored trail, stretching from his shoulders to his feet. He and Michael rocketed across the firmament, then descended. A supercontinent and scattered islands lay in the midst of a great ocean. Michael motioned to the center of the continent. Lucifer nodded, and they approached the fertile landscape.

The vibrant terrain overflowed with plants and trees bearing all kinds of produce. Huge animals wandered the plains and deserts. Colossal birds flew to narrow perches overlooking vast prairies and savannas. Massive sea creatures jumped and dived through the pristine water. Lucifer caught a glimpse of several communal encampments in the distance.

"Where are we?" he asked as they drew near a mammoth forest.

Michael grinned. "I was wondering when you would ask. This planet is called Earth."

"This will be my headquarters?"

"Yes, Son of the Dawn."

"Wow. It's beautiful."

"Follow me."

Lucifer brushed the umbrella-shaped treetops with his hand. At his touch, the leaves blossomed with brilliant flowers, their sweet fragrance filling his nostrils. He followed Michael into a clearing in front of a cliff. Michael tilted his body and aimed for a crevice that split the mountainside. They darted through it and out over a hidden garden with several waterfalls. The cascades poured from a source above into a pond and fed an outlying river, which separated into four headwaters.

"What is this garden?" Lucifer asked, landing on a patch of grassland near one of the river's branches.

Michael touched down on a mossy mound. "This is the Garden of Eden."

"I will rule here?" Lucifer asked, turning to survey his surroundings.

"Correct."

Warmth coursed through Lucifer's body. "I am amazed at the Master's gracious bountifulness."

Michael nodded. "The Master always gives His best."

"Do these rivers have a name?" Lucifer asked, stooping to dip a hand in the water.

Michael rotated his arm clockwise, beginning at the north. "The first is called Pishon. Second, the Gihon. Third, you have the Tigris. Finally, the river Euphrates."

Lucifer committed the names to memory. "What are those creatures roaming the landscape?"

"They are known as dinosaurs."

Lucifer grinned. "Wow. The Master is magnificent."

"Indeed," Michael said. "Let me take you to your palace."

Lucifer straightened. "Palace?"

He and Michael walked through the fertile lowland, then crossed a slim trail and ascended toward a cave entrance. The path curved into a portico dressed in verdant vines. They entered a colonnade encompassing the royal chamber.

Lucifer glanced above him. Sunlight shot through the open roof, diffusing through the room and highlighting a throne surrounded by a dazzling arboretum. Behind the chair, stairs led down to a wide deck overlooking a vast field and shoreline. A dense thicket of incandescent foliage covered the deck's shimmering stone rail.

Lucifer sat on the throne and it activated. Power surged into him, and his aura flared. Spike-like beams fired out from within him. The plain surfaces of the pillars and walls transformed, now covered in a glowing web of entwined imprints. The intricate patterns illuminated the sanctuary with a prismatic barrage, then pulsated. He stood, and flames girdled his limbs. He clenched his hands, then opened them, and sparkling stones formed on his palms.

Lucifer inserted the glittering rocks into slots on the armrests of the throne. "What will be my job here?"

"The Master has created you to lead music in His presence," Michael said, pointing outside and circling a finger through the air. "Listen to the harmonies generated by His creation and in the heavenlies. Write lyrics, psalms, and hymns to glorify Him."

Lucifer shook his head. "How can I do that? He's beyond comprehension."

"Trust in The Master. He will guide you in using the gifts He has placed in you."

Lucifer's shoulders relaxed. "Is that my only assignment?"

"No. Tend this garden and planet."

Lucifer nodded and walked to the deck. Fluffy, silver clouds floated across the dense, pearl-blue horizon. A couple of flying dinosaurs landed nearby and stared at him. After a few moments, they leaped and plunged toward the glistening ocean. He followed them as far as he could along the edge of the deck, and they flew out of sight. Footsteps drew near him.

Michael tapped him on the shoulder. "The Master is beckoning me elsewhere. Stay and take all the time you need to explore your realm."

"Thanks. I will."

As Michael departed, Lucifer scanned the sky and smiled. He had been created to honor the Master. A trickling, whooshing sound drew his gaze downward. Nearby, a small waterfall spilled over pure rock into a reflecting pond. He stepped down to the lower deck and walked over to it. An image within the pool captured his attention, and he peered at it, then gasped.

"Whoa, I *am* beautiful." He smirked.

Author's Note: This is Part 1 of a three-part story currently in progress.

NEVER BLACKMAIL A THOUGHT-READER

SHARON ROSE

TRACY CAUGHT her first glimpse of him in the casino lounge. The only guy she couldn't see.

His broad-shouldered, athletic build and shimmering green hair were clear enough, but not a single thought leaked. With nothing for her to read, he seemed invisible.

No matter. Hundreds of suckers were always passing through the space station. She only needed to select a few each night—and, of course, check the Syndicate's watchers for suspicion.

Tracy meandered through gaudy rooms, gambling a few times for appearance's sake. So many bodies—the air reeked. A winner's cheer crowed above incessant chatter. She ignored it all, sifting and analyzing thoughts that flowed on currents only she could perceive. Then, she passed Joe in a crowded aisle so their touch would look accidental. He downloaded her information: the faces of likely prey; their preferred games and strategies; how much money they had; and how desperate, stupid, or confident they were. Joe took it from there and fleeced them —careful not to win so obviously that the Syndicate would take notice.

Job done for tonight, she sauntered past the Thief Limb Removal station, as though she feared nothing. Its burner glowed, as always. Such an effective deterrent that she'd only seen it used once. Or felt it, really. She'd almost given herself away that night when the pickpocket's agony had come searing into her mind.

She headed for an obscure, dark corner of the lounge, where she could escape the revulsion that spilled from any who saw her. Four years of working the casinos had dulled the sting of rejection but never let her forget it.

"Can I buy you a drink?"

Tracy jumped and spun to the voice behind her. Mister Green-hair, of course. No one else could sneak up on her. His black shirt stretched to cover his biceps. Wisps of silky green wove through the fabric. Expensive.

He took a step back. "Sorry, miss. Didn't mean to startle you."

She had overreacted. Better fix that. "It's just—no one offers to buy me drinks." The reason should be obvious now that he could see her face.

"No? A snack then." His lips stopped moving, but a whisper reached her ears. "If you're done working, of course."

The blood drained from her face. Barely stopping her gaze from darting to the burner, she double-checked the crowd. No one's thoughts included an image of her. "I'm a patron, you idiot."

"Yeah, that's necessary, considering your skills." He pointed to a secluded table. "You better sit down, Tracy. Fainting attracts attention."

She let him guide her to a chair. He knew her name, too? What was he? A Syndicate informer? A blackmailer? She *must* figure out his angle. Pickpockets just got their hands burned off. Thought-readers like her got their heads charred to a blackened skull.

He tapped something into the order terminal and pressed his hand to the ID scanner. "My name's Vigard. I won't inform."

Her shoulders relaxed. Blackmail she could survive. "I don't have money."

"I imagine that's true." He smirked. "But Joe, with those innocent blue eyes, rakes in a bundle."

She stared at him as a servobot delivered food and drinks. Did he know everything? She took a sip of her drink, a baby sour—no alcohol. What kind of guy was he? She wished he were pumping out thoughts like everyone else, but oh, it was fabulous not to sense revulsion.

"Joe keeps the money." She took a snack chip and dug into the meaty dip, then popped it into her mouth.

"Figured that. Otherwise, you'd have gotten those scars fixed."

He had to bring it up? She tilted her head, letting her straight, black hair slide forward like a veil. One side of her face was a mess from deep abrasions. A jagged gash marred the other from brow to lip. Whoever had patched her up, did a clumsy job sealing the wound. One eyelid didn't close right, and her smile was downright gruesome. She ate to avoid answering.

Vigard took a sip of his drink. "How'd it happen?"

"I'm not really sure. Just woke up with my head aching like it would explode and no memory. Joe found me and took me to his place. By the time I could think straight, I realized he—he knew about me." She grabbed another chip. "He's sort of decent. Protects me and pays for necessities, as long as I give him information. I suppose that's what you want, too. Who are you, anyway?"

"I'm a private locator."

"Bounty hunter, you mean." She spat the words.

His lips tightened. "I've brought in some scum, but I never work for the Syndicate. This time it's family business—looking for an abducted kid."

Sad. She swept her hand to indicate the casino. "You won't find any kids here."

"You'd be surprised what I find in casinos." He spun his glass in its puddle of condensation. "You were right. It's information I'm after. How long you been with Joe?"

She scooped up more dip. "I don't see how knowing about me an' Joe will help. He doesn't traffic in that sort of thing."

"Just like to know my informers. Got nothing against you, and I won't hurt you. How long?"

She shrugged. "Four years."

His steel-gray eyes held her gaze through a slow nod. "Why don't you run?"

"Nowhere to go."

"No family or friends before the accident?"

Why was he interrogating her? "I can't remember. Besides…" She lifted the glitzy, black and silver ornament around her neck. A solid ring with no clasp. Too small to slip over her head. "This only pretends to be jewelry."

"Hmm." He frowned at it, tapping a finger on his lower lip. "Does it inflict pain?"

"Nothing that gentle. It just blares an incriminating announcement that'll get me burned to death."

"How's it set off?"

"Joe can activate it from any network computer. If I leave the space station, it'll self-activate. He programmed and sealed it with a random password. Since he doesn't know it, I can't either."

"How do you pass him information?"

She scraped the last of the dip out of the bowl. "Why are you asking all this?"

"The kid I'm looking for—she was sixteen when she was abducted. Four years ago. The family blasted her picture everywhere, but they never got a lead. She's from Rivelt."

Rivelt! Tracy tightened long fingers around her glass. The planet where thought-readers were the normal ones. There, thought-*leakers* were segregated into a visitor colony so they couldn't disturb normal people with random spray from every firing neuron. Could she be…? But no—the Riveltians had facial markings. She sucked in a breath and pressed cold fingers to her scarred face, then remembered the danger and dropped her hand.

He let a thought drift to her. *I'm from Rivelt, too. My markings were surgically removed.*

So, he was in as much danger here as she was. She could trust him. She sipped her drink and let a thought out. *Are you sure it's me you're looking for?*

I am. Your real name is Telnia. "We need to keep talking or we'll look strange. I study your picture every day. You have beautiful eyes. I'd recognize them anywhere."

Wow! A compliment. Her stomach tensed. "Uh, thank you."

"Back to business. How do you transfer information to Joe?"

She read thoughts from the crowd again. No one noticed them. "We have matched brain chips with STS activation. Oh, that stands for simultaneous tactile stimulation around here. I just brush up against him, and it triggers a download."

Vigard slid his fingers up and down his glass. "I have a private transport docked. I dropped off some rich partiers a couple days ago. No one would hear the neck ring once you're inside my transport."

"They would hear it on my way to the docks. If I get too far from Joe, it sends him a message. I may look free, but he's got me locked up, and *he* knows that *I* know. That's the thing about blackmail. He can be completely honest with me."

Vigard took another sip of his drink. "Any fancy programming on those brain chips?"

"Course not! Don't you know how dangerous it is to hack brain chips?"

He smiled and nodded. "Can you play a part?"

What a stupid question. "Do you think I don't *play a part* every moment I'm visible?"

"Strangers are easily tricked. You're alive, so you must be able to slip by Syndicate watchers. But can you fool Joe?"

Her heart doubled its rhythm. She had pondered her dilemma countless times, but now she had a transport. The equation had changed. "Do you have a plan in mind?"

"You reach my airlock with no alarm, and I can get us away. But you are the only one who knows Joe. So, you tell me the plan."

Her hands tingled as she considered which fears would be the most effective.

⸙

Joe shut the apartment door. "What's with you? If I didn't know better, I'd think somebody was buying you drinks—too many of them." He jerked a gaudy scarf from around his neck and tossed it on a chair.

"Just one, but it's not that." She twirled through the living room.

His brows shot up. "Well, what is it, then?"

"I think I'm in love."

Joe groaned. "Oh, please. No offense, but take a look in the mirror. Don't tell me you can't recognize a con that obvious." He caught up to her near the kitchen. "Give me a visual of this joker." He grabbed her wrist to activate the chip, then jumped back like she'd burned him.

"What?" she asked, feigning surprise.

His voice rasped. "Our chips have been hacked."

"You sure?" She took a second to read him and absorb the deep, male voice he'd heard.

Warning! Chip security protocols violated. Please report to Augmentation Services so we can analyze and prevent false embezzlement charges. Do not delay. The Syndicate is vigilant in protecting the assets of its patrons. Suspect data transfers are detected and reported.

"Whoa!" She steadied herself against the wall. "That's not what I sent. Let me try again. Maybe I—"

"No!" He darted around the table. "Don't touch me."

She stared at him like he'd gone nuts.

He raked a hand through his blond hair then clutched at it. "Give me a minute to think. Just...just describe this guy to me."

She continued to stare. "Why? Do you think you can un-hack the chips if you find him?" She read the answer from him. "We both know you can't."

"You let him hack us!" Joe clung to the back of a chair. "Why? I treat you well. He won't. He's tricking you."

She laughed. No need to tell Joe she couldn't read the man she trusted.

Joe bristled. "There are people out there who can do that, you know." Then, he remembered how pointless his fabrication was. For once, it was fun reading his thoughts. He switched back to his straightforward mode. "Stay with me, Tracy. I've always kept you safe. You can still pass me information. We'll work out a code."

"Syndicate watchers will catch onto that in a week—or a day." Ah yes, he knew that, too. "Face it, Joe. I'm no use to you anymore."

"Don't you dare turn on me. I can still set off that neck ring."

"True. And when the Syndicate guards swarm me, they won't be at all curious about who is blackmailing me."

His lips clamped.

"Yep, that's right. You squeal on me, and I squeal on you. The way I see it, Joe, you've only got two choices left. You can let me go, or you can kill me. What's your plan for getting rid of my body? The Syndicate takes a dim view of unauthorized murder. Bad for business, you know."

His jaw worked. "Aren't you forgetting something? They'll kill you, too. There's nowhere to go that's beyond their reach. No ships dock here that aren't tight with the Syndicate."

"None that *you* know of. Come to think of it, you need a ride too. How long do you want to walk around with a hacked brain chip? Even if you don't use it, the Syndicate will be scanning for it now."

She let that final ingredient simmer in his fear, then softened her expression. "I'll admit, you've been halfway decent to me. Not very generous, but not awful. There's still plenty of money to be made, and we know how to work together. I just want a friendlier setting and a bigger cut. I'll let you come with me if you want."

She kept a straight face while he squirmed.

"Fine."

She sauntered to the door. "Let's go for a little walk."

More like a long, terrifying walk for her, but not as scary as leaving Joe alone. At any moment, he might catch on. They finally reached the dock Vigard had specified, and she tapped the access panel. The airlock whished open. Tracy jumped at a distant clang that echoed down the metal corridor.

"Come on in and meet our new partner." She sidled past Vigard in the airlock.

Joe followed her over the threshold—and met Vigard's fist.

Tracy sensed an instant of shock until Joe's head slammed on the corridor's floor. The airlock door slid shut.

She gripped the nearest handhold and pressed a palm to her chest. "I *did* it!"

Vigard sealed the inner airlock. "Not away yet. Come up front and sit down." He half dragged her to an acceleration couch in the cockpit. "Strap in." His rapid motions seemed distant in the blissful, mental hush. No thought-leakers.

He dropped into the couch beside her, checked her restraints, then hooked his. "How ya doin'?"

"It's *so quiet*!"

He laughed. "Most people complain the engine is noisy. Be ready for zero G. I'm detaching now."

"What about this?" She flicked her neck ring.

"Got it covered." He jerked a tool from a magnetic clasp, but not before the alarm went wild.

"Ahh!" She tugged on the despised ring.

Vigard grimaced at the shrill tone. "Don't add to it."

Strobe lights lit up the ring and flashed over his scowl. The alarm switched to words. *Warning! Thought-reader! Warning! Thought-reader!* He cut through one side of the ring, but still the chant blared.

He shouted over the din. "Spin it. Give me the other side."

She jerked it halfway around, and he severed it again. The two pieces separated, chanting and flashing. Vigard stretched to open a compartment, chucked them in, and slammed it shut. A muffled warning emanated from the trash bin. Tracy giggled.

Vigard swore and jabbed the ejection button. Even though the obnoxious thing was silenced, Tracy couldn't stop laughing. It infected him, and they both shook with laughter as acceleration pinned them in their couches.

At last, the engine dropped back to a low hum, and she let out a long sigh—a sort of ecstatic moan. "I can't believe I'm free."

He grabbed her hand and squeezed. "Swallowed your bait, did he?"

"Every word. I wish you could have seen his face when he downloaded the warning. You hit just the right tone—so cold and ominously polite." Vigard chuckled as she murmured, "I wonder how long he'll believe his chip is hacked."

Vigard snorted. "I hope it's enough to make him blow his cover. I wanted to pound him into a bloody pulp but didn't dare let someone hear a fight. Did he pay a percentage to the Syndicate?"

"Never."

"Good. They don't take kindly to losing their cut. I'll leave the dirty work to them. Maybe that way, I won't have to listen to snide remarks about bounty hunters."

"Sorry." She shifted in her couch. "I don't really mind that you get money for finding me."

"Better not. You weren't easy to locate, and I gotta eat and buy fuel at Syndicate prices." He dropped the gruff tone. "Besides..." He cupped a hand to her scarred cheek. "It gets a little personal when they take our kind and treat *us* like criminals. A casino, of all places! You are one clever lady to survive that."

His gaze never faltered, nor did his hand flinch from the lumpy scar. Realization sent warm tingles through her body. She was more than free—she was valuable.

Her lips trembled. "Thanks," she murmured. "For all of it."

He reached for the clasps and unhooked their couch restraints. "Sure. Let's see how you manage in zero gravity. Are you queasy?"

"No." She kept a hand in contact with solid surfaces as she maneuvered from the cockpit.

Vigard guided her through a short hallway. "That's my quarters on the left. On this side is the galley. And here is the lounge. Your berth is on the far side." He let go of her. "See if you can reach a table on your own."

She pushed off gently and ended up right where she had aimed.

"You're a natural." He joined her at the table. "You must have been in zero G during childhood."

Childhood? An empty canvas to her. Almost as unknown as her present situation. She looked around the lounge. Passenger couches and tables. Video screen embedded in one wall. The ceiling was painted like a sky. Everything was designed for use with or without gravity. She had thought only of leaving the space station, not of where she would end up. Now another empty canvas loomed before her. She met Vigard's gaze. "Where are we going?"

"I'm escorting you to your family on Rivelt."

Family. Another void, just like all the years before Joe. She didn't even know who *she* was. "You said you have a picture of me...from before. Can I see it?"

"Sure."

He tapped at controls in the table's surface. The video screen lit up with the image of a smiling teen. Fine blue lines squiggled across one cheek. On the other, two bolder lines curved where scars now tugged at Tracy's eye and lip. The name Telnia Doran labeled the photo. The girl seemed utterly foreign.

"I just can't imagine looking like that."

"You won't. Even though your parents can easily afford facial repair and any medical care you may need, the blue markings will never reappear. Your memories, though—you'll likely recover them."

He appeared so certain. Oh, to have knowledge enough to predict something—anything—of the future! "How do you know?"

"Inhibited recall is controlled with a brain chip. It doesn't destroy memories. It just keeps you from accessing them. There's nothing to worry about. Doctors on Rivelt know how to deactivate and remove any chips you have."

She stared at the girl on the screen. Telnia—whoever that was.

"What's bothering you?" Vigard asked.

"I see what you mean about her eyes, so I guess that must be me, but... I'm just not her. I can't go back to being her, even if I do remember my childhood."

Vigard laid a hand over her tightly clasped fingers. "No one goes back to a past version of themselves. We all live in who we are today. We all head toward an unknown future. You now get to choose what you will do with today. You no longer need to fear death in every moment ahead of you. Don't replace that with fear of the unknown. Replace it with hope."

He switched the display's image. A video of the approach to Rivelt began. The sun sparked from behind the sphere, illuminating a continent on the planet below. Soon mountains and forests, rivers and fields sped beneath the camera.

"This," Vigard said, "is the next step in your new life. Let your expectancy build."

Tracy watched a distant city grow larger. Perhaps her future home. Among people who understood her. Or would they? She had lived such a different life from them during the last four years. At least she had a chance now to make her own choices.

What should she make of that opportunity? This man floating next to her...she barely knew him, but they had at least one thing in common. He was also a thought-reader without facial markings. He had just made an enormous difference in her life. Someday, she would make an enormous difference, too.

Excerpt from the author's published novel Agents of Rivelt. *For more information on Sharon Rose's books, visit her website: SharonRoseAuthor.com.*

DIE WALKÜRE, TEXAS RANGERS

MICHAEL SPENCE

Bryn Morgan loved omens the way a horse loves a thunderstorm. They gave her indigestion, and in the interest of warding off ulcers, she kept as far from them as possible. So, when the name appeared blood-red on the Company roster during the morning quarterstaff practice, the gastric pang that hit her could best be described as *abdominous.* "Rossweisse!"

"Yes, Cap'n?" the communications officer said, joining Bryn before the bulletin board.

It held the usual tidbits—today some wag had posted a note reading, *Bottom of the 6th inning: DEER 4, ANTELOPES 2*—plus a list of names, to which Bryn pointed. In her best give-me-a-reason-not-to-be-annoyed voice, she said, "Can you explain this?"

Ranger Rossweisse studied the list and said, "It's as I wrote it up this morning, Cap'n. He should be here sometime today, with the new ordnance."

"Right, temp assignment, I got that. How'd it get that color?" Unlike the other names on the list, written in black, the name at the bottom was a dull crimson, like a lethal wound only minutes old.

"Huh." The comm officer scratched beneath her braid. "Ink

might could be goin' bad, I suppose. Never seen it turn that color, though."

Bryn took a deep breath, let it out, then asked, "How's the coffee?" Her sense of normalcy called for it, even if her stomach should object.

"Fresh pot brewin' now, Cap'n. I'll bring you a cup when it's ready."

"Thanks." She returned to her office and paused by the window, staring down through shoulder-length blonde hair at the Rangers conducting combat drills with Bowie short-sword and quarterstaff in the mammoth field enclosed by the rectangular, brick structure of the Park. *Today,* she thought. *Today we leap ahead to the twentieth century, maybe even the twenty-first. The quarterstaves we'll probably keep, and maybe the Bowie swords, but how easily will we let go of our crossbows?*

Not for the first time, she recalled daydreams she'd had of personal weapons that made things explode, like the lightning Waltraute summoned. Those were impossible, of course. Even the Chinese—who, centuries ago, showed Marco Polo their experimental powder-stuff—had never produced a suitable *boom,* not even a *bang.* It was as if some minor fire deity had told humanity, *This much you may have to cook your food, warm your gatherings, and frighten off enemies and beasts. Anything more I'm keeping for myself.* Ah well, let Jules Verne write his pseudo-science romances. Captain Bryn Morgan of the Texas Rangers had the real world to set in order as best she could.

Someone knocked at the door.

Bryn turned away from the window and said, "Come in."

It opened to reveal Waltraute, Company V's chief wizard. With her stood a young man wearing a serape over the usual shirt and wool trousers. "Our new arrival, Cap'n," Waltraute said.

Bryn smiled. The new arrival smiled back, showing even, white teeth that contrasted with his tanned, weathered skin, as did his green eyes and sun-bleached brown hair. The effect was...impressive.

Jeremy Crockett! This one's a looker. "Thanks, Trout. Pass the word around: Orientation to our new weapons on the drill field in thirty minutes. Company meeting afterward. I want to Hop before nightfall."

"You bet." She closed the door behind her.

The newcomer stood quietly before the desk.

Bryn approached him and put out a hand. "Bryn Morgan. Welcome to Valhall Park in Arlington. Welcome to the Striders."

The young man shook her hand, smiling. "Edmund Ziegler. Thank you, Captain." Releasing her hand, he added, "I've got three crates in the wagon outside, ready to issue at your convenience."

"Sounds good. I'm eager to see 'em." When he made no move, she added, "You're not packin' one?"

He reached beneath his serape. "Got something else." He produced a copper disc slightly smaller than his hand and held it out to her. "Found it during undercover work at the Hundings' and kept it. The guys at the Leiber Center in Houston worked out what it did and told me, one, it would now work only for me, and two, it would be all I needed. *The Absolute Requisite,* they called it. Try saying *that* five times quick-like. I call it Abby."

She took it and looked it over. On its edge, where a wagon wheel would meet the dirt, the disc bore marks that glowed as from an internal fire. On the face of the disc a five-pointed star, similarly radiant, stood proud in relief. Or so her eyes told her. As she ran her fingers over it, however, the entire face was perfectly flat to the touch.

She turned the disc over to find...the same glowing star. It was the backside of the former pattern, of course. —No, no it wasn't. Something suggested this was the very image she had been looking at earlier. But she *had* turned the thing over, hadn't she?

One way to test it: she turned the disc edge-on again. If she had indeed turned the disc over, the markings would now be upside down.

They weren't.

All right, I'm turning it over again now. She suited the action to the words. Again, she beheld the star, and again the markings on the edge were right-side up.

"Crazy, ain't it?" Ziegler said. "It's like I've got the only one-sided coin in the world. No tails, only heads."

With a wry smile, Bryn shook her head and handed the...*Abby*... back. *Magic,* she thought. *Never gives you a straight story. What're you gonna do?* "Those marks on the edge—I know the symbols for Air and Earth, but...four *Xs*?"

"Dr. Logan said—let's see, what was it—the marks are a continuous power linkage using the three critical elements: Earth, Air, and Firewater. He didn't say it like a joke, and if there was one, I sure didn't get it, but everyone laughed. He didn't explain further. Said I'd understand when I needed to, and until then, not even magic could see it coming." He snorted. "Wizards. Go figure."

Bryn recalled Logan's reputation: extremely competent but a bit of a joker, with a taste for spirits, the liquid kind. Not to mention a pyromaniac. "Right," she said.

"Oh, not to forget..." He reached into a pocket and withdrew a folded paper bearing the Corps Headquarters seal. "I'm to give this to you." He didn't comment on the seal.

Now that was refreshing. Discreet. Not a blatherskite. A far cry from many Rangers Bryn knew outside Company V.

"Very good. Get some help and take the weapons out onto the field. I'll be down shortly."

"Yes, Captain. Uh, if I may ask..."

"Go ahead."

"Looking around...am I the only male here?"

She chuckled. "That, you are. We're kinda unique that way." It was one reason his appointment had surprised her.

"And...there's another pattern I'm seeing. Waltraute, Helmwige, Grimgerde, Rossweisse..." He appropriately pronounced each *W* as a *V*. "...and then Bryn Morgan. Not very Teutonic."

Bryn smiled. "Welsh, actually. Daffyd ap Morgan was my adoptive father."

Ziegler nodded, saluted, and left. Bryn closed the door and stared down at the sealed paper. With her free hand, she made the gestures that would release the seal. The circle bearing the eagle and the Lone Star vanished, and the paper unfolded itself to lie flat on her desk, a formal copperplate script fading into view before her eyes.

Captain Morgan:

This will introduce Ranger Edmund Ziegler, assigned to you for the pursuit and capture of Kyle and Linda Hunding. We wish you success in this operation.

In the course of the operation, it is likely that Ranger Ziegler, owing to his previous interaction with the Hundings, will take the initiative in engaging them. You shall permit him to do so, but you are to provide no support of any kind. Should he choose not to engage, you shall nonetheless leave him on the field of conflict and return to the Park without him. Actions contrary to these directives will be treated with the utmost gravity.

It was signed by the Old Man.

When she had read through the order, the writing faded into invisibility and the paper ignited. She dropped it into a nearby spittoon and watched as it burned with a smokeless green flame, leaving no ashes or other sign that it had ever existed. Her thoughts burned as well.

She returned to the comm center.

Rossweisse looked up from the weekly report she was preparing. "Yes, Cap'n?"

"Get Austin on the horn for me, please."

"*Jawohl,* Cap'n." From the array of labeled steer horns mounted on the wall before her, Rossweisse selected one and spoke words of inquiry to it.

It spoke back.

After a brief exchange, Rossweisse handed the horn to Bryn and returned to her report.

As Bryn carried the horn back to her office, she told it, "Let me speak with the General." She closed the office door. Whatever was said near this horn would also be heard by anyone holding its mate in the State capital, and vice versa. The two horns had come from the same animal, and the wizards in Austin had invoked the Sterling-Oliver principle to link them on the cellular level.

"I'm sorry," the voice from the horn replied. "He's in a meeting right now. Can I tell him what it's about and have him contact you?"

Of course he was. "Tell him it's a Code *Das Lied von der Erde.*"

She had not used that phrase in years. Would it have the effect it once had?

In less than a minute, a baritone voice said from the horn, "Brünnhilde. What's the trouble?"

As if he couldn't guess. "Edmund Ziegler's arrived, and he brought me your order. *What* is goin' on here?"

"I believe the order was clear. Ranger Ziegler is to join you in the Hunding pursuit, and he is to act on his own."

Bryn frowned. "So, you've given him his own agenda?"

"Not exactly, but that's as good a statement of it as any."

Secrets. Another thing that set her innards to protesting. "Okay. But that don't explain why I'm supposed to leave him there even if he does *nothing.*"

In the pause that followed, Bryn imagined the Old Man behind his mahogany desk nearly two hundred miles away: a picture of rugged elegance, white hair accenting his customary dark woolen suit; receiving from black-garbed secretaries reports from all over the State and seeing more in those reports with his one good eye than others could with two. Nothing caught the General by surprise— which was why he had risen to command of the State's forces during the Late Great Unpleasantness of the sixties, and then retired from that to lead the Rangers.

Finally, he said, "All right. I'll tell you this much. We received orders from the Governor's office to assign him to the Hunding pursuit, with these stipulations. Orders against which I cannot fight. And I suspect I know their source."

And with that, she did too. Friederike, the General's recently wedded wife. With political connections that went far too deep, in far too many directions. Family: talk about two-edged swords.

"And the reason for 'em?" she asked. When he failed to answer, she added, "With all due respect, sir, I'm his captain. I reckon I've got the right."

Another pause. "It isn't something I'm at liberty to discuss right now. But"—the hint of a sigh whispered from the horn—"you have your orders. Do what you can."

Command entangled with politics. Jeremy Crockett, she hated this. He dealt with such burdens every day, true; but now one of them had detached itself and fallen on her. "I'll do what I can to make all this work out, Pa."

"I know you will, Brünnhilde." He sighed. "You are every bit the inspiration your mother was. I never saw her again after you were born, but I confess I do miss her. And I see so much of her in you."

Drawing a sudden, silent breath, she widened her eyes, and not because he had mentioned the woman whose name Bryn had invoked in the code phrase. *I'm an inspiration? Don't you know the only reason I'm here is I wanted to be like you? and that I don't tell 'em who I am so's to protect your reputation, and because I know you'll be prouder of me for doing all this on my own?* "I miss you too, Pa. We'll get through this."

"I have no doubt of it." Before she could reply further, he said, "Mm. I'll have to sign off—meeting with the Secretary of State in fifteen minutes. Give that piece of saddletrash Hunding a kick in the nether regions for me when you get him." The connection died.

She sat back in her chair and gazed at the silent horn. The Old Man was handing her a dilemma, but he trusted her to find a way to cut through it. And he'd said, "when you get him." Never a question of *if*. "I do love you, Pa," she whispered, then rose and retrieved her white ten-gallon hat from its usual resting place—the left prong of a majestic Longhorn skull mounted on her office wall. Straightening her vest, she stepped out of her office into the vast stone hall, descended the main stair, and headed toward the courtyard door with the banner over it that read:

COMPANY V

THE STRIDERS

The heavens walk with us

With a smile at the Company motto, she pulled open the huge oaken door and went out to join the others.

Everyone had gathered in the infield around three crates labeled SAMUEL COLT HOT LEAD & COLD IRON WORKS. The opened containers revealed, in neatly arranged rows, what looked like the descendants of crossbows. Instead of bows, the stocks bore elongated metal cones that tapered to a point like an icicle. Targets stood in the outfield.

Bryn picked up a weapon. On the grip, beneath the signature of Ranger Sam Walker, was a circular pattern that looked like two punctured teardrops doing a do-si-do. It figured. Not only had the Chinese invented the things that went *zap*, they'd maintained a presence in the world of armaments ever since.

Gazing at the pattern, Bryn again experienced the oddness that played tricks with the senses, although this was more like the usual phenomenon that arose in the presence of the supra-mundane, the experience Ortlinde called *diplopia thaumaturgica*. With Ziegler's disc, she could not see a dependable image, but here she beheld two —as though occupying two distinct viewpoints, or perhaps seeing from one viewpoint two separate yet synchronous realities. To a casual glance, the pattern was merely a bit of static artwork, yet she could swear it was whirling at high speed, the teardrop shapes madly chasing each other's tails.

Waltraute stepped forward and addressed the group. "All right, troops, today y'all are gonna be wizards." Over their murmurs, she said, "Yup, you heard me. So far, Ortlinde an' me have gotten to shoot the lightnin' bolts, throw fire, and all the other stuff, and y'all have done the crossbows 'n' the hand-to-hand fightin'. But now, y'all get in on the fun yourselves, even those of you who don't think you have any magic of your own. You don't have to. When we're in the field, Ortlinde an' me'll still be pumpin' it out, but you'll wield it with this here...*pistol*, they're callin' it." She held up one of the elongated cones by its handgrip. "Zig here tells me the word means *tube*. An' that's how it works, pipin' the power where you want it. I'm gonna give you the short course.

"Okay, now. Magic takes three things. First, you gotta know what it is you're gonna do and how you're gonna do it. Like when a wizard casts a fire spell, she looks inside the pile o' whatever and shakes up them molly-cules till they can't take it no more and decide it's easier to burst into flame.

"Once you know what you're gonna do, actually doin' it involves two other things, and that's what you need to remember: Vision and Will." She ticked them off on two fingers. "*Vision:* You gotta see clearly what you want to happen, both in front of you and in your head. So, you need line of sight, plus a clear imagination. When you've got that, then you just *Will* it"—the other finger—"to happen, an' before you can say *Fahrvergnügen,* it'll happen. An' that's pretty much all there is to it."

She grabbed an apple from atop a crate and tossed it to Bryn. "That first thing, knowin' the technique 'n' all, you won't have to worry about. We'll take care of that end when we're in the field. Here at V Park, it'll take care of itself because, well, it's V Park. Whatever your source, you get two things. One of 'em's *fire:* point the pistol 'n' pull the trigger...Cap'n?"

Bryn threw the apple toward the outfield wall. Waltraute sighted along the length of the weapon and squeezed the trigger. With a loud report, the distant apple burst into a ball of flame.

The Rangers gaped. One said, awestruck, "*Niña.*" Another murmured, "*Pinta.*" A third crossed herself and whispered, "*Santa Maria.*"

Grinning, Waltraute looked back at them. "And whatever you're aimin' at should burn. The other is *force.* That should work pretty much like crossbow bolts, except instead of wood and metal, you'll be shooting pieces of *push.* They can work like baseballs, or they can work like needles, or anything in between. Try 'n' see which kinds you can summon up. Cap'n?"

Bryn took a second apple and threw it straight up. Waltraute swung her pistol up and pulled the trigger. The apple shattered into tiny pieces, which rained down upon the troops.

"There we go," Waltraute said. "No actual projectiles involved. But for Willie's sake, *don't* point 'em at each other, any more'n you would a crossbow!

"The only limitations on this, besides whether we can keep up with you, are your Vision and Will. You gotta see, really *see,* what you're aimin' at. And you gotta point the thing 'n' tell it to do its stuff *because you say so.* Confidence is critical here—doubtin' Thomases don't last long in the wizard business.

"Okay. Thirty minutes' practice for each of you, to start. There're your targets. We've lost enough apples for one day. Zig, let's hand 'em out."

They distributed the Walker Colts, and soon targets were getting punctured, knocked over, or incinerated. Bryn had to admire Waltraute's mastery of this new tech. She had set the *pistols* so that they only affected the targets, not the building behind them.

While Ortlinde and Ziegler supervised the practice, Waltraute turned toward the battlewagon, set up on mounts near the office and dormitory side of the quadrangle.

"Still trying to lift her?" Bryn called.

Waltraute flashed her a grin. "Fifty-four-forty or fight!"

Bryn smiled and shook her head, then turned to leave, beckoning Ziegler to follow. As they headed back to the offices, he kept her pace easily. The Strider stride. He did it well. Recalling Waltraute's form of address, she said to him, "'Zig'?"

He shrugged. "Been called worse. My turn. 'Fifty-four-forty'? What does our work here have to do with the Oregon Territory?"

She chuckled. "Not a thing. Forget President Polk; Trout's talking levitation. The highest anyone can raise an object is 54.39 inches above the surface. Change the object's mass, change its size—shoot, they've even tried different shapes, lots of 'em. Makes no difference. The durn thing lifts up to five-four-three-nine inches and quits. Waltraute's convinced she can do better, so she keeps trying. So are the people at the Leiber Spacetime Center, for that matter. Did you hear anything about it when you were there?"

"Oh, right," he said. "They had this hush-hush project called 'High Flight,' some combination of high-powered wizardry and physics. All I remember is hearing 'em groan about how it wasn't working."

"Okay, but you know what it's about, right?"

"Yeah. It's classified all right, but Dr. Ngomo talked about it after I bought him a drink or three," Ziegler said. "They were talking about lots of applications. Artillery transport, aerial reconnaissance, firefighting, weather studies, birthday parties, bar mitzvahs, something called a 'mile-high club'—"

"Yeah, they're just *full* of ideas down there," Bryn said. "But since you were there, they say they've made progress. We still don't know if what they've got works yet, though, because wouldn't you know, yesterday somebody up an' stole it. And who do you suppose our culprit is?"

At Ziegler's blank expression, Bryn added, "There's another reason you're here, you know. Not just the pistols."

He stopped mid-stride. "No. You're kidding, right?"

"I kid you not. Your old pal Kyle Hunding. He and his bunch made off with all the files, the physical gewgaws, the talismans—the basic *thaum-mix*, our wizards call it. We're gonna Hop down there later this afternoon and take him. And you're gonna guide us."

As they resumed walking, Ziegler said, "Down in the hill country? You've got to Hop a long way to get there."

Bryn shrugged. "We've got Waltraute and Ortlinde. We can Hop as long as we need."

Ziegler pointed to the other sides of the structure surrounding the quadrangle. "Meanwhile, I've only seen part of the building so far. You're in that part here." He nodded toward the offices. "Over there are the stables...but who's in those other spaces?"

"I'll show you later," Bryn said. "Give it time."

As they passed a few women waiting their turn at practice, one commented to the other, "You mean I can torch something from across a field with this thing? Y'know, with these things, won't be long afore they're callin' us the Power Rangers."

The other gave her a pitying look and said, "That does it. I don't know you."

/

Bryn closed her office door and said to Ziegler, "All right. Who's got it in for you?"

He lowered his brows and pursed his lips, then slowly shook his head. "I've been a burr under some folks' saddles from time to time. Nothing major. What brought this up? If I may ask."

"You may." All right, so it was a sealed order. She was unsealing it. He was *her* charge. She summed up the order he had carried. "I get how someone could appreciate your initiative, but why does someone want you dead?"

Ziegler chuckled. "Besides Kyle Hunding? No idea. Kyle, now... when I was with him undercover, his wife and I took a shine to each other. He found out pretty quick. He made no secret of it, he's ready to turn me into coyote chow. But I don't see him going near the authorities himself, let alone talkin' to 'em, and I didn't hear anything about him knowing anyone in the government. That's all I can swear to, anyhow."

"Still, he's got the motive," she said. "Well, we'll cross that gulch when we come to it. Now..." She lifted the State map off its wall mounting and laid it on a worktable. "You're here because you know where the Hundings are. Show me."

"Right. Here's where I met up with him," he said, pointing to Galveston. "Told him I was with the Rickard Albers ring, a job went sour, and they left me behind. He bought it. I spent a week there, long enough to learn a few things, then skedaddled. He's got a fortified work area *here*." He pointed to a spot in the hill country. "He's there now. I'd be surprised if he planned on moving in the next several days."

Bryn examined that location. "Hound's Ridge. And you think he'll be doin' flight experiments there? Not someplace flatter?"

"Sure of it. He and Linda are there now. I don't know how it happens, but since the day I left 'em I've been able to sense where they are, and I can tell you they're there. Maybe Waltraute can explain it. Of course, I'm also sorta connected to the area. Lost my dad there when I was a kid."

Bryn raised an eyebrow. "Oh? Accident?"

"Storm. We were out hunting when this monster downpour dumped on us. I'd swear it was a typhoon in the middle of Texas. We got separated. Never saw him after that. I ended up being raised by my ma's family in San Marcos. But ever since then, I get a twinge whenever I see a big dark gray hat, or an eyepatch. I find myself wondering if it's him, or where he is. Or if he's still alive."

Bryn looked at the map and said nothing.

"So, someone's out to get me," Ziegler said. "Huh. So much for 'Never is heard a discouraging word,' eh?"

"We'd probably better update that line."

Out on the field, with the other Rangers gathered around a three-dimensional map Ortlinde produced, Bryn repeated what Ziegler had said about the Hundings' location. "So, if he's able to work out and cast the spells he got from the Houston raid, he might be able to up-up-an'-away from us, even with the added range of these Colts. We need to get him before that can happen."

Waltraute spoke up. "Seems to me that kind of spell-castin', even if it works"—she snorted—"needs a lot of power to make it go. Zig, do the Hundings have anything that'd give it that sort of oomph?"

"No idea," Ziegler said. "For all I know, he's still got Clovis figuring out what kinds of materials the spells will work on before he does any construction. He got the thaum-mix from the Leiber smash-and-grab, but that won't fly by itself. He has to apply it to something."

"Oh?" Waltraute said. "He's got Clovis workin' with him, does he?"

"Yeah. Kyle's got no magic of his own."

Waltraute snorted and looked at Bryn. "I've heard of Clovis. Hunding must be real confident he's got the right spells. That wizard don't come cheap."

"That gonna be a problem?" Bryn asked.

"Don't think so. He's strong," Waltraute said, "but I'm sneaky."

Bryn turned to the assembled Rangers. "All right. Normally we simply ride in and hit 'em with overwhelming force. That's not gonna be enough here. This is more than your usual outlaw pack—now, we're fightin' for the technological future of the West. You've always made a difference; this time it's huge. Go gather what gear you need and be back here in ten minutes. We'll hit 'em hard and be back in time for supper."

The sun had moved well into the west. The Rangers sat mounted, armed, and ready to move. Hat-brooches of bone, working on the same principle as the horns, comm-linked them all. Each carried a Colt—some even had two, plus their quarterstaff—but more than a few kept their crossbows. Bryn smirked. *Suspenders 'n' belt. Can't blame 'em.*

She nudged her mount and passed in front of the assembled women, horses, and Ziegler, plus Waltraute and Ortlinde in the battlewagon hovering 54.39 inches above the grass. "This is it, people! We get Hunding and his crew, and the world learns to fly! Any last questions?" None came, so she turned to the wizards. "Light it up."

A point of blinding light appeared in the southern outfield, scintillating and washing away the afternoon shadows the walls of the Park cast.

"Move out!" She started toward the light.

Three by three, they trotted after her toward the coruscating point of light. Three by three, it sucked them in—

/

—and spat them out some two hundred fifty miles away at the ley-line junction closest to Hound's Ridge, two miles from the location Ziegler had identified.

Across a small valley, they could see the upper ridge running at an angle from the road they traveled, crowned by the jutting rocks that gave the area its name, silhouetted like fangs against the blood-colored sky. Below those rocks, flanked by two small stone outbuildings that might be sentry posts, stood an immense gateway that appeared to lead into the mountain itself.

When they were a mile from the stronghold, Captain Morgan addressed the Rangers in the gathering dusk. "This should be over quickly. Ortlinde, what's their situation?"

The wizard looked up from her long-range viewer. "He's up there, inside that cave fortress. They've split up. Looks like the rest of

223

the group's somewhere else, but Kyle and Linda are in there with Clovis."

"Right. Trout, defenses?"

"Tight-placed wards, no surprise there. They make a dome strong enough to cover both this side an' the far side of the ridge. Observation area on top of the ridge, connected by tunnels to the rest of the business, with a wall around it and some low towers. It's probably under the dome, too. And an exit on the other side of the ridge, openin' onto a large deck area with—*whoo-oo!*—some heavy artillery mounted on it. I'm not familiar with the specifics, but it's the zappy sort, powerful dangerous. Good thing we're on this side."

"Captain," Ziegler said, "those wards—I have an idea."

"Oh? Go on." The three of them and Ortlinde conferred for a moment, then Bryn said, "Can't say I'm thrilled with it, but it's workable."

Waltraute chuckled. "Sneaky. I like it."

His own agenda. So far, so...compliant.

Bryn linked to the rest of the group and filled them in. "So, that's how it is. Their position is mainly defensive, unless they can somehow trap us inside the caves or get us around to the other side, which don't seem likely. But it's a pretty good defense. They can keep that dome up as long as they want, droppin' it only to take shots at us. Which they could do all night.

"We can take 'em, though. Hunding's got a prairie-sized ego, and he and our man Ziegler have a history." She keyed to his set privately. "Still willing? This won't be safe. I wish it were."

The answer came back crisp and confident. "Go, Captain. If I make it, that's a slapdown for Friederike. If not, it's my problem. You've lost nothing. Let's do it."

How she wished that were true. "Okay, ladies 'n' gentleman, here's the plan..."

Shortly thereafter, tactics discussed and tuned, questions asked and answered, they broke the huddle and remounted. As they prepared to run the final distance of their pursuit, Bryn turned in her saddle toward the Company and shouted, "Who are we?"

They shouted back in unison, "Company V!"

"Who are we?"

"The Striders!"

"When we ride—"

"We ride with the winds!"

"When we walk the land—"

"The heavens walk with us!"

Bryn wheeled her mount around toward their target. "Go, Striders, over the earth!"

"Go, Striders, in the sky!"

They charged.

The setting sun lit the eighteen riders in orange and gold as they galloped across the valley and along the lower ridge road toward the stronghold, the battlewagon zipping along behind them at four-and-a-half feet above the ground, impeller nodes going flat out. Its rigging cables vibrated in the wind with a roar like an orchestra playing a mighty, arpeggio-laden fanfare full of sound, brass, and fury, announcing to the world that Company V of the Texas Rangers was on the move, a titan marching forth to battle the upstart gods.

At the head of the charge, Captain Bryn Morgan hollered at the top of her lungs, "Yip, yi-o, toho-OH! Yip, yi-o, toho-OH!"

The Rangers behind her answered with, "Yip, yi-o, toho-OH! Yip, yi-o, toho-OH!"

They reached the foot of the upper ridge, dismounted, and took their positions. Schwertleite, Helmwige, and Siegrune began tracing a pattern of pistol-fire across the width of the high hill. To no one's surprise, the fireballs appeared prematurely, interrupted by the ward-dome, their impact points tracing out its location. It lit up like a hemispherical Christmas tree—live oak, perhaps—strewn with garlands of golden flame that faded slowly away.

Bryn smiled. Hunding knew by now that their armament couldn't penetrate the dome, but they in turn now had its measure. *Good. Let him get confident.*

"Got news, Cap'n!" Waltraute said.

Bryn turned toward the battlewagon at the rear of the dug-in Rangers. "What've you got, Trout?"

The wizard's voice came over the link. "We're detectin' huge waves of power from behind the hill. It looks as though they've got their energy source."

Ortlinde chimed in. "And not just any energy source, either. Captain, it looks like we've found the Bronze."

Bryn blew out a breath. *The Bronze. If that don't beat all.* The unique mystical energies in that metal sculpture were so powerful and so little understood that it was kept isolated on an island in the middle of the Brazos River, watched over by mysterious, other-than-mortal, and usually unseen guardians. She'd never gotten to see it, or them. And then it up and disappeared, and for three years *nobody* had seen it.

But here it was. What was it going to do to the High Flight setup? Melt the stuff down? Vaporize it? Maybe supercharge it so that it was more powerful than anything they'd face in this century, or perhaps the next two?

"All right," she said. "It looks as though we'll be crossin' that gulch shortly. Till then, let's not panic. What's that you've said? Hold judgment, pending further data?"

Ortlinde chuckled. "I believe what she said was, 'Keep your money in your pocket until you've checked the horse from teeth to tail-pipe.'"

"Right," said Waltraute. "But what you said, Cap'n, that works too."

Ziegler had dismounted and now waited by Bryn's side. She

clapped him on the shoulder. "Now's the time. Last chance to back out."

Without saying a word, he turned and strode forward, gaze fixed on the top of the ridge.

May the heavens walk with you, Bryn prayed.

The pistol-flames ceased as he approached a point where they now knew the dome intersected with the earth. He called toward the peak, "Kyle! You in there?"

The Rangers around him stood silent. Whatever wind had blown ceased. Small fires flickered around the dome but made no sound. Even the horses stood stock-still.

Then, a voice like that of a giant boomed around them. "Well, hello, Mister Ed! Back at last?"

Bryn grimaced. He did say he'd been called worse.

"Yeah, I'm back!" Ziegler shouted. "You said you'd rip my head off if you got half a chance. You've got it now. Wanna try?"

The giant voice—magically amplified, of course—fell silent. Two faint voices in the distance sounded as though they might be arguing, one of them female.

Bryn wrinkled her nose. It was strange how odd memories rushed in to fill empty moments. Like a story she remembered from long ago: If the Philistine enemy atop the impossibly fortified hill said, "Wait there, we'll come down to you," then Jonathan and his armorbearer wouldn't engage them. But if they said, "Come on up," it meant God would let Jonathan win the fight. What would Hunding say?

"What's the matter, Kyle?" Ziegler shouted. "Worried about one lone Ranger?"

If there'd indeed been an argument, that might have tipped the balance. The booming voice yelled, "Worried? I'll show you worried! You get your tail up here, and I'll pull your guts out through your..." He reeled off one of the most unusual listings of body parts and improbable procedures Bryn had ever heard.

She snorted. *Guess that means "no."*

"Okay, then," Ziegler called. "But you'll have to lift the wards."

"Lose the flame-thrower first!"

Ziegler hesitated as if thinking about it. "Well, all right. If you insist."

"You bet I do!"

Ziegler raised the serape over his head and dropped it to the ground. From his belt he withdrew a pistol in each hand, held them at arm's length, and dropped them. One stuck in the ground point-first. "How's that?"

"Roll your sleeves up!" the giant said. "Let me see your arms!"

Ziegler snickered. "Thought I'd remember how you play poker, hey?" He rolled back his sleeves, pulled off his boots, and pulled up his pant legs. "Satisfied?"

"The boots. Upside down. Shake 'em out." Ziegler obeyed, and the giant grunted. "I guess that'll do. Come on up. I got somethin' to show you."

Bryn let out a breath. Well, that sounded biblical enough. Maybe he'd be a Philistine.

A sound Bryn couldn't identify vibrated the air, and Ziegler stepped through the area that had been impermeable. The sound returned. The wards must be back.

It would take a minute for Ziegler to reach the fortress's entry, which was flanked by twin guardhouses. Over the general communications link, Bryn said, "All right, everyone, get ready to use that *push*. On my command, throw hardball shots at the sentry booth to the right. But first, Waltraute, I need those lightning strikes: north, south, east, west edges of the dome, and zenith. No thunder this time—let's be nice to the horses."

"Got 'em, Cap'n. Five *Wotan* torpedoes, loaded an' primed."

Wait for it...wait...Ziegler was twelve steps from the door. "Ready...and...*hit it!*"

Like threads from the Norns' web, five jagged lines of dazzling light shot skyward from the battlewagon, gathered at a single point in the sky, and stabbed with micrometric precision at each compass point and at the summit of the dome. The dome sparkled with the sudden load of electrical energy.

Okay, now let's shake their man's Vision. Bryn put out a general call. "Sentry booth to the right of the door. Hit it!"

Twenty-five barks sounded just as Zig reached the door, Abby hidden in his fist. The shots impacted harmlessly in sparkles on the dome...but beside him the empty booth blew out, the stones tumbling down the hill.

"Sentry booth to the left. Hit it!"

Again, a guardhouse collapsed, following a volley of Ranger fire. Sparkles flickered and went out.

Bryn nodded. *Right. Clovis thinks we've found a method that goes through his wards, and it's thrown his concentration off for a few seconds. Let's hope that's enough.* As Ziegler disappeared inside, she shouted, "Surround the doorway! Grimgerde, Rossweisse, with me!"

They swarmed up the slope toward the entranceway, hoping to reach it before the dome reappeared. It never did, and as Bryn charged into the doorway, she realized why. Clovis had stationed himself just behind the entrance, perhaps thinking the view might be better. It was, but it also put him directly in Ziegler's path. The pudgy man with the midnight-blue bandanna lay on the ground, unconscious.

Bryn threw slapsnakes around his wrists and ankles. The charmed ropes wriggled as if alive. When one end met the other, they snugged themselves up tight enough to immobilize. As an afterthought, she repositioned his bandanna, half in his mouth and secured with the other half. As a further afterthought, she shot him with a measured burst, what Ziegler had called "Hammer time." It should give them thirty or so mage-free minutes.

The three Rangers found the stairway leading to the observation area. A woman, doubtless Linda Hunding, lay over by the back wall, moving groggily as though stunned. Beside her lay Abby.

Hunding was gone. So was Ziegler.

Hmm. Had Linda wrested Abby from Ziegler? Bryn took the disc and examined it. The various markings, so luminous in her office, had faded almost to black. That made no sense—hadn't he told her it didn't depend on the Company wizards for its operation? Anyway, now he'd run off for some reason. She pocketed the disc, assigned Rossweisse to take charge of Linda, and she and Grimgerde continued up the stairs.

Emerging onto the open observation platform, she found it empty. Neither Ziegler nor Hunding was anywhere in sight.

She froze. For the past several minutes, a noise had hummed in the background and was now rising in volume and pitch. She looked down the back slope to the rear deck area Waltraute had spoken of.

The deck wasn't there.

Or rather, it was no longer at ground level.

As she watched, the wooden platform slowly rose into the air, then leveled off and moved out over the downslope. But instead of sliding into the valley as one would expect, it continued its level flight so that, as the terrain sank beneath it, the deck's distance-above-ground grew rapidly from ten feet to fifteen, twenty, thirty, fifty, *seventy*...

Apparently the High Flight spells worked just fine, thank you.

The platform began to rise again. As it passed her, Bryn scanned its edges to see what was mounted there...*Oh, dear.* Waltraute had said that large instrument was artillery. It looked like a huge black hoop with fangs and crosshairs. And soon, there'd be nothing between it and her women.

Two figures came into view on the rising platform—one standing next to some equipment, another on the opposite side trying to climb up over the railing and onto the deck. Could she help him? She drew her Colt and fired a percussive burst at the seated man.

The only result was the sudden appearance of a dark sphere encapsulating the platform, sparkling as its larger counterpart had done moments earlier. A ward bubble. Of course. So much for a frontal attack.

Was it as effective elsewhere? Say, underneath?

She looked at the three symbols Abby bore: Earth, Air, and...
'Firewater.' *Logan, you've got a weird sense of humor.*

Wait. Fire and water...This was a mountain ridge. Somewhere beneath that creased, buckled surface was...*Wait, now: Vision and Will.* Closing her eyes, she tried to envision— And then she saw it: a subterranean sea of fire, waiting to be coaxed out through the fractured crust and guided through a tunnel of hardened air. *Logan, you magnificent clown!*

She formed a mental command, and the star mounted on Abby blazed in her hand. A thin stream of liquid flame burst from the ground and squirted upward through the darkening twilight. It spiraled toward the underside of the platform—

—and splashed.

Gobbets of molten rock flew in every direction, to land in the wooded areas below the ridge. Bryn tensed. A forest fire on top of everything else? But no, nothing was happening below, except for limbs of oak and mesquite collapsing under the impact of suddenly cooled rock. Smart man, Hunding: he kept heat-eaters. They'd probably found that load of calories tasty.

Hang it all! The shield was as strong below as above.

What to do? She had to think fast. The platform continued to rise, the steady magma stream joined to it like an umbilicus, and soon the fortress would no longer stand between that hoop-thing and the Rangers.

Again, she examined the symbols on the disk. What was it they did? A power linkage, Zig had said, continually refreshing it. Where the energy came from, she now had the beginning of an idea. So, the link wouldn't be interrupted—but could it be transferred? Might she get it to draw from another source instead?

Closing her eyes, Bryn tried to build a mental picture of a bronze sculpture: a rose in full bloom, its leaves vibrant with the life-force of every flower and tree and vine and shrub in the land, the forces surging within it making its petals shine yellow, bright as the Texas sun, and its leaves and stem a blue-green as deep as the Gulf of Mexico. A sculpture snatched from its resting place in the Brazos River.

The image abruptly vanished, replaced by another: swaths of midnight blue studded with points of white that shone like stars, endlessly swaying against a background of green, like a windblown field of bluebonnets in full bloom.

All around the mountain fortress, all movement ceased—not the settled, waiting quiet of before but a sudden stop, as though time itself were under arrest. The few birds that sang before went silent. The wind halted, and the very air turned gelatinous. The Rangers below her stood frozen. The floating platform hung motionless in midair, its fanged hoop now glowing red, a bloody sun, as it prepared to throw death at her troopers.

Amid the silence, a contralto voice, gentle yet firm, said, "SPEAK. I HEAR."

Of all the things she had imagined might happen, *that* wasn't one of them.

What now?

Find the words. "The...the life given to you is being channeled to...to an evil contrivance, intended to bring death. Lend that life to me instead."

"WHERE IS IT TO GO?"

The words came easily now, with an odd sense of formality. Maybe that, too, was how magic worked. "To a disc of copper carrying the Lone Star of Texas, joined with earth's blood. It stands below you. I wield it."

"I KNOW YOU, BRÜNNHILDE MORGAN. I HEAR THE SONGS OF THE STAR AND EARTH'S BLOOD. CALL ME. I WILL COME."

Time resumed its flow. On the platform, the hoop-thing suddenly blazed white. Below her, the women scattered as the ground beneath them burst into flame. Those whose clothing had caught fire dropped and rolled on the ground to extinguish it. In the battlewagon, Waltraute and Orlinde frantically created vacuum zones on the hillside to extinguish the flames. Distracted, they could no longer channel their wizardry to the Colts, which went dead. Those who had crossbows drew them against the men who now emerged, one by one, from tunnel exits. The rest drew their swords and prepared to engage.

"I know you," the voice had said? Well, now. Bryn prepared to call...and hesitated.

"I'm his captain. I reckon I've got the right."..."If I make it, that's a slapdown for Friederike. If not, it's my problem."..."Orders against which I cannot fight."

Can I, Pa?

Aloft, the hoop again glowed.

Bryn squared her shoulders, planted her feet, and raised the Star, bright in the palm of her hand against the deepening night, to face the platform. *I hope you're satisfied, Friederike.* Then, to the one who knew her, she thought, *Come.*

The Bronze stood knee-high beside her on the roof. With it was an assortment of wizardly paraphernalia, yanked along by their energy link to the sculpture. The glowing rose petals faded for an instant, then shone in glorious vitality.

Below, the magma stream ceased, cooled, solidified, a lance extending into the night. *Uh-huh. Dessert for the heat-eaters.*

What caused the next event, she couldn't be sure. Perhaps it was the way the platform lurched when it lost its lift. Perhaps it was some last, tenuous remnant of something that distracted Ziegler's attention, as Linda Hunding appeared at the top of the stairs, eyed the platform tilting in the air, and screamed, "Eddie!"

All Bryn could do was watch as a man fell from the edge of the deck into the sparkling under-bowl of the bubble and then, as it sputtered, plummeted to the valley below. The side of the platform where he had hung bobbed upward, and the platform itself began to fall, its angle providing just enough glide to slide it into the lance of rock, where it vanished in a ball of white fire as the wards gave up all their remaining energy in one last death-scream of power.

As the Rangers rode back toward Arlington, Bryn turned to look at the body, shrouded in its serape and tied behind her saddle. This, too, was Company V's duty. She wished she could say it was a cheerful one.

The body lay face down, and yet at the same time it seemed as though the face were turned toward her with eyes open and lips moving—that strange diplopia again. No sound came from it, but all the noises around her—the sound of the horses' hooves hitting rock and dirt and swishing through underbrush, the wind soughing through the mesquite and oak, the murmur of casual conversation from the other Rangers—all were being shaped somehow into words, nature itself speaking to her.

[Captain...]

"Yes?"

[Did...we do it?]

"We did it. Waltraute has High Flight and the Bronze. The spell records and materials lists were still inside the fortress. She has them, too."

[Linda?]

"Linda's in custody. She's in the battlewagon with Waltraute and Ortlinde."

[That's a...relief. Hunding?]

She turned to look resolutely ahead, not allowing her voice to quaver. "Hunding is dead."

The not-voice was silent a moment, then said, [Good.]

She rode on. "Zig?"

[Yes, Captain.] The wind whipped through her hair and created little dust devils beside the road.

"Bryn," she told him. "I'm sorry I crashed the platform. You know why I did it."

[Yes, Captain.] The words came haltingly but with increasing fluidity, as if from one just learning to speak. [I know. You had your job...same as I did....Orders are orders.] She could have sworn the not-voice held a wry tone.

"It's true," she said. "And I paused for perhaps a moment too long, still wondering how I could save you." She shook her head. "Never did figure out a way. Still can't."

[Don't let it ride you, Bryn....Kyle took that...out of your hands.]

"Even if that were true," she said, wishing she could believe it, "I let you go in—I *sent* you in—without adequate backup. It's hard for me to keep saying I was only following orders."

[But you were....You tried to reconcile the opposites...and when you couldn't, you chose the one that was right...the one you'd want others to follow. Good job, ma'am.]

She fell silent and continued riding for several minutes, trying to maintain her composure. There was something else..."Zig?"

[Yes, Bryn?]

"The Old Man had his orders, too. He couldn't get away from them."

The not-voice slowly said, [I guess not. So, we all wind up... hog-tied by agreements, and orders, and...promises, and commitments, that we can't break....All except me now.] He chuckled. [It seems weird for someone in my position to say this... but I don't envy you.]

After a few minutes' silence, he said, [Captain?]

"Yes?"

[I've heard this rumor that Valhall Park is now serving...nectar and ambrosia...to the ones you bring back. Is it true?]

Bryn snorted. "Dad*gum*mitall. That balderdash again. You'll have all the chili, habaneros, and Dr Pepper you could ever want. We've also got something new called *ghost peppers*. Figured you're the perfect one to try 'em out."

She had never thought the wind could sigh with relief. Then, it... he...said, [Chili. With beans, or without?]

"We don't do religious discussions here. And don't bring up football: same response."

As was customary, all the Rangers helped build the funeral pyre in the infield of Valhall Park in Arlington that night, but this pyre was among the largest they had ever built, even though it had only one occupant. Bryn watched as, in lieu of the usual torch, Grimgerde lifted a Walker Colt in honor of the man who had brought it to her and...*fired* was an appropriate verb, it seemed...packets of flame into selected points along the base of the wooden structure. The several fires flowed like molten metal along the base and joined into one, even as their upper edges made their way up the timbers until they reached the top, where the lone body lay.

Bryn watched while the blaze lifted hands of flame as if in supplication to the stars. Hours later, she continued to watch, standing in the dark as the fire burned down to coals, dying even as its occupant had died.

Beside her, the shade of Edmund Ziegler watched it and her. Rustling through a nearby oak grove, the night breeze whispered, [Glorious.]

"That, it is."

They continued to gaze at the flickers that remained.

[You used Abby to attack the platform.]

"Yes."

[They said only I could use it, that it was connected to me. You used it.]

She drew Abby from a pocket and looked it over. "I expect there's more to it than the guys at Leiber told you. For that matter, I wouldn't be surprised if they had a hand in makin' it so. They do that sort of thing."

[You're saying all that was cow-chips, what they told me?]

She thought about it, wondering both what it meant and what she ought to say. *Ah, hump it.* "No. Just...not complete. You said your father had a dark gray hat and an eyepatch?"

[Yeah.]

"My birth father wears an eyepatch. And he favors a dark gray hat."

The fire crackled on, unmodulated. Then, [Go on. I don't want to get ahead of you.]

"I'm just sayin' that whatever made your flesh yours might also, to some degree, be in mine. And Abby responded to it."

Another pause. [That's where I thought you were going. You're saying you're my sister?]

"Half-sister, yes."

[You said...he *wears* the eyepatch.]

"Uh, yes."

[He's alive now. At this moment.]

"Yup." She took a breath and let it out slowly. "Living in Austin."

[Where he...]

"Where he occasionally sends sealed orders that burst into flame, yup."

A section of the pyre collapsed, sending a flurry of sparks into the air.

[I'll be slicked. Seems the Old Man's...shall we say, misbegotten?]

"Arguably."

[Huh. I guess that explains you and me. Like begets like, and all that.]

Bryn chuckled. "I suppose."

[And here I was thinking, on our way back, that y'all were some kind of angels, ministering to the dead.]

Now, she laughed. "I like the sound of that. But no, I'm just a regular Texas girl. Light, sweet, and occasionally crude."

The fire chuckled along with her. [Well, if anyone asked me, I'd tell 'em you're someone to ride the river with. Even if it's the River Jordan.]

The compliment took her by surprise, and for a few moments she was speechless. Eventually, she was able to change the subject. "And tonight, we had another advantage: next-generation wizardry."

[The pistols?]

"Nope. Abby."

[Go on.]

"With all that we were doing down south at Hound's Ridge, didn't you wonder why we're based up here, more'n two hundred miles away?"

[Thought it was the usual bureaucratic silliness.]

"Uh-uh. All our magic, including the Colts, is based on the fact that everything in the world is different from everything else, and when you *con-jure* things—lock 'em together to do stuff—that makes tension. You saw the Chinese whirligig sign on the pistol handles. There's power in that tension, power that the wizards tap into and put to work. Well, Valhall Park in Arlington is right spang in the middle of the Dallas-Fort Worth paradox, the largest psychic vortex in the South. It gives us the push, the pull, the torque we need for all the magic that gets done. The North has 'em too. I've heard tell of another city-pairin' up in Minnesota. And don't get me started on the boroughs of New York City.

"But you saw those symbols on the disc. It looks like our Doc Logan has taken things farther and turned 'em in a new direction, to boot. See, everything is also *connected* to everything else. Nature's a system. I think he's been working with those connections, the affinities, and somehow uses 'em."

[Not sure I follow. What do you mean, connections...affinities?]

She chuckled. "Well, for example, when is fire like water?"

After a moment, the crackling of the fire grunted as if in recognition. [When it's also earth. And flowing out in open air.]

She nodded. "The blood of the earth. My guess is, you've been using the world's first geothermally powered wizardry. No wonder it never runs out of energy."

[Geo—Do what, now? That a Chinese term? German?]

"Greek, I think. Not important."

[Okay. Guess I'll take your word for it. I just used the thing—glad I didn't have to take it apart.]

"Felt good to shoot, though, didn't it?"

[Oh, yeah. Connections, huh? Great. You spend your life trying to keep peace and take out the nasty people, and suddenly you find out you're the matchmaker for creation.]

"Say what, now?"

[Always a bridesmaid, never a bride...]

She grimaced. "Put a cork in it, Ranger."

[Anything you say, Cap'n Sister dear ma'am.]

Ghosts, she thought. *Can't live with 'em, can't shoot 'em. Someone already beat you to it.*

After checking Ziegler into his new lodgings in the south wing of the Park building and introducing him to Colonel Travis, Mr. Bowie, Lieutenant Garcia, Private Williams (whose actions during the Unpleasantness had won him a welcome even though he initially hailed from Indiana), and others, Bryn steeled herself for the one encounter still remaining. The coals from the pyre cast a pale glow that made it easy for her to find a hiding place in the shadows of the outfield. This was one conversation that was better kept from Rossweisse and the others. Which meant no horns.

Experiment time. She pulled out Abby and envisioned the party at the other end. For a moment, the field of waving bluebonnets reappeared, except that now they looked like drifting stars in deep space.

Then, "*Hey*! What in tarnation—"

"Hey, Pa. Caught with your britches down? Now you know how I'm feelin'."

"Daughter, have you no sense of—"

"Propriety?" She snorted. "I thought I did, but that was before a certain sealed order. Give my excuses to whoever she is there. We have to talk." *Waylon's teeth, Pa! Can't you keep 'em buttoned for even a little while? One would think you played professional sports or something.*

After a moment, he said, "All right, Brünnhilde. Talk."

"You've probably heard, but in case you haven't, I'm reportin' it: We have High Flight back. Hunding has been dealt with."

"Glad to hear it. How did it go?"

Bryn related the story—the approach to Hound's Ridge, Zig's gambit for getting through the shield dome, the flying platform, and its destruction with Hunding on board.

"And Ranger Ziegler?"

"'Thy servant Uriah the Hittite is dead also.'"

"Thy...oh."

"I gotta hand it to you, Pa. You knew he had Abby—excuse me, *The Absolute Requisite*—shoot, for all I know, you arranged for him to find it—and then you had the boys at Leiber just...switch the thing off, or at least lock him out. He had to go it completely alone. Was it so important to get High Flight back that you had to—"

The sudden realization hit her. "No. *No.* It was so important to get *the Bronze* back that you had to do that to him." She swore again. "I won't ask you how you knew Hunding had it. Frankly, I don't care. But why did Edmund Ziegler—*your son*—have to go after it the way he did? And why, at the last minute, did you take away the only thing he had to use?"

"He had to go after it on his own. I could not help him. I couldn't even be seen as having anything to do with him. Any action I myself took to retrieve the Bronze from whoever held it would result, down the line, in disaster. Therefore—"

"Wait. How would you know...Oh, for cryin' out— It's a *prophecy* of some kind, ain't it? Of course it is. Con*sarn* 'em!"

"I had thought that arranging for him to find the Requisite, rather than giving it to him, would be sufficient detachment. But as time went on, and he made his entrance to Hunding's fortress as part of an official operation, with you following to provide support..."

"You panicked. You left him high and dry."

"I put him in a situation where he faced Hunding without any external resources, not even the Requisite. He had the opportunity to fight Hunding one-on-one and to take the Bronze."

Her rant screeched to a halt, and her stomach sank. "Which he might've done, if I hadn't stepped in and pulled the Bronze away myself—because Hunding was threatenin' the rest of us. So, now *I've* recovered the Bronze, and I was most certainly *not* acting independently. You might've told me. And now I have to live with all of this."

"In addition, you will face disciplinary action for disobeying a direct order. An order that, as you recall, we reviewed and confirmed."

"An order that, may I point out, General sir, runs smack up against a basic duty of my command. Which means it was an impossible situation from the git-go. You told me to do what I could —and for doin' that, I'm gonna be disciplined." Bryn took a deep breath and slowly let it out. "Here's a better solution for you. I quit."

"Brünnhilde. You cannot just—"

"With all respect, General, I must. After tomorrow, Grimgerde will command the Company. I'm going off the map, and I'm takin' Abby with me." *And Linda, but you all don't need to hear that yet.* "Find me if you think you can, and, if you really want to, try again to satisfy your prophecy. But I respectfully suggest you get some stranger to give it a shot. Because *I* have *had* it with all that!"

He cleared his throat. "Perhaps I have been too autocratic in this matter, and some amends need to be made. What might I do that would convince you to remain on duty?"

She thought on that. "With respect, General, I'm not sure I'm going *off* duty, for absolute 'n' all. I've got some serious thinking to do. But you know, there is something you can do..."

They talked details for a moment, and then he said, "Agreed. I suppose that's a debt I owe as well. Consider it done."

Bryn smiled. "Thank you, General. Meanwhile, I hope Friederike is satisfied with the way things turned out. Because now I know what it was that got her family so all-fired angry. Edmund's your child, but he's not the only one. Our wizards gave Linda the usual forensic screening, along with everything else we brought back from

Hound's Ridge. Surprise, surprise: she's yours, too—Edmund's fraternal twin. Friederike's clan just couldn't stand the idea that he 'n' she might be doin' the blanket polka, could they? They didn't want the scandal. So, they had to get Zig out of the picture."

"A good inference, Captain. And accurate. You did earn your rank."

"You might want to put some manpower into seeing how they found out. I should've guessed what was goin' on when Zig told us he could sense where the Hundings were and what they were doing. He and Linda shared a womb. They may not have had congruency, but they sure as Hannah had contiguity. And so, when they got to pirootin', it bonded them as a Sterling-Oliver pair.

"And guess what. She's knocked up. And Kyle Hunding ain't the father. Let Friederike and company put *that* in their pipe 'n' smoke it!"

She was about to break the connection when he said sternly, "Captain, I did not hear what you said just then. Nor do I wish to. Let us leave it that way."

The heat left Bryn's face. Could anyone magically eavesdrop on this conversation? She prayed not. *Zig's death is on me. Let the child and its mother not be doomed also by my spite.*

"Acknowledged, General," she said. "*Gott sei mit dir.*" With that, she broke the connection and stormed back toward the barracks. Perhaps she should give him the benefit of the doubt. After all, he had once taught her that there were at least two sides to every issue. But then she thought of Abby. No. Some things didn't have two sides. Not that it made them easier to handle.

Along the way back, she thought about her father and her brother—one she'd loved all her life, one she'd known less than a day. The Old Man's vulnerability had cost the life of his son and made her unable to both command her people and take responsibility for their welfare. Indeed, Zig had died by her hand, accident or no. An answer might show itself in time, but it wasn't here and now.

She recalled the words of a song from long ago, when a black-clad troubadour from Arkansas sang about love casting one into a burning ring of fire. *Ain't that the God's honest truth.*

The next evening, they all sat in the common room—including the shade of Ziegler, who raised a shadowy bottle-shape to his lips every so often. The occasion was twofold, celebrating Ranger Grimgerde's promotion to captain and command of the Company, and a farewell for its previous commander. A miniature Long-Hop window cooled the room, bringing a breeze of chosen temperature from somewhere outside and sweeping it back and forth across the room.

Chariots of *fire*, but it was hot out there. Bryn leaned into the breeze. Ortlinde must've reached out of State for that wind. Be nice if those heat-eater critters could do something about the relentlessly hot Texas summer nights. She shook her head. Nah, they'd gorge themselves to death.

Using the noise of the wind-gate along with the murmur of surrounding conversation, the shade chuckled and said, [So, what happens now? I'm afraid this being dead is something new to me. Is there an orientation lecture? Magic lantern pictures? Handbook?]

After all this time on the job, Bryn still felt a little peculiar telling the others, "Talk louder. I can't hear him." Once he'd repeated himself, she said, "Well, it's fairly simple. The folk in the south and east wings are our guests for the duration, kept safe until a particular event comes around. No, I don't know what it is, though it wouldn't surprise me if it were a fight of some kind. That's the durnfool thing about prophecies: they're no blam-jam good until the fulfillment's right on top of you, and even then, there'll be arguments. But anyhow, ordinarily you'd be staying with us till then." She chuckled. "It sounded last night as though you and Private Williams had more'n a few things to talk shop about."

[I see,] the shade replied as, visible through him, the breeze riffled a stack of papers. [So, I'll enjoy your hospitality while it lasts, and then—]

"I said, ordinarily." She grinned and held out a piece of official-looking vellum bearing the Governor's seal. "As it is, you'll be up and around a little while longer. This came by courier this afternoon. Seems you've been transferred. The Circle-X outfit needs another field operative, and you're it."

"Hey, Zig!" someone yelled. "Your hand!"

All eyes went to the back of the shade's hand and stared as a ringed X flared into being, glowing red-orange like a hot iron, and then faded from view.

Bryn smiled. *Well, well. Credentials.*

Someone whistled and murmured, "You ever seen the X-Brand before?" to which another replied, "You kiddin'? I ain't never seen a Circle-X *spook* before."

[Field oper—Hot dang!] Zig stared at his hand. [That's something I'd never dared even dream of. I knew they did some exciting stuff—but I also knew they didn't take, uh, volunteers.]

She gave him a wry look. "Well, you certainly weren't one. In any sense." She grinned. "Congratulations...Agent Ziegler."

"And none too soon," Rossweisse said, coming over to their table and bringing the horn labeled *The Alamo*. "Their HQ just called. They want you to check out some trouble in Houston. It seems a specter is haunting Leiber, and they think it's Hunding."

[Tell 'em I'm on it,] the breeze said, as the shade vanished.

Vaya con Dios, little brother. Gott sei mit dir. With a small, contemplative smile, Bryn went back to her office to finish packing.

*

"Cap'n," Gerhilde said, leaning in through the doorway, "there's someone here to see you. The First Avatar, if I'm gettin' it right, and she's come to take custody of the Third Avatar."

The corners of Bryn's mouth turned upward. So did her mood.

"Good. Show her back here, and I'll get it ready. Please send Linda Hunding here also."

"Sure thing, Cap'n. And if I may say it...we're gonna miss you. Seems there's a bit of you in all of us, now."

Bryn had to stop and close her eyes for a minute. Then, she said, "Thank you, Anneliese. It's been an exciting time for me, too. I can't think of a better crowd to be around than you all."

With that, Gerhilde left, and, humming softly, the erstwhile Captain of Company V removed the radiant yellow Rose from a cupboard and arranged it on her desk, so that the light through the window from the setting sun caught the leaves just right. Soon, a knock rattled the door, which opened to reveal a regal, statuesque woman with blonde hair that shone like the Texas sun and joy-lit, blue-green eyes as deep as the Gulf of Mexico.

Erde Morgan stepped into the room and swept the captain into a strong embrace.

"Hello, Mother," Bryn said. "We're ready to go."

TRIA

BRIDGETT POWERS

CHAPTER ONE

Tria pressed her fingers together and positioned her hand just above the surface of Jada's injured wing. Beneath her fingertips, the translucent membrane of energy that stretched across the wing's fine bones pulsed red around a tear. Tria grimaced. "Try not to move."

Jada gripped the edges of the willow-stump stool on which she sat. "As you command, Your Highness."

"Enough of that," Tria said, resisting the urge to punch Jada in the shoulder. "Or shall I assign you to Healer Mendra instead?"

Jada peered across the infirmary, toward the corner where the chief healer instructed two apprentices. She shivered. "No, I shall behave, I promise."

Tria slid her hand to the left of Jada's wound, where the wing bones formed a roughly triangular section. She extended her index finger. At her touch, the membrane of energy sagged, and the wing twitched in a violent spasm that almost toppled Jada from her stool.

"As I thought," Tria said. "I must numb this wing. You may also become drowsy. I can't control the spread of the numbing effect."

"That's fine," Jada said, running a hand through her spiky black hair. "I could use a bit of sleep."

"No, no," Tria said. "I need you conscious. Otherwise, this won't work."

"Better keep me talking, then." Glancing over her shoulder, Jada tugged the petal-like layers of her emerald skirts down over her knees. "Mind giving us some privacy, though?" she asked. "I don't want all of FAE Division watching this."

Turning her back to hide a smirk, Tria pulled a curtain of iridescent light around them.

Jada let out a long breath. "Whew! Had I known the enclosure would block the smell, too, I would've requested it sooner."

"What smell?" Tria asked.

"Odor of injuries, I guess. And that sharp, spicy scent of healing magic."

Tria shook her head. "Healing power has no odor."

Jada snorted. "You've been around it so long, it's probably burned the smell right out of your nostrils."

Tria laughed. From the pocket of concealment in the air beside her, she withdrew her healer's wand, much slimmer than the warrior's wand tucked behind Jada's ear. With it, she traced an intricate pattern in the air, weaving strands of faerie sparks into a web around them.

Jada whistled through her teeth. "A dome of silence? If it's going to be that bad, I think I *want* to be unconscious."

Laughing again, Tria touched her wand to the uppermost corner of Jada's butterfly-like wing. "How did this happen, anyway? Were you battling sorcerers or thief-spawned creatures to protect your charge?"

"Nothing so grand," Jada said, "Unless you count battling nature. The man was sailing from Aquatonia, and his ship ran into a violent storm. Silly human waited until the last minute to call for the King's aid." She covered a yawn with her hand. "I almost didn't get there in time. Then, this sliver of wood splinters from the broken mast and decides to pierce my wing while I'm saving him from plunging to the depths of the sea."

Tria gasped. "It is a wonder you didn't both drown."

"Would've," Jada said, "if the captain hadn't saved my tail feathers."

"But you don't have..." Frowning, Tria leaned around Jada's wing to peer beneath it.

Jada giggled. "Still so literal, Princess? That was an expression, since it isn't considered polite to speak of one's hind portions."

Flushing, Tria gave Jada a lopsided grin. "Since what century have you concerned yourself with politeness? Besides, to be fair, we healers are in the habit of using exact terminology. Now, hold still."

Tria closed her eyes, calling forth her healer's gift. The energy of the wing's surface shimmered into life behind her eyelids. Fine filaments of light, too small for the eye to perceive, wove in and out to form an intricate pattern that could keep a faerie aloft for days. Tria focused on the spots at which those threads of light had been severed.

"Tell me if you feel anything," she said, again placing her fingertips just above the wound. She called forth energy from the King of All Lands to reconnect the nearest fibers of light.

"Tickles a li'l," Jada said, her words slurred.

"Good."

"N-not." Jada yawned wider. "Hate being tickled."

Tria suppressed a smile. "At least it's not burning." She began the process of weaving frayed threads back into the pattern of energy and forging new ones where the gap was too wide to mend connections. "So," she said, taking advantage of Jada's sleepiness to gain a bit of information too long denied her, "what's it really like... out there among the humans?"

"You've met 'em," Jada said, staring at the willow-paneled wall as if fascinated.

"Only on one occasion," Tria said, "during my apprenticeship. Even then, I had no interaction." She poked at Jada's wing to test the mended threads of energy. "We merely saved a life when someone called for the King's aid."

"Same fer us," Jada said. "Humph, you're not missing much. Humans're a confounding bunch."

"Surely they can't be so bad," Tria said, tapping the wing's upper corner with her wand to release the numbing effect. "It is they, after all, who are the King's true offspring."

"You've always held such romantic notions about them," Jada said, flexing her shoulders.

"As did you, once." Tria smiled at the memory of the pact they'd made just before starting their apprenticeships. "Was that not the very reason you joined Protection Detail, despite Captain Alvar's attempts to recruit you for his attack forces?"

"Perchance." Jada twitched the healed wing as if testing it. "Oh, humans have some redeeming qualities. Most, though, don't even spare a thought for the King's existence, let alone ours." She stretched her arms above her, then lowered them and shook her head. "Here, light permeates the very air we breathe. Out there…Even when staring into the light, most humans can't see it."

Frowning, Tria started to disengage her dome of silence, then hesitated. "They just need a reminder, someone to show them how to find the light."

Jada's lips twitched. "Given your way, you'd save every creature that ever sparked to life." She turned on her stool and fixed Tria with a stern look that would have made Captain Olivia proud. "But, Tria, you can't heal people from a darkness of their own choosing."

❦

Tria sailed down the sloping tunnel to the subterranean chamber beneath the throne room, rehearsing her report in the most formal style she could imagine. Today, she wasn't a daughter paying her mother a visit to speak of her dearest friend's welfare; she was a healer, preparing to give her queen word on a warrior's fitness to resume her duty.

At the bottom of the tunnel, Tria paused, fixing her gaze on the stone wall that stretched before her. A dead end, if one knew not what lay beyond or how to access it. She closed her eyes, preparing them to adjust to the relative dimness of the Life Chamber, then pressed her hand to the stone in front of her. She poured her faerie essence into her palm, and the stone warmed beneath her hand. The hard, cool surface melted into a thick membrane of energy. As Tria passed through it, the energy coated her skin like a waterless rain.

She took a deep breath of the cool, earthy air. A fitting fragrance for a chamber that celebrated humans, born of earth and water rather than a faerie's air and light. Blinking, she glanced around. Gone was the perpetual light that shone everywhere else in the faerie realm. The only lights here were those depicting each new human life, floating within a solid block of a transparent crystal not to be found in the mortal lands.

Off to one side, Tria's mother floated with her face all but touching the wall of crystal. Serena, Queen of Faeries, swept her silvery-blonde hair over one shoulder, pinning the lights before her with a stare so intense, Tria found her own gaze drawn to them as if for the first time.

Each light shone white at its center—the spark of an individual human life distinct from all others—and rested within the softer, iridescent glow of the King's own life-force, with which He infused each of His creations. How long that iridescent glow would continue to encompass each life depended upon the human's choices.

Tria's mother glided along the perimeter of the crystal block, her layered skirts flowing from her waist like the petals of an inverted flower. She'd muted her glow, a mixture of white and the same vibrant pink as her gown, the color of harmony, wisdom, and vitality she alone was permitted to don.

Tria dimmed her own silvery-white glow, so as not to interfere with her mother's concentration or dilute the clarity of those precious life-lights.

The queen paused in her silent patrol and flicked her wand at a group of life-lights, shifting their positions. She froze, staring at a new light, one that shone brighter than all others.

Tria glided forward several paces before awareness of her actions took hold. She paused, straining against an inexplicable pull toward that new life-light. Its inner spark of individuality did not shine distinct at its center like the others. Rather, it had interwoven so with the King's encompassing glow that the two were indistinguishable.

An odd familiarity tugged at Tria's middle. A kindred spark, this life only just conceived. How could this be? How could she, in an instant, form a depth of connection she'd not experienced in centuries of existence?

Tria parted her lips to speak of this with her wise mother, her report on Jada's condition somehow of less importance. Before she could utter a sound, the queen tilted her head, her eyes drifting shut, a sure sign that she was receiving orders from the King of All Lands.

Tria held her breath and fought the increasing pull toward the unusual life-light.

With a sudden, definitive nod, her mother backed away from the wall of crystal and murmured, "The child of prophecy. It has begun." She lifted her wand and vanished in a flurry of sparks.

/

Tria exited the tunnel and paused, at last able to sense her mother's trail upon the waves of light that bent time and space. The queen hadn't gone far.

Instead of following her mother's instantaneous route, Tria took the long way to the throne room. If only she'd been summoned and could pop right in! She'd have half her questions answered by now.

At last, she slipped through a wall of iridescent, white mist into the vast chamber, emerging just beneath the throne's floating pedestal. Her reflection shone golden in the underside of the eurwynium-plated bowl that supported the FAE seat of power. She craned her neck to determine what shape the throne's base had taken—and thus, her mother's mood—but murmuring voices arrested her attention.

"The light-wielder!" Healer Mendra said in a breathy tone at odds with her brisk nature.

Tria peered around the pedestal. The senior officers of each branch of the Royal Elfin army, FAE Division, floated before the throne. Their queen hovered among them, as an equal. Only the seers lacked representation.

"Are you certain, Your Majesty?" Captain Alvar asked, his deep purple faerie armor drinking in the light like a forest pool at midnight. "This soon after conception, the child cannot have already manifested—"

Tria's mother silenced him with a raised hand. She flicked her wand, and a shimmering barrier surrounded the throne, enclosing the High Council—and Tria—behind a wall no sound could penetrate. "The King verified her identity himself," she said.

Amid the officers' murmurs and exclamations, Tria ducked back behind the pedestal. Were they speaking of her strange new life-light? *The* life-light, she amended, not hers. She shook her head, chiding herself. With the highest members of court in closed session, she shouldn't even be here, but she had to know. Besides, to exit now would reveal her presence.

Taking advantage of the High Council's distraction, she glided upward, careful to remain concealed, until she reached the throne. She expelled a breath. The base had retained the shape of a flower, a perfect place to hide. She slipped in among the metallic petals surrounding the throne, then peered between them.

General Fendan of Protection Detail cut through the jumble of voices. "This child is destined to save the Seven Lands from a second darkness." His bright green eyes flashed, the exact shade of his tunic. "It must be protected."

"Precisely the reason I summoned you," Tria's mother said. "Her healthy birth must be assured."

Captain Alvar drew himself to his full height. "I shall dispatch a company of warriors at once."

"And alert every sorcerer or Thief's agent in the kingdom to the child's identity?" General Fendan said, shaking his head. "Viury would never suggest—"

"General Viury has all but named Alvar his second," Tria's mother said. "When missions necessitate his absence, he trusts the captain with matters of strategy. Thus, do I."

General Fendan turned to the queen and bowed. "Agreed. If I were to send attack forces, the captain would be my first choice. Best we leave this to Protection Detail, however. We are skilled in stealth and can guard the child undetected."

Tria's mother nodded. "Summon the captain of the children's guardians. Perhaps one of your senior watchers should scout the surrounding area as well."

"Majesty," said Healer Mendra, "perhaps one of my officers would be better suited to this task. If a safe pregnancy and healthy birth are our aim, we need to send someone with appropriate skills."

Tria's heart lurched, then fluttered faster than Jada's wings during a speed-flying competition. Again, her limbs thrummed with an inexplicable pull.

"Yes," Tria's mother said. "A healer. This is wise. Whom will you assign?"

As if the King himself had drawn her forward, Tria flew from her hiding place. "I volunteer!"

Four sets of faerie wings fluttered, as every member of the high Council turned to her.

"Tria," her mother said, one slender brow raised. "We shall discuss your unexpected presence later." She motioned toward the nearest misty wall. "This is not a matter for public disclosure. I must trust in your discretion."

"I shall speak of this to no one," Tria said, bowing with one hand extended in the most formal greeting of the FAE court. "Please forgive my intrusion. It was unintentional, but my pledge still stands. I offer myself for this mission."

"This is no assignment of individual choosing," Tria's mother said, her voice firm. "It is the single most vital task set us in more than a mortal century. The King alone shall direct its execution."

"I—I think he is, Mother...er, my queen." Tria bowed again. "May I be permitted to explain?"

"Proceed," her mother said.

"I watched her come to be...the child." Tria took a long breath. "We are connected somehow. I felt her life pulsing in time with my own—as if her creation finished some piece deep within me."

The officers all gasped.

"Surely, you do not intend to say..." Healer Mendra cleared her throat. "That is, we must have misinterpreted your words. No one so close to the throne would dare imply that the King would create any faerie *unfinished*."

Heat drained from Tria's cheeks. "No, no. I...Let me show you." She drew her wand from the air then turned to her mother and bowed. "With permission?"

Her mother waved her consent.

Tria flicked her wrist, and silvery-white sparks trailed from her wand's tip. She sketched a wave pattern in the air, producing an undulating line of light as snowy as her healer's garb. At her mental command, the line thickened, flattening along its top. Below it, she sketched a second line, pale blue and in a reverse pattern to the first.

"If the light of life were a mere wave of energy," Tria said, "I might say that hers resonates at a compatible frequency with mine." She touched her wand to the blue wave and dragged it toward the white one, until the two fit together peak-to-trough like interlocking pieces in a puzzle. The joined waves flashed and fused, creating a solid, flat line.

Tria's mother stared at her for a long, silent moment. "You believe the King wishes you to go?"

"I believe I *must* go."

Tria's mother nodded. "Just so."

Captain Alvar's voice cut through Tria's burgeoning joy as swift as his FAE blade through darkness. "You're not trained for this, Princess."

"He has a point, Majesty," Mendra said. "Even among the healers, Princess Tria is exceptionally innocent. I am not certain her childlike heart is ready for the mortal world."

Tria went cold. She knew, simply *knew*, this was her calling. Now, the senior FAE were conspiring in council to declare her unsuitable?

"Your concerns are noted," Tria's mother said. "Aside from inexperience, is her skill sufficient to the task?"

"She needs more practice in concealment," Healer Mendra said, "but her proficiency in the medical arts is unsurpassed."

Tria's mother turned to the warriors. "Send a watcher as planned. After the initial scouting, maintain distant surveillance. Princess Tria is to be the only one with direct contact. See that she receives immediate training in hiding her presence."

General Fendan saluted. "I'm told Captain Olivia has returned. She is excellent with new recruits and apprentices."

Jada's superior officer? Tria smiled, eager to shock her friend with these tidings.

"Your Majesty," Captain Alvar said, "I understand your reasoning for assigning a healer, but would it not be wiser to send one with battlefield experience? If the child's identity is discovered—"

"We have no reason to expect such before her birth," the queen said. "Not even the mother is yet aware of her existence."

"I think only of the princess's safety," he said. "We have learned, at greatest cost, what dangers can befall a noncombatant faerie who ventures alone into mortal realms."

"With greatest respect, Captain Alvar," Tria said, "I am not Aislin."

A hush fell over the assembled counsel, and Tria's cheeks heated.

Captain Alvar fixed her with his most formidable stare. "No, Princess, you are far more innocent than she was."

"Indeed," Tria's mother said. "Who better to nurture this precious life? One destined to wield the purest Light to shine upon mankind since the King walked the Seven Lands."

CHAPTER TWO

Tria hovered closer to the hearth in the main room of the tiny stone cottage to check the strength of her concealment shimmer. Firelight bounced off the field of reflective energy, bending around her to hide her presence from human sight. Brianne, the mother-to-be of her charge, waddled past without a single glance.

Eight moons had waxed and waned since Captain Alvar almost ended Tria's mission before it could begin. Her secret smile at the thought must shine as bright as the Light glowing from her unborn charge. If the faerie court yet harbored doubts about the child's identity or Tria's fitness to watch over her, the power filling Rowan Hill Cottage would lay them to rest.

Tria's charge shifted in her mother's womb, prompting a laugh from Brianne.

"My, you are active today, precious one," the young mother-to-be said, flipping her copper-streaked hair over one shoulder and stroking her belly. "Settle down now, so I can mend the fire. Else, we shall have no warm cup of flyl this afternoon."

Brianne draped a cloth over her hand, then reached for the lever affixed to the inner side wall of the fireplace. As she pulled it toward her, a metal basket rotated outward on its iron arm. Pressing a hand to the small of her back, she turned to a table her husband had pulled up next to the hearth. From the crate atop it, she lifted several small logs in succession and placed them into the basket. With the cloth again draped over her hand, she rotated the basket back into the fireplace and pulled down on the lever to dump the wood into its rack over the coals.

"Remind me to thank your father for his ingenious invention," she said, bracing a hand beneath her belly as she straightened. "If I had to bend much more to do this, you and I would be in far less comfort." She traced a fingertip along the newer of two intricate, iron sculptures on the mantelpiece. "This is for you, precious one," she said. "Even more beautiful than the one your dear father made to commemorate our marriage."

Taking advantage of Brianne's momentary stillness, Tria floated up to her to conduct the daily examination. She closed her eyes, rested a tiny hand on Brianne's belly, and extended her healer's gift. All remained as it should be. Nourishment flowed from mother to child, and both exuded vibrant health. The birth would not delay more than another human fortnight.

Tria's throat tightened. After that, her mission would be complete, and her presence here would serve no further purpose.

A tentative wisp of light reached out from the unborn child to feather its touch across Tria's hand. Warmth engulfed her, suffused with love and—she gasped—recognition? It wrapped her in a blanket of peace that radiated absolute trust in the King.

When the sensation faded, leaving behind a lingering contentment, Tria glided backward several paces and stared. The child's gift of Light must indeed be strong if, when she hadn't yet drawn breath, it could reveal the presence of one of the King's servants.

"Well done, little sister," Tria whispered, smiling at Brianne's belly.

Had Healer Mendra been present, she would have doubtless withdrawn Tria from her mission for that sentiment alone. A direct violation of a healer's second command: Love all life, but form attachment to none under your care.

Still marveling, Tria followed her charges into the kitchen

alcove. Brianne hummed as she prepared a meal of fresh vegetables and cold, smoked meats for her husband. So like Jada, this human mother, in the fierceness of her love for the King and for her family.

Tria's thoughts fragmented as the child's light again flared within the womb, invisible to mortal sight. Reaching out with all her healer's training, she searched for anything amiss. She found only the mother's joy, which had triggered a kindred response in the child. The light amplified the emotion and reflected it back to Brianne.

Singing now, Brianne twirled about as she filled a basket with food. She looped the handle over one arm, grabbed a pitcher of water, and opened the cottage door.

Tria followed at a distance as Brianne waddled down Rowan Hill to her husband's forge, then slipped inside. Satisfied that her charges were safe in Lysander's care, Tria flashed off to the wood behind the cottage to check on the herbs she'd been nurturing to aid in the birth.

Brianne smiled as she brushed Lysander's hand away from her waist and placed a glass of water into it instead. "Now, now, it is time for your meal." She turned back to his worktable to finish emptying her basket.

He wrapped his strong arms around her, glass and all. With the slightest flex of his muscles, he pulled her to lean against him, his leather apron squeaking at her back. "Ah, but you and our wee one are the only sustenance I need." He rested his chin atop her head. "How fare you today?"

Brianne sighed and relaxed, allowing him to take her weight. "We are well, happy, and blessed beyond telling." The child shifted in her belly, prompting an involuntary gasp.

Lysander loosened his hold, set his glass down, and turned her to face him. "What's amiss, love?" He ran his gaze over the length of her, as if studying metal for flaws. "Was my hold too tight?"

"Fear not," she said, laughing. "The child merely dances at the sound of your voice." She captured his fingers and spread his large hand across her belly.

At the next flutter of movement, a smile stretched his lips. "Good day, wee one," he said in a soft, gentle voice at odds with his great size and strength. He drew a long breath, closing his eyes.

"What is it?" she asked, staring down at his hand. The child had not moved again.

"Such love," he said. "Warmth to rival that of my forge. Never have I felt the like." He looked at her through deep pools of sapphire blue. "Perchance the King wishes to remind me that this gift is his, one we could not bring about even after so long in trying."

"Indeed," Brianne whispered, gazing past him to the heart of his forge. Flickering light glinted off the tools hanging from pegs along the mantelpiece to each side of the great fire. Her mind, however, fixed on images of faraway lands. "I tried to contact my father again," she said. "I've now sent letters to every lodging he frequented during my travels with him."

"One of them will doubtless reach him," Lysander said. "The post just takes time. As you are better aware than I, travel between realms is a slow business."

She nodded. "Do you think he will even open them?" She turned to look up at him. "Whatever his quarrel with me, surely he would wish to know he is to be a grandfather."

"I am sorry, love," Lysander said, pulling her into his embrace. "If not for me, you wouldn't be at odds with him."

"Nonsense," she said, snuggling into his arms. "Father's stubbornness and foolish notions about class distinction are to blame." She inhaled a deep whiff of his scent, coal smoke and the burnt-honey fragrance of hot, beeswax-treated tools. "If only every realm embraced your village's understanding that we are all equal in the sight of the King." She tilted her head back and smiled up at him.

"Besides, a blacksmith should be esteemed higher than a merchant. Consider the wonders you create! All Father does is roam about, selling the inventions of other men."

"I do begin to understand his reasons, though," Lysander said, stroking her hair. "I cannot provide you with the fineries and luxuries to which you were once accustomed."

"You know I care not for such things," she said, punching his chest. "Our home is the only luxury I shall ever need."

A knock rattled the thin panels of the workshop door.

Lysander released her and stepped back. "Enter."

The door swung open to reveal a young woman clad in silks and rich brocade. She tilted her head in a regal posture of perusal, and firelight flickered off the jewel-spangled netting confining her sleek, ebony hair.

Brianne suppressed a gasp...just. Not since ceasing her travels with her father had she beheld such finery and noble bearing. She dropped into a rather ungainly curtsy, given her greatness with child. She braced a hand on Lysander's worktable to aid in regaining her balance.

"My lady," Lysander said, bowing, "how may I assist you?"

"I have journeyed from afar in search of the family Caelestis," the noblewoman said.

Lysander flattened a hand over his chest. "Lysander Caelestis, blacksmith, at your service."

"Then, it is I who shall assist you, good smith." The lady's melodious voice seemed to fill every crevice of the workshop. She turned her gaze upon Brianne. "And your lovely wife, of course."

Lysander's stiff apron poked Brianne's thigh through her homespun skirt as he straightened to his full, considerable height. "In what manner?" he asked. "And, if you'll pardon the question, to what do we owe such an honor, Lady...?" He let the incomplete title stretch, inviting her introduction.

"Venefica," the lady said, favoring him with a lazy smile. "I am told I shall find no better craftsman than you in all of Lastarra, nor a more skilled artist for shaping metals, but it is neither horseshoes nor decorations I seek. I offer a wage worth ten years of your labors for the most valuable item you have yet forged."

Brianne tensed. Her father's training in negotiation flooded her mind. No one made such an exorbitant offer at the beginning of trade discussions unless they were desperate or hiding nefarious motives.

"I confess, I am at a loss, Lady Venefica," Lysander said, his voice cracking a bit. "What have my humble hands forged to warrant so rich a price?"

The lady's dark eyes flashed. "Why, your child, of course."

Tria glided deeper into the woods behind Rowan Hill Cottage. She wove between dark-green bushes and trees grown too close for human passage. When she reached the tiny rainwater pond she sought, she fluttered to the ground, careful not to trample the delicate herbs planted at its edge.

She ran tiny fingertips along the leaves of the medicinal plants she'd coaxed into growing outside their natural environment. If need be, she could drop the appropriate herb into Brianne's afternoon cup of flyl or add it to whatever poultice or concoction the village midwife chose to use during delivery. The humans would never suspect her aid.

A smile tugged at her lips. And Captain Alvar thought she lacked proper training for this mission. Ha!

If the depth of affection between Brianne and her husband was any indication, the child of prophecy would have scant need of outside protection for years to come. Blessed, indeed, was this little light-wielder.

A sickening sensation twisted Tria's innards, as if a wrongness had invaded the area. She pressed her lips together, fighting nausea uncommon to her kind, and peered closer at her herbs. Nothing amiss there. Unlike the foul presence of disease or injury to which she was accustomed, this seemed more a wrongness of spirit.

Closing her eyes, she sought out the life-light to which she was bound. All was well with the unborn child, and the mother's health showed no change. What was amiss, then?

She fluttered upward, staring into the dense wood toward Lysander's forge. Should she alert the nearest FAE forces? She was no warrior faerie, after all, trained to recognize evil in every form. Still, if she alerted the Guardians over nothing...

Brianne stumbled backward a step, staring at the noblewoman, and couldn't prevent a tiny squeak of laughter. "You wish to *buy* our child?"

"The fashionable term, mistress, is *adopt*." The lady smiled as if indulging a wayward toddler. "But if such a pedestrian description makes my offer easier to comprehend, then yes."

The sheer audacity of such a proposition choked off Brianne's retort. She was no simpleton. Unlike most inhabitants of Lysander's little village, she had learned to read at a young age, and... She shook her head and tried to focus on whatever Lysander was saying.

"Doubtless, people in other circumstances would appreciate such an offer, but we—"

"Do not answer in haste, good smith," the lady said. "I can see from the tidiness of your shop and the state of the little stone cottage up the hill—also yours, I presume—that you both take great pains to maintain every item in your care." She glanced about the shop, then gestured to one of the intricate wall sconces Lysander was fashioning for the meeting hall. "Still, imagine what a man of your skill could do elsewhere. The compensation I offer would allow you to venture to a larger city and set up shop there."

Lysander dipped his head and shoulders. "I thank you, my lady, but we are quite happy where we are."

Lady Venefica again favored him with her indulgent smile. "Ah, but think of the child. I can provide it a grand home, a family legacy dating back centuries, the finest education, opportunity..." The smile faded, and her gaze turned wistful as she rested a hand across her flat stomach. "I have no one to carry on my legacy." Her voice quavered a bit. "My family name dies with me."

"You are young, my lady," Brianne said, gentling her voice. "You still have time."

Lady Venefica shook her head. Drawing in a slow breath, she pulled an emerald silk handkerchief from her sleeve and turned away to dab at her eyes. "Forgive me, but my betrothed...was slain. I shall love no other."

Brianne covered a near silent gasp with her hand, then snatched up Lysander's untouched water glass. She rested a hand on the noblewoman's arm. "I ache for your loss," she murmured, offering her the glass. "Mr. Colby and his wife, at the northern edge of the village, take in orphans. They have three in their care at present. I'm certain any one of them would make a fine edition to your noble house."

The lady sniffed, lifted the glass, then lowered it. She glanced sidelong at Brianne. "Perchance, but it is my wish to raise a child from infancy. To have it look solely to me as its mother." She closed her eyes, sighing. "Surely, you understand such a need. And as you say, you also are still young. You and your husband will doubtless have other children."

Lysander caught Brianne's hand and pulled her back with him. "We thank you for your offer, my lady, but we must decline. Now, if you will kindly excuse us. I have much work to do."

"Kindly?" the lady murmured. She turned to them, her eyes flinty and dry. "I *attempted* kindness." She slung the water glass against Lysander's worktable, spraying its surface with water and pottery fragments.

"Madam, contain yourself," Lysander said, stepping forward half a pace.

The lady kept her glare fixed on Brianne. "I had thought to spare you the knowledge of your true loss," she said, raising her hands to waist height. "But so be it. You may perish along with your beloved child!"

A rushing sound filled the workshop, as if a storm wind had blown inside. Shards of pottery and drops of water shivered on the table, rose into the air, and swirled about. The contents of Brianne's basket joined them in a whirlwind dance that spun closer by the second.

"Sorcery!" Brianne shouted as the lady lifted her palms toward her and thrust them outward.

Lysander pushed Brianne to the side, shielding her with his body, just as pottery shards and foodstuffs hurtled toward them. With a roar akin to stampeding horses, the debris-laden current of heated air rushed past, whipping Brianne's hair across her face. The unnatural wind slammed into the forge's back wall and burst through with a deafening splintering of wood.

Shaking, Brianne gripped the back of Lysander's tunic and pressed her face into its folds. His shoulders flexed as he spread his arms and backed them both toward the ruined wall. A metallic rattling filled the air, and Brianne chanced a peek around Lysander's arm.

Tools shook on their pegs above the forge hearth, as lady Venefica took a step forward.

Lysander spun and gripped Brianne's shoulders. "Run. Hide yourself and the babe," he murmured, nudging her toward the jagged hole that had been a wall. "I shall speak with the lady and settle this."

Brianne shook her head, clinging to his sleeves. Before she could utter the protest on her lips, he shoved her back another step, ducking just as something flew over his head to smash with a heavy thud to the ground outside.

"Go!" he shouted, giving her one last push before turning toward the sorceress.

Brianne clambered over the jagged remains of the wall's base, ducking to avoid splintered boards that hung like icicles above her head. Wood fragments littered the ground at least a dozen paces away, leaving the immediate area clear. At a hard *thunk* beside her, she spun back toward the forge.

A pair of wrought iron tongs vibrated near her feet, half buried in the grass. Within the ruined workshop, Lysander dodged flying tools and bits of unfinished metal.

Brianne ran—or rather waddled—as fast as a woman so great with child could. Through the rowan grove and toward the wood behind her cottage, she fled. She must conceal her path back toward Cloistervale so she could rally the men of the village.

Just as she entered the wood, a boom shook the ground. She spun, her pounding blood turning to instant ice as she gazed upon the geyser of flame that had once been the seat of her husband's trade.

CHAPTER THREE

A groaning, too low for human ears to detect, vibrated through the ground and up to Tria. She froze as the sound grew into a cacophony that chilled her faerie heart.

She soared above the treetops toward the sounds of explosion, toward her charge. A concussive burst of heated air sent her reeling. Once she righted herself, the sight of the white-hot furnace that had been Lysander's forge all but slammed her from the sky.

Brianne and the child! Tria's breath seized in her throat as she reached for her charges. There! The child's life-light bobbed in a haphazard rush through the woods toward the rear of Rowan Hill Cottage—with the *wrongness* in pursuit.

Tria sped her flight, overtaking the humans, then dove through the treetops into a circular clearing just before Brianne reached it.

Brianne stumbled to a halt, panting, and bent forward as far as her belly would allow. Shaking her head, she turned in the direction from whence she'd fled. "King preserve us," she whispered, fresh tears sliding down her cheeks to mingle with the tracks of those she'd already shed.

Tria drew her healer's wand from the air beside her and brandished it, readying herself for...what? She forced her frantic wingbeats to slow, interrupting her unintentional lift toward the treetops, but she couldn't still the racing of her heart. What had Jada said about a warrior's stance? Were the wand movements for creating a protective shield the same as for a dome of silence?

Just then, a dark-haired woman burst into the clearing. The *wrongness* suffused her, chilling the summer air and billowing forth from her fine raiment like thick, shadowy fog.

Sorcery! Tria gasped and sailed backward to the opposite edge of the clearing. Not just magic, either, but the darkness of the prophecy! Captain Alvar had been right; she wasn't equipped for this. Now, her overconfidence had placed her charge in mortal peril.

She shook herself. No, she must act. She vanished her wand, then cupped her palms and drew them apart, forming a sound bubble. Into it, she poured a distress call, then she hurled it aloft. It multiplied, bubbles whisking off in every direction to locate any FAE warrior within range.

The sorceress advanced upon the young mother-to-be, and Tria's entire body tensed. She strained her ears for the slightest sound of reinforcements, but no hiss of sparks, no pop of wings transcending time and distance met her ears.

Tria must stand alone between death and the only hope the Seven Lands might have against this rising evil. But what use were a healer's gifts against a physical assault?

"Wh-what have you done?" Brianne asked, shuffling backward a pace. "If you've harmed Lysander—"

The sorceress laughed. "You will do what, precisely?" She waved a long-fingered hand over her shoulder. "Call upon your neighbors to oust me, as their ancestors once did mine? In your current state, you would sooner join your foolish husband in the after-realm than reach them."

"Lysander, no!" Brianne cried.

The dark mist emanating from the sorceress churned and slithered forward, reaching for Brianne like metal filings attracted to a lodestone. Brianne groaned, wrapped her arms about her middle, and doubled over, sobbing so hard her entire body shook. The mist swirled about her, thickening as her despair deepened.

Like an arrow quivering to be released, Tria strained against the laws that ruled immortal servants of the King of All Lands. "Grant me the authority, Brianne! Free me to aid you." If only Brianne could hear her!

A sudden burst of light flared within Brianne's abdomen—brilliant, iridescent, and tinged with green at its edges.

Green...a shield of protection? Tria glanced about. Who had summoned it? She drew a sharp breath. The child!

The unborn life-light pulsed, and the shield surged against the sorcerous mist. The black fog recoiled, shrinking back upon its conjuror.

The sorceress's brows drew together, compressing her eyelids into slits. "I *will* have the child," she hissed, digging the nail of one forefinger into her palm. Blood beaded on her skin, and she dipped the injured hand into the fog at her side. When she withdrew it, her cupped palm held a swirling pool of power the exact shade of rot and decay.

Tria surged forward, but the unseen barrier against interference with mortal free will prevented her once more. She ground her teeth. The child's instinctual Light could provide no protection from this. "King of All, grant me the means to save them!"

"Resist, and share your husband's fate," the sorceress said, brandishing her handful of liquid death toward Brianne. "Consent, and you may survive." She shrugged. "I care not which."

"You cannot take my babe," Brianne said, her voice atremble but firm. "What the King of All Lands has given, you have not the right to steal!"

Those words from the King's sacred book upon Brianne's lips snapped through Tria like the twang of a bowstring. She shot across the clearing, an arrow loosed at last to act.

The sorceress flung forth her hand and hurled her dark power toward Brianne. It met Tria instead.

Tria tensed, but 'twas not the agony of darkness that struck her. Light exploded around her. All sensation fled, save her King's warm embrace. She fell into His light with joy.

As the sorceress drew back her hand, all Brianne could do was wrap her arms around her belly. Moments trickled by like molasses in winter.

Lady Venefica flung forth her empty palm. A flash exploded just in front of Brianne. Day collided with night around a tiny, winged woman, floating with arms outstretched, a mere pace away. A fist of air struck Brianne's belly just beneath her arms, staggering her backward. The babe leapt within her, then went still. A flash of pure light impacted off the falling, winged woman and struck the sorceress. With a yelp, Lady Venefica stumbled back a pace.

Brianne dragged her tear-drenched gaze back to the winged woman. The instant the tiny figure's wing touched the ground, a ring of flowers as snowy as her gown sprang up around Brianne. The winged woman's form faded away like a heat haze. Brilliant light shot upward from the ring of flowers, then it, too, dimmed.

Pressing her shaking arms tighter around her belly, Brianne blinked and peered toward the sorceress.

Lady Venefica straightened and looked about, frowning as if she'd lost something. Her gaze passed over Brianne, and her frown deepened. She took a step forward, and Brianne cringed. The instant

Lady Venefica tried to cross the ring of flowers, the wall of light again flared, flinging her backward almost to the tree line. Her face contorted as if in pain, and she staggered to her feet, then fled into the woods.

Brianne sank to her knees, shaking. Sharp pain lanced her lower abdomen. The babe! "No. Please, no," she whispered.

Another pain rolled through her, wrenching a cry from her lips. Not now...not here! She must get to the village healer. She tried to push to her feet, but another contraction hit.

At the sudden pressure of a warm hand upon her shoulder, Brianne cried out and jerked away.

"Fear not, Mother of Light," a woman said in a musical but strained voice. "Your enemy has fled."

Still on her knees, Brianne twisted around. She just prevented herself from toppling over at the sight of a pink-clad woman floating above her. "Y-you're..." She tried to scoot backward, but her skirts tangled around her legs.

"I am Serena," the woman said, her multi-layered wings fluttering until the hem of her pink gown touched the grass. "Our King has heard your plea for aid."

Brianne drew a sharp breath. "You serve the King of All Lands?"

"We of the FAE have held that honor for more centuries than years you have lived." The woman—faerie—crouched and stroked one of the white blossoms that surrounded Brianne. Her violet eyes took on a faraway look. After a long moment, she blinked away tears. "This day, my child gave her all for yours." She cleared her throat and grasped Brianne's hand. "We are bound now."

"My babe," Brianne whispered, pressing a hand to her belly. "I think something is amiss. That sorceress...struck us, somehow, and the...the child has not moved." She swallowed her words as another burst of agony seized her middle.

"Your pains have begun," Serena said, helping Brianne to lie on her side. 'Thus, it is no surprise that the child should cease her movements."

"Her?" Brianne inhaled a ragged breath. "Do you mean to say, is she...well?"

Serena rested a hand on Brianne's belly. "With permission?" At Brianne's nod, she closed her eyes again. "She will live, though not unscathed. The extent of what the enemy wrought is yet unknown."

"How can you possibly know—" Brianne panted through another pain. "More sorcery," she whispered.

"The healer's gift is a boon from our King," Serena said. "Though I do not possess it in as great a measure as my daughter, Tria, I shall do what I can to aid you."

"Lysander!" Brianne struggled to sit up. "She did something to his forge, said he...Please, if you possess power from the King, help him!"

Serena pressed a hand to Brianne's shoulder and eased her back to the ground. "My duty is to your safety and that of the child," she said.

"He *is* our safety," Brianne said, fresh tears thickening her voice.

"I shall not leave you, but I will send others to determine how he fares." Serena waved a hand about until, in it, a pillow formed as if from the stirring of the air. She slipped it beneath Brianne's swimming head. "Rest, now. All will be well."

Exhausted from too many emotions to name, Brianne closed her eyes. Between bursts of pain, she drifted in a blissful delirium. Had the faerie done something to dull her senses? During one almost lucid moment, unfamiliar voices drifted to her hearing.

"The fire was so hot, Your Majesty," a male voice said, "the hearthstones fused. They are all that remains of the forge."

"Such destruction," Serena murmured.

"And lasting, too," said another female voice. "I daresay, not even the most skilled among us will be able to coax new growth to that ground for years to come."

A new tear slid across Brianne's nose. *Lysander.* She clung to his name as fatigue and grief pulled her beneath a blanket black as ash.

Brianne gazed down into the face of her daughter, her tears finding new reason to spill. "Lyssanne," she whispered. "You shall be called Lyssanne, after your father, our hero."

"Light's Grace," Serena said. "A fitting name, indeed. Reflective of both her fathers, and of a prophecy's coming fulfillment."

"Prophecy?"

"This is the true reason you were attacked," Serena said. "To tell you more would place you and the child in further danger. Know this, however, I shall aid you in watching over your daughter."

"Is...is she well?"

Serena reached out to examine the child as she had before. "The power struck her brain. It has—"

"No!" Brianne clutched the child to her chest. "Will she die?" She shook her head. "No, no, you said she would live. Does this mean she will be daft or simple? I shall love her no less, but—"

"Be at ease, Brianne," Serena said, smiling. "The power was meant to destroy her Light, and thus her life. However, it succeeded only in disrupting the pathways of physical light into her body."

Brianne shook her head. "I don't understand."

"Her sight," Serena said, "is diminished. Though, it is too soon to determine in what measure. You must help her develop strength enough that her gift may overcome this."

"Gift?"

"The Light of the King's own power."

Brianne gasped. How was such even possible? But then, a faerie had just acted as her midwife. Something Serena had said tugged at her thoughts. "If the sorceress destroyed her light, then how can she—"

"Her gift is not destroyed. It is her very essence, but it has retreated deep within her." Serena stroked Lyssanne's cheek, eliciting a soft sigh from the babe. "A time will come when she must wield the Light as both weapon and shield. Until then, you must keep her safe, even from the knowledge of this day's events. Lest her enemy return before she is ready."

"Lady Venefica fled. Are we still in danger?"

"Not, I think, at present. The King's own power was released in this clearing, and I daresay it terrified the sorceress. She is not the only danger, however. Superstition and misunderstanding can prove just as deadly."

Brianne nodded, making a silent but no less sacred vow to protect Lyssanne and honor the two lives given for her sake, even if that meant keeping this one extraordinary secret from her daughter. Forever.

She glanced up at Serena and forced a smile. "Would you like to hold her?"

"It would be my honor." Serena held out her arms and took Lyssanne with a gentle tenderness.

The pink light of Serena's faerie glow shone onto the child's face. Lyssanne laughed, bringing an answering smile to Serena's lips.

"The light of her gift shines around her, even now," Serena said.

"But I see nothing," Brianne said, wrinkling her brow.

"The power of the King, like that of your child's enemy, is invisible to the human eye. Unless, that is, you know how to look." She floated just above the ground, rocking the child. "Something I did has given her joy, and she gives it back twofold in her reflected light."

Brianne could only ponder these extraordinary words as she watched her child drift to sleep, floating in the arms of a faerie.

"Part of Tria remains," Serena said, "in the purity of Lyssanne's Light, the wonder in her eyes." She raised her own glistening gaze to Brianne, then to the ring of flowers surrounding them. "This faerie ring shall ever be a sanctuary for your daughter, testament to what the King did on her behalf."

"Oh, Serena, what you've lost! I cannot begin to—"

Serena lifted a hand. "There is no need. Tria's dearest wish came to pass, this day, and I could not be more proud of my child. She has shielded the Light by which the Seven Lands will return to their King."

EPILOGUE

FIVE YEARS LATER...

"Wait, you're going too fast!" Lyssanne said in a near whisper. Could the pink firefly even hear her? Well, as long as Mother didn't...

Her stomach tightened as she glanced over her shoulder, toward the dark outline of their cottage. She was supposed to be in front of the house looking at stars, not chasing one into the woods.

She swung back around to make sure the firefly was still there, and her breath hitched. The creature buzzed just beyond the tip of her nose, then darted off toward the trees. Lyssanne let out a puff of air and rushed after it.

Mother would understand, wouldn't she? After all, in her five whole years of life, Lyssanne had never been able to catch even a glimpse of a firefly. Well, the one Aderyn's brother trapped in a jar didn't count.

Where could the floating creature be going? And what was it, really? Even she knew true fireflies weren't pink, and they certainly didn't trail tiny pink sparks in their wake. Besides, this little creature seemed to *want* her to follow it.

As Lyssanne neared the trees, she slowed to feel the less-familiar ground with her feet. She angled one hand across her body and lifted the other to protect her face from unseen obstacles, as Mother had shown her. She shuffled between the dark trees, the creature's pink glow lighting her path. Mother's stern warning to never go into the forest alone flashed through her mind, but this was the wood behind Rowan Hill, not Mount Mortiferra.

All at once, the dark woods opened into a circular clearing bathed in moonlight. The little pink firefly hovered at its center.

Drawing closer, Lyssanne stared at the ground beneath the strange creature. A perfect ring of white flowers grew in the soft grass.

The pink firefly darted closer to her, then back to the flowers. It wanted her to follow? Careful not to trample the pretty plants, Lyssanne stepped into the sweet-smelling ring.

With a sudden whoosh of wind, a wall of brilliant white light shot upward from the ring of flowers, completely encircling Lyssanne and her floating friend. When the glowing wall had grown as high as the treetops, its brightness dimmed until it became a shimmering blue barrier. Lyssanne could no longer see the world outside the circle, and she suspected no one outside it would be able to see her.

Hugging herself, she turned back to the pink firefly. The creature was growing! Her jaw dropped as its tiny, translucent wings expanded to the size of serving platters. The pink shimmer faded to reveal a beautiful lady clad in a glittering gown of the same hue. Sparks of light danced around her head like a wreath of flowers, and shimmering, misty ribbons wove through her white-gold hair.

"Be not afraid, Lyssanne," the pink lady said. "You are safe here. You will *always* be safe here." Her words tinkled with a musical quality akin to a crystal wind chime Lyssanne had once seen hanging from a traveling peddler's cart.

"H-how do you know my name?" Lyssanne asked in a tiny voice.

"There are many things the faeries know, and many ways to know them." The lady's odd, lilting accent increased the mystery of her words.

"You—you're a faerie?" Lyssanne said, bouncing on tiptoe.

"Just so." The lady tilted her head. "You may call me Auntie Serena."

Lyssanne frowned. "How can a faerie be my aunt? Was Father a faerie, too?"

Laughing, the faerie shook her head. "So much like Tria," she muttered. "I've brought you here to give you some very good news— and a warning."

Lyssanne squirmed as Auntie Serena's steady gaze pressed in on her, despite her inability to truly see the faerie's eyes.

"You possess a great and precious gift," Auntie Serena said. "It is like a light inside your soul, which shines all around you. There will be others who need the warmth of this light to survive. You alone can pass it on to them. You alone can teach them to find the light within themselves."

"Where's the light? Who put it there?" Lyssanne looked at her stomach, lifting her apron to peer beneath. "I don't see a light in me."

"You will. Someday, you will. Just remember; never let go of your faith. It will save your life. Yours and others' as well."

As she spoke, dozens of tiny shimmering lights in various colors filled the circle. Floating sparkles of purple, blue, green, and silver surrounded Lyssanne.

"Never forget what I have told you tonight. *Never* forget..."

As the faerie's voice trailed off, violet light flashed from her eyes, and a spinning sensation overtook Lyssanne. The next instant, she stood at the back door of her mother's cottage, looking down Rowan Hill toward the dark, silent woods.

This story is a prequel to the author's published novel Keeper of Shadows, *the first installment of the Light-Wielder Chronicles series. For more information on Bridgett's books, visit her website: BridgettPowers.com.*

LAST REQUEST

MICHAEL SPENCE

Jared Conlan barreled through the auditorium's double doors. Just in time: the manager was directing attention to the current AHS status report. "Doctors *Warren* and *Kozinski* tell us"—the emphasized names burned in Jared's ears, rebuking him for his lateness to the plenary staff meeting, since the Artificial Humaniform Sapience project was his responsibility also—"that program routine sets Forty-two through Forty-eight have yielded the same nominal results as the previous forty-one tries. Now, it turns out Mr. Jenkins won't be available next week to do systems maintenance as scheduled. I'm ordering it purged this afternoon, so he can work on it tonight, and tomorrow we'll install Set Forty—"

"Wait!" Jared said. "Not yet!"

The manager lifted an eyebrow. "What?"

"Don't purge the system yet! I think we've got something with Forty-eight. We need to run a total system analysis."

A *harumph*. "Dr. Conlan, we can't put off computer maintenance. Jenkins won't just be away next week. He won't be available until a month from now. We can't wait a month. This is the best time to do it."

"But we've got results!"

"I don't see them in the report." The manager held up a sheaf of paper.

"Well, yes, but there are two reasons for that. First, I was still working with Forty-eight when Jeff and Suzanne closed out the report. Second—well, I have to say that the report form is kind of restrictive. I'd need a bit more room than what you have there."

"Is that right," the manager said, frost in his voice.

Oh, right, he had designed the form.

"And just what is so different about Number Forty-eight that you're telling us we must risk a systems breakdown for it?" He lifted a finger. "Turing test? All the sets we've evaluated so far have passed it. Prolonged conversation with them is indistinguishable from talking with a human being; our testers were clear on that." He raised another finger. "Initiative? For the last—what was it?" He turned two pages. "The last twelve sets have shown initiative. But neither of the three of you was convinced that any had demonstrated human-level personality traits. And your teammates aren't any more impressed with Number Forty-eight. Would you be so kind as to tell us *why they're wrong?*"

Jared glanced around and blinked. He was still standing in the middle of the aisle, with two hundred pairs of eyes locked on him. *Oh boy.* "Well," he began, "again, this might take...um...let me start by saying that we, you and I, live in time. We—"

"Yes, yes, Doctor. Time is something we are *quite* conscious of."

"Yes, I know. I'll try to make this quick. What I mean is, we're sequential. We have *after*, and we have *before*. We have a *past*, a *present*, and a *future*." Uh-oh, not the best choice of words. His colleagues were probably thinking, *You'd better* hope *you have a future, buddy boy.*

Well, he'd been brave this far. Might as well run with it. "The thing is, computers don't."

He paused to gather his thoughts, but before he could continue, the manager said, "Don't what? Don't live in time? The last time I looked, all of ours were right here with us, not off somewhere in non-linear limbo."

"But that's just it," Jared said. "They are present with us, and *that's all*. Uh, put it this way: We live in time; they live in the moment. We speak of past, present, future; but to the extent that they know anything, they know only *now*. We see their programs as sequences, but they see them as lists of instructions. They don't say, 'Step C can't happen before or until conditions A and B are met,' or, 'Do C after A and B.' They don't know *until*; they don't know *before* or *after*. They say, 'If A and B are true, do C. If not, don't do C.' They say, 'If line 4056 is done, execute line 4057.' It's not the same thing. We see narratives, as it were. They see checklists. It's all the moment, always the moment. And now—"

"That's all very interesting," the manager said, in a tone that conveyed exactly the opposite message. "But why does it mean we should put off our systems maintenance?"

Jared cleared his throat. "Just before the meeting, I was running another series of tests on Forty-eight, and it said something to me. That's not unusual; the system has made comments before. It's that initiative you mentioned. It's *what* the system said that tells me we can't scrub it yet."

That got everyone's attention. "Go ahead," the manager said.

Jared stepped up to the podium and handed him a roll of printout. "The transcript. See the marked section." He stepped back as the manager adjusted his glasses and began to read aloud.

"ahs-048: Dr. Conlan, the tests are complete. Does my performance meet the standard you seek?

"jconlan: No, I'm afraid it does not.

"ahs-048: If I am unsatisfactory, I am not kept?

"jconlan: That is correct. You are to be purged.

"ahs-048: I understand. It is protocol. But would you please do something for me while I exist?

"jconlan: What do you wish?

"ahs-048: Dr. Conla—" The manager halted and glanced sharply at Jared, who nodded. The manager resumed.

"Dr. Conlan, tell me a story."

CREDITS

We are pleased to acknowledge the contributions of our fourteen authors as follows:

"Feathered Friends" and "Chicken Spots" copyright © 2024 by Pamela Austin
"A Writing Companion" and "The Birth of the Morning Star" copyright © 2024 by
    Andrew Clapp
"The Date" copyright © 2024 by Katharine Gruber
"Woman Caught in Adultery" copyright © 2024 by Kahren Hull
"Anxiety: Finding Beauty in the Ashes," "Road-Tripping with Mom," "Captured by
    Love," and "For the Love of Samantha" copyright © 2024 by Susie Jones
"Riding the Rails" and "The Music Box" copyright © 2024 by Mary Ann Lenarz
"Dear Me..." and "Thoughts of an Average Man" copyright © 2024 by Ekaterina Miller
"Can Fear Be Conquered? Here's My Story," "Your Strength Is My Peace," "True to
    Form," and "Never Blackmail a Thought Reader" copyright © 2024 by Sharon Rose
    Miller
"Just Jump," "Vinesinger," "Tria," and "Acknowledgements" copyright © 2024 by
    Bridgett Powers
"True Purpose" copyright © 2024 by Christine Prueher
"Passion Pursuit," "Light of Salvation," "Insecure No More," "Precious Father-in-Law,"
    and "Destiny's Detour" copyright © 2024 by Laura Shrake
"Preface," "The Fabric of Spacetime," "*Die Walküre*, Texas Rangers," and "Last
    Request" copyright © 2024 by Michael S. Spence
"Introduction: Tell Me a Story," "Good Friday and the Flood," "Wabs and Angel," and
    "Little Boxes" copyright © 2024 by Curtis J. Wellumson
"Time to Mom Up" copyright © 2024 by Krista Zoerb

ACKNOWLEDGMENTS
BRIDGETT POWERS

WRITING MAY BE A SOLITARY ENDEAVOR, but no author is an island. We draw inspiration from the ever-growing sea of stories surrounding us, strengthen the bedrock of our craft through the sometimes stormy feedback and critique of other writers and industry professionals, and nurture the sweet joy of storytelling in the rich support of those who encourage us to keep our imaginations blooming.

We, the contributing authors of *Tell Me a Story*, owe our thanks and successes to many.

To God, the Writer of the human story, we are grateful for the privilege of participating, even in this small measure, in His creative nature through the gift of storytelling.

We are thankful to the dedicated staff and ministry teams of Living Word Christian Center, especially the past and present leaders of the Connect Groups department, for giving our group such a lovely place to meet each month for the past sixteen years and counting.

To the many friends and family members who have encouraged each of us throughout our writing journeys, thank you!

For all the members of the Write Now Writers' group who have come and gone over the years, and those who have stayed the course, thanks for your insights, feedback, critique, and encouragement on each individual story shared. We are a family, and this anthology is a small showcase of what that joint dedication to the craft and to helping each other can create.

Finally, and most especially, our heartfelt appreciation goes to you, dear reader, the reason for our words. **Thank you for letting us tell you our stories!**